Adoption Memoirs

MARIANNE NOVY

Adoption Memoirs

Inside Stories

TEMPLE UNIVERSITY PRESS

Philadelphia • *Rome* • *Tokyo*

TEMPLE UNIVERSITY PRESS
Philadelphia, Pennsylvania 19122
tupress.temple.edu

Library of Congress Cataloging-in-Publication Data

Names: Novy, Marianne, 1945– author.
Title: Adoption memoirs : inside stories / Marianne Novy.
Description: Philadelphia : Temple University Press, 2024. | Includes
    bibliographical references and index. | Summary: "In this volume,
    leading scholar of Literary Adoption Studies Marianne Novy complicates
    the all-too-often essentialized popular perspectives of adoption through
    a critical comparative analysis of over forty adoption memoirs"—
    Provided by publisher.
Identifiers: LCCN 2023050359 (print) | LCCN 2023050360 (ebook) | ISBN
    9781439925898 (cloth) | ISBN 9781439925904 (paperback) | ISBN
    9781439925911 (pdf)
Subjects: LCSH: Adoptees—Biography—History and criticism. | Adoptive
    parents—Biography—History and criticism. | Adoption in literature. |
    Families in literature. | Adoption.
Classification: LCC HV875 .N689 2024 (print) | LCC HV875 (ebook) | DDC
    362.734092 [B]—dc23/eng/20240403
LC record available at https://lccn.loc.gov/2023050359
LC ebook record available at https://lccn.loc.gov/2023050360

∞ The paper used in this publication meets the requirements of the
American National Standard for Information Sciences—Permanence
of Paper for Printed Library Materials, ANSI Z39.48-1992

Printed in the United States of America

9 8 7 6 5 4 3 2 1

In memory of my two mothers
And for all who have gained or lost family through adoption

Contents

Acknowledgments   ix

Introduction   1
1. The Women Who Couldn't Forget   16
2. Same-Race Identities: Seeking Ancestry, Exploring Relationships   43
3. Constructing Racial Identity: Seeking Ancestry,
    Exploring Relationships   88
4. Many Ways to Be an Adoptive Parent   137
    Concluding Thoughts   184

Notes   191
Works Cited   213
Index   223

Acknowledgments

The second part of Chapter 2 is slightly revised from "Class, Shame and Identity in Memoirs about Difficult Same-Race Adoptions" by Jeremy Harding and Lori Jakiela, which appeared in the online open access journal *Genealogy*, vol. 2, no. 3, 2018. Chapters 2 and 3 are expansions and revisions of "New Territory: Memoirs of Meeting Original Family by Seven Adopted Americans," *Adoption & Culture*, vol. 3, 2012, 124–40. I am grateful to Emily Hipchen, the editor and then publisher, for permission to reprint, with many changes, and for much more.

After Emily joined what would become the Alliance for the Study of Adoption and Culture (ASAC) at a meeting of the Modern Language Association (MLA), she transformed it. She hosted ASAC's first conference, at the University of Tampa in 2005, and established a precedent for biennial conferences. With her help I hosted the next at the University of Pittsburgh. Many others followed throughout the United States, constructing a diverse and challenging intellectual community. Meanwhile, Emily began ASAC's publication of *Adoption & Culture*. Under her guidance and editorship, the journal was eventually taken under the wing of the Ohio State University Press. Several articles I published in *Adoption & Culture* after this transition included material revised for publication in this book: Chapter 3 includes some material from "Transcultural Adoption Literature for Pediatricians and Parents," vol. 6, no. 1, 2018, 135–61; Chapter 4 includes some material from "Teaching Changing Families to Get Adoption into the Curriculum," vol. 7, no. 1, 2019, 43–66; passages from "Memoirs and the Future of Adoption," vol. 9, no. 2, 2021, 308–24, appear slightly revised in Chapter 3. In addition to providing me a venue for publishing about adoption, Emily read and commented on a draft of this book. And I thank her especially for helping me connect with Gretchen Sisson.

Emily organized a panel at the 2023 MLA convention where I met Gretchen. After learning more about her book, *Relinquished: The Politics of Adoption and the Privilege of American Motherhood*, I asked her if she could send me a prepublication copy electronically for me to read as I was finishing my own book, and she did. It made a powerful impact on my thoughts.

I would also like to thank Carol Singley and Margaret Homans, who both connected with me through the MLA about adoption in literature, cochaired ASAC (Carol in its early days and Margaret later), and read and commented on a draft of all or part of this book. As scholarly and insightful adoptive mothers, both of them expanded my perspective. So did Barbara Katz Rothman, Molly Shanley, Judith Modell, and Janet Mason Ellerby (who read the birthmother chapter, in which her memoir is discussed). Jill Deans, Margot Backus, Cynthia Callahan, Marina Fedosik, Rosemarie Peña, and the late Martha Satz also made important contributions to ASAC from which I benefited.

During the last third of my forty-five years teaching at the University of Pittsburgh, I often sought administrative help in planning adoption-related events on campus—films and talks by creative writers and scholars as well as the second ASAC conference. I received administrative support especially from Nicole Constable and Kathleen Blee, successive deans of Pitt's Graduate School of Arts and Sciences, and from English Department chairs, the late, much missed, David Bartholomae, and Don Bialostosky, and Nancy Glazener, former director of graduate studies and of the literature program, all of whom approved many of my requests to teach courses on adoption in literature and culture. Under Dave's guidance, the English Department also supported help with the ASAC newsletter by Tara Lockhart, Katherine Kidd, and Amy Whipple.

Jennifer Kwon Dobbs, as a graduate student at Pitt many years ago, introduced me to the world of Korean adoptees and I have enjoyed seeing her become an internationally recognized poet as well as Chair of the English Department of St. Olaf College. Frayda Cohen connected me with Pittsburgh Families with Children from China. Paula Kane alerted me to Soojin Chung's *Adopting for God: The Mission to Change America through Transnational Adoption* (NYU Press, 2021). Pediatrician Sarah Springer, whose practice includes many international adoptees, taught me about medical issues while we taught mini-electives on adoption and foster care to Pitt medical students. Social worker Kelly Ryan-Schmidt and activist Kitty Griffin Lagorio, who focuses on the problems of postinstitutionalized children, spoke to this mini-elective and also taught me. So did Suzanne Polen, Liana Maneese, David

Schoenewolf, Libby Ferda, Penny Edwards, and Ali Patterson, who along with Lucy Fischer especially helped with film and video events.

As a professor emerita, I still benefit from the Pitt Office for Equity, Diversity, and Inclusion through its sponsorship of affinity groups, which now include the Pitt Adoption Community for Education. One group member, Joanna Mittereder, gave me references to social work articles about open adoption. Libby Ferda directed me to Angela Tucker. Other members, especially Christina Newhill, Tim Ziaukas, Lori Jakiela, and Katelan Hudson, also helped. And I thank many people from the larger world of adoption writing and scholarship—Ned Balbo, Bert Ballard, Elizabeth Bartholet, Jan Beatty, Wayne Carp, Danae Clark, Lorraine Dusky, Jane Elizabeth Edwards, Ellen Herman, Tobias Hubinette, Eleana Kim, Barbara Melosh, and Lise Wesseling—for sending me their writings. Some others who helped me on my journey to the publication of this book are Mike Dietrich, LeAnn Fields, Laura Lovett, John McLeod, Laura Portwood-Stacer, and Linda Seligmann. Thank you for helping me on my journey to the publication of this book with your assistance.

In a sense, preparation for this book started in 1975 when I began searching for my birthparents with the help of three influential adoptee memoirists (all of them now deceased): Betty Jean Lifton (who spoke in Pittsburgh that year), Jean Paton, Florence Fisher, and Nancy Fair, who ran a local support group, Pittsburgh Adoption Lifeline. I also owe debts of gratitude to many other people I met from the world of adoption reform support and activism, especially Janine Baer, Mary Ann Cohen, Katie Lee Crane, Ann Fessler, Sheila Ganz, Michael Phillip Grand, Marley Greiner, Pam Hasegawa, Susan Ito, Joyce Maguire Pavao, Adam Pertman, John Raible, and Rickie Solinger. I would also like to thank loyal friends Susan Andrade, Anita Mallinger, and Liane Norman for their interest and support.

My husband, David Carrier, has listened to every detail of my progress on this book for years and has staunchly believed in its importance. I am grateful for the constant gift of his intelligence and love. Our daughter, Liz Carrier, and her wife, Rowan Shafer, as well as, in the past two years, our granddaughter, Logan, have contributed enormously—though from Vancouver, British Columbia—to the joy in our lives.

Adoption Memoirs

Introduction

Adoption stories often make the popular media, but features about dramatic moments, such as custody transfer, reunion, or finalization of a transnational adoption, don't really show what those immediately involved feel at the time, let alone their long-term experience. As adoptee Nicole Chung writes in her recent memoir, *All You Can Ever Know*, the usual stories about adoption on TV, movies, or novels don't show "what happened *after* the tears or the hugs or the accusations . . . the unvoiced questions, the quiet drama of the everyday."[1] Adoption memoirs tell inside stories of adoption. At least, they tell some of what one person involved with adoption experienced over a long time, during which they and their relationships may have changed a great deal. But this book will provide even more insight by putting contrasting inside stories together.

There is no single story of adoption, no single story for either birthmothers, adoptees, or adoptive parents. My book discusses forty-seven memoirs, one perhaps partially fictionalized, with the author's real name still unknown; two of them films rather than print. The memoirs are mostly by U.S. authors, with three adoptees—Jackie Kay, Jeanette Winterson, and Jeremy Harding—from the UK and one (Jenny Heijun Wills) from Canada, all of whose stories resonate in some way with U.S. readers.

As Barbara Melosh summarizes, in the United States since the end of World War II, adoption has often been seen as the "best solution."[2] Its image has been a win-win or, rather, a win-win-win, with the birthmother escaping stigma and poverty and the adopted child and parents living happily ever after together. This is the image that the Supreme Court majority relied on in *Dobbs v. Jackson Women's Health Organization*, its recent revocation of *Roe v. Wade*, making abortion more difficult to obtain in the hope of increasing the number of adoptable children. But since the 1970s, not just melodramatic media stories but also memoirs complicate this view, as Melosh shows and this book demonstrates in depth, revealing social justice issues in adoption.[3] From the end of World War II until 1973, more than one and a half million young women, in what journalist Gabrielle Glaser calls a "reproductive- and human-rights story," were "funneled into an often-coercive system they could neither understand nor resist."[4] The memoirs discussed in my book's first chapter support her view. Though these birthmothers in important ways contrast with the woman on whom she focuses, they also do not forget relinquishment but often remember it with pain. In later chapters, we see that while some adoptees recall close and happy relationships with their adoptive parents, others do not or find those good relationships shadowed by racism or by lack of knowledge of their origins. Adoptive parents often write that they could have used more education or more specific information to prepare them to raise their adopted children, and many adoptees agree. Getting past the secrecy imposed by closed records to meet birthparents does not in itself solve these problems. Most of these memoirs show that relationships between adoptee and birth family may be rewarding but can take work and sometimes turn out to be impossible to maintain.

Reading memoirs by adoptees and adoptive parents together demonstrates that some adoptive parents are still practicing the denial that many adoptees' memoirs have been calling out for years, while others, especially concerned about adoptees' and/or birthparents' needs for continuity, are changing adoption practices for the better.[5] This book shows how much some adoptees appreciate parents who encourage discussions of adoption and how frustrated others feel by parents who don't. It provides cautionary narratives, pictures of generosity, and stories of mistakes, learning, and forgiveness. Adoption memoirs of all kinds often reveal irresponsibility, deceit, and/or cruelty by adoption agencies, social workers, orphanage directors, doctors, and, in the background, state legislators who keep birth records closed.[6] Many of these memoirs thus provide what Kimberly McKee, writing especially of those by Asian American adoptees, calls "counterstories" that "dislodge one-dimensional portrayals for multi-dimensional, nuanced realities."[7] These memoirs show that while transracial adoption is often considered antiracist, it may expose children to overt racism and implicit bias.[8]

Adoption memoirs are also revelatory about gender issues. Not only do women predominate as authors in all genres of adoption life writing, as Barbara Melosh writes, but most of the authors who led both the movement to adopt and the movement to open closed adoption records have been women.[9] The first is mainly because women are traditionally more involved with child-rearing, the second partly because, in the United States at any rate, more girls are adopted than boys and also because, correlating with child-rearing, an interest in family relationships is psychologically more likely and culturally more expected for women, so women are more likely to search and to write about the search and its aftermath.[10] These memoirs show the persistence of prejudice against women's and girls' sexuality, evident in the treatment of birthmothers and occasionally of female adoptees, and not only the still predominant gendering of child-rearing as feminine but also sometimes an impossible ideal of the Good Mother. Memoirs by adoptive fathers often meditate on how different their behavior is than that of their own fathers, and many adoptive mother memoirists take it for granted that it is their responsibility to deal with their children's emotional needs and their fault if they cannot.[11]

These are often fascinating narratives, but in addition to this they are important because people involved with adoption often feel like they cannot tell their story publicly. Some memoirists, particularly early ones and adoptees when discussing their birth family, use pseudonyms. Like some other adoptees, I was told, as a child, not to talk about being adopted and I broke that commandment only rarely even as a young adult. It may take a lot of courage to tell individual or family secrets. Yet if these are not told, stereotypes about adoption, idealizing or melodramatic, may go unchallenged and too many people may make life decisions without the help that some of these stories could give them. It is remarkable how many memoirs by adoptive parents and birthparents as well as adoptees say, in effect, "I was not prepared for how difficult my life would be." Reading about these memoirs may provide some preparation for others.

In the 1960s, after years in which the experiences of adoptees and birthmothers were considered too secret to write about for publication, two pioneering narratives appeared. Adoptee Jean Paton published *Orphan Voyage* under the pseudonym of Ruthena Hill Kittson. A woman whose identity has never been discovered wrote about a birthmother's experience in *The House of Tomorrow* under the pseudonym of Jean Thompson. A few books from the seventies, especially Betty Jean Lifton's *Twice Born* and Lorraine Dusky's *Birthmark*, helped lift the curtain of shame. Memoirs by adoptive parents had less shame to deal with and began earlier. I mention some in the chapter on transracial adoptees, but parents' memoirs have their own chapter. More memoirs by members of all three groups were published during and since the memoir boom, which began in the late 1980s. The earliest adoptive parent memoir I discuss in detail is Michael Dorris's *The Broken Cord*, from 1989, though I briefly discuss Helen Doss's *The Family Nobody Wanted* (1954) in Chapter 3.

Few statistics on adoption are collected by the U.S. government. The Adoption History Project website estimated, a few years ago, that there are about 5 million adoptees in the United States.[12] The U.S. population is now about 330,000,000. This would mean that around 1 in 66 people in the United States was adopted. In 2020, according to the Children's Bureau, there were 95,306 domestic adoptions in the United States, many of toddlers or older children, with about 19,658 infants adopted privately, out of about 4 million infants born. (This is between two and twenty times the number of domestic adoptions in other developed countries, adjusted for difference in population.)[13] A fairly recent calculation is that every year in the last few decades, 0.5 percent of infants born in the United States are relinquished for adoption, though the judges who overturned *Roe v. Wade* expect those numbers to be soon increased. In 2020, only 1,622 children from other countries were adopted by parents in the United States; those children who were adopted transnationally when the numbers were higher (e.g., nearly 23,000 in 2004) are now approaching adulthood and exploring especially complicated identities.[14] The U.S. census of 2010, according to the National Center on Adoption and Permanency, estimated that 4 percent of families with children under eighteen are adoptive families. Adoptive parents might, statistically, have a better chance of connecting than those with other relations to adoption, if they wish to.

Birthparents and same-race adoptees and adoptive parents are invisible minorities. Birthparents have significant stigma to face and so very seldom disclose their identity to others outside of their families (sometimes even to others within their families, as we will see). Adoptees, whether same-race or transracial, may well grow up not knowing anyone else with that status, and sometimes this in itself leads to a sense of alienation. Not only do they have a different ancestry than their parents, but they may also feel different within their community. Same-race adoptees cannot identify other same-race adoptees by their appearance or by their names. If my experience is at all typical, adults rarely disclose being adopted unless they are professionally involved with the issue, are searching or are explaining their relationship with a birth relative or commenting on a recent news item, film, or bestseller related to adoption—and sometimes not even then. It is comparatively recently that some have found communities with other adoptees, and memoirs and memoirists helped these form. Currently the internet is a large resource for such communities.

Adoptive parents of same-race children may avoid disclosing this status, though the stigma of infertility is less in the United States than in the past, and adoption is so often praised. On the other hand, if they want, they might find a support group, especially if they adopt through an agency. If they adopt internationally, there is almost certainly some kind of support group available, at least online, for when their children are young, and there may even be a local chapter of this type of organization, such as Families with Children from China. But from the evidence of these memoirs, many adoptive parents do not get the support that they need.

Telling Adoption Stories

Adoption stories are particularly complicated to tell because every adoptee's story is also in part the story of their parents, biological and adoptive—and every adoptive or birthparent's story is also in part the story of an adoptee. Each person starts by seeing their own side of the story. They cannot speak their truth without telling something about how they are affected by other people's words and actions, so they must narrate some of those other words and actions. Sometimes all they can do is speculate. Some memoirists, such as adoptee Jeremy Harding, birthmother Margaret Moorman, and adoptive father Ralph Savarese, try very hard to understand other points of view. Adoptive parents, when writing about children who are teenagers or older, may ask them to write a chapter or a shorter piece for their book.

John Raible writes of transracial adoptees' "continual negotiation and performance of fluid racial identities over the course of a life span."[15] Some psychologists believe that all adoptees go through phases in their attitude toward adoption.[16] However, the presence or sequence of those phases can vary enormously. Many adoptees, looking back over their lives, see their parents differently than they did in the past and may guide the reader through forming an opinion and then changing it also. Following a memoirist's change of views over time–this also includes observing birthparents and adoptive parents discovering how inaccurate their expectations have been and/or reacting to adoptees' changes—is one of the ways in which reading a memoir can lead to more understanding than reading an interview or the answers to a questionnaire, the tools that journalists and social scientists most often use. Each of these memoirs is the story of a multifaceted and changing individual who is not reducible to their opinions about a list of contested issues. Writing a memoir is a more public version of creating a coherent narrative of one's life, which, as Harold Grotevant has pointed out, is the process through which adoptees, birthparents, and adoptive parents can develop an identity that incorporates adoption.[17]

In a previous book, *Reading Adoption*, I constructed a partial history of how adoption has been represented in literature—classical Greek drama, Shakespeare, the eighteenth- and nineteenth-century British novel, and twentieth-century American novel and drama.[18] In its introduction, I told part of my own story and located myself in relation to issues of family, identity, and others important in the dialogue around adoption. In this book I will show how many other people have so located themselves in their writing. In that book I discussed memoirs by Jean Paton and Betty Jean Lifton largely in relation to how they used Sophocles's *Oedipus*. In this one, I am taking memoirs more seriously.

I begin with birthmothers' memoirs because their voices are less often heard than those of adoptees and adoptive parents; because they are more publicly stereotyped as either sluts or angels; because they can tell an earlier portion of the adoption story, that beginning with conception, than any of the others; and because they are often supposed to forget their relinquishment while memoirs show that they do not forget but instead often find the experience traumatic. Birthmothers' memoirs challenge stereotypes, and by introducing their stories early in the book I hope also to increase readers' understanding of some birthmothers discussed in subsequent chapters. Then I proceed to adoptees' memoirs, since their experiences too are still less often heard than those of adoptive parents, although adoption is supposed to be for adoptees' benefit. The experiences of same-race and transracial adoptees are different enough, though they share much also, that I give each a chapter of their own. And finally I turn to memoirs by adoptive parents. Some have clearly learned from the writings of adult adoptees, and others have not.

Adoption has changed in recent years, and this book shows some of those changes, with most of its memoirs coming from the twenty-first century. There are fewer children adopted now than in the 1960s, but adoption is more visible because more adoptees are transracial and/or transnational. For transnational adoptees, visiting their country of birth is becoming more common. Transracial adoptees still usually live in communities where no one else looks like them. Searching for birthparents is now more common, and DNA testing can help.[19] There are now more adoptions by gay people than in 1999 when Jesse Green published *The Velveteen Father*. And there are more adoptions that are open not just in the sense that the adoptive parents and birthparents have met but also in the sense that they keep in contact.

How Memoirs Speak to Each Other

Barbara Melosh's chapter, "Adoption Stories: Autobiographical Narratives and the Politics of Identity," discusses memoirs from all three relations to adoption, as I am doing, but this is unusual.[20] Since Melosh, only Margaret Homans, in *The Imprint of Another Life*, considers issues in all three types of memoirs.[21] As in the lives of many adoptees, birthparents, and adoptive parents, important conversations are thus left unspoken. This book will help us hear them.

Reading memoirs from several different viewpoints together is instructive. The memoirs discussed in this book often speak to each other. Several birthmothers and a few adoptive parents write about the effect that reading memoirs by adoptees has had on them. Many adoptive parents and adoptees agree that adoptive parents should have more education about their children's history and about the issues they must deal with, especially if they are adopting transracially. Had Jaiya John lived and written his memoir, *Black Baby White Hands*, earlier, Douglas Bates might have better understood the Black daughters he discusses in *Gift Children*. Birthmothers, adoptive parents, and adoptees complain about closed state records, the failure of orphanages and agencies to give or share information, and even more unethical behavior, such as allowing neglect or abuse, representing one child as another, or giving children to parents who are severely depressed or whose child-rearing practices are known to be problematic. Transnational adoptees and adoptive parents sometimes discover that birthparents represented as dead are still alive and thought that what they were signing was permission for a child to be educated elsewhere.

More strikingly, sometimes memoirs speak to each other by way of contrast. Transracial adoptee Rebecca Carroll's *Surviving the White Gaze* speaks directly to birthmother Jan Waldron's version of their story in *Giving Away Simone*, especially its neglect of racism. All the transracial adoptee memoirists find it important to learn about their heredity or at least their ancestral culture, and adoptive parent memoirists such as Jana Wolff, Sharon Rush, Emily Prager, Kay Trimberger, and Jeff Gammage agree. However, Green, whose sons are white but Latino, disagrees, and Theresa Reid, Claude Knobler, and Jeanne Marie Laskas at best underplay and at worst deny this importance. On a parallel issue, same-race adoptees differ among themselves, and sometimes vary at different stages of their memoirs, about the relative weight of nature and nurture, as do those with other relations to adoption. Lorraine Dusky notes her daughter's differences from her adoptive family, while birthmother Janet Ellerby sees her daughter's upbringing as much like that of the children she raised. Adoptive father Bates is, for a while, anxious about whether his children are doomed to the disorganized behavior of their birthparents regardless of their nurture, while adoptive father Knobler believes in letting his son's nature emerge instead of being anxious about nurturing him. Adoptive mother Trimberger, who had believed in the dominant power of nurture, revises her views as she observes her son and draws on behavioral geneticists' analyses of interaction between nature and nurture to understand his development. But after Jaiya John's memoir, a reader may feel that all three of these parent authors miss some of the impact of racism.

Jeanette Winterson says, in *Why Be Happy When You Can Be Normal*, that adoptees feel unwanted; others such as Sarah Saffian relate a very different experience. Chung, however, writes that a transracial adoptee may feel loved, may feel that in her situation "adoption was truly the best option in a sea of imperfect ones" (198) but experience "years of wondering and confusion" (202). A few refer to the question of whether adoption in itself should be considered traumatic, argued influentially by Nancy Verrier in her book that names separation from the birthmother as the primal wound (which she also takes as the book's title), but most of the adoptees whose memoirs we read, and some described by their adoptive parents, have experienced much instability, sometimes including neglect and violence, in their early years, and this, more than adoption in itself, might be the cause of feeling wounded. And, as Katarina Wegar has argued and as Lori Jakiela's memoir especially shows, adoptees' discomfort may often come at least partly from stigmatization: "experiences of being adopted in a culture that defines adoptive kinship as inferior."[22] In cases of transracial adoption, the more obvious kind of stigmatization comes from racial prejudice.

Religious language has often promoted the win-win view of adoption. Pearl Buck and Bertha Holt, who both wrote influential mid-twentieth-century books promoting transnational adoption, saw it in relation to the universality of God's love, though Buck had an ecumenical approach and Holt's emphasis was on giving children the right religious training.[23] Catholic and evangelical Protestant cultures especially promote the view that the birthmother is doing a good deed by giving a child a secure family and a couple the child they want rather than having an abortion.[24] We see this in the Catholic social worker Amy Seek consults. Holt's agency is still functioning, and as discussed in Kathryn Joyce's *The Child Catchers*, for many evangelicals today, as for the agency's founders, adoption is a way to deal with an orphan crisis around the world and a chance to convert the heathen.[25] Jane Jeong Trenka's memoir shows some of the problems with this approach.

The win-win view of adoption persists in secular as well as religious terms in the still influential belief that adoptees are lucky. This adjective is especially likely to be applied to transnational, transracial adoptees. Jane Jeong Trenka critiques the designation by noting all that she lost although she gained an education and some freedom, while others, such as Lori Jakiela, Jackie Kay, Nicole Chung, and Mei-ling Hopgood, find luck in their particular situation—Jackie Kay and Mei-ling Hopgood because their adoptive parents are so extraordinary and Nicole Chung and Lori Jakiela because they appreciate their adoptive parents by contrast to extremely difficult birthparents. Some adoptive parents feel that the choice of a particular child for them was fated by God or "the universe" or particularly well-chosen by the orphanage: Chung points out problems with invoking God, and the separated twins discuss the issue of fate. Religion can appear in these memoirs as a source of shame, especially for birthmothers and some adoptees, but it can also provide a connection to eloquence, rituals of inclusion, or language for gratitude.

Many adoptees' memoirs conclude by acknowledging what they have received from both their heredity—perhaps their actual birthparents—and their adoptive parents or from both their country of birth and the United States. However, these conclusions frequently follow troubling feelings of double identity combined with disconnection from their ancestry, especially for trans-racial adoptees. Transracial adoptee memoirists Trenka, John, and Catherine McKinley complain about their parents' attempt to repress their emotions, but Kay's and Hopgood's parents are far from cold, and we see passionate and understanding sympathy also in adoptive parent memoirists such as Wolff, Savarese, and Prager.

Secrecy and Openness

The United States formalized permanent legal adoption at an earlier date than many other countries, though many other countries have long had informal adoption practices and some, as well as some American cultures, still do. It was largely legalized state by state, with Massachusetts in 1851 passing what is considered the first modern adoption law. What makes the current U.S. adoption system most problematic for many adoptee and birthparent memoirists is that it legally removes the birthparents' parental role, as opposed to giving a child a greater number of caring people. Reinforcing this legal move, most states in the United States (to some extent) and some Canadian provinces and other countries also separate the adoptee from his or her original parents by keeping their names and the adoptee's name secret.

In the UK the names have been available to adult adoptees since 1975. The memoirs of UK adoptees Jackie Kay, Jeremy Harding, and Jeanette Winterson, all authors widely known in the United States, reflect this difference, though much of their family and search dynamics have partial parallels here. Many adoptees find the search process frustrating because of closed records. For Harding, as well as for Jean Strauss and A. M. Homes, going through records that are public eventually gives a feeling of inclusion in larger histories. With the extensive current interest in genealogy and genetics, they share their quest with many others.

As adoption historian Wayne Carp and legal scholar Elizabeth Samuels have shown, in a significant portion of the twentieth century, the names were supposed to be available to an adoptee who had reached adulthood.[26] Over the past few decades, after much political advocacy, some states have returned to that level of availability, but some only for those born after a certain date or not prohibited from knowledge by a veto from their birthmother. And some adoptees have made contact through DNA analysis or social media.

On the other hand, many adoptions today do involve early contact between the adoptive parents and the potential birthparents, and sometimes this contact continues and includes the child, as in Wolff's memoir *Secret Thoughts of an Adoptive Mother* and Amy Seek's *God and Jetfire*, or resumes before adulthood, as in Carroll's *Surviving the White Gaze* and Waldron's *Giving Away Simone*. The openness always intended by Wolff and Seek, from their different perspectives, is probably in part a consequence of adoptees speaking out about the positive impact of meeting their birthparents as adults by contrast to their years of wondering. All four memoirs, however, show that an open adoption, even in the best of circumstances, which Seek has, is still emotionally challenging. Like some memoirs that continue after reunion, they reveal that it is often hard for birthmothers and adoptive mothers to avoid feeling that they are in competition. Furthermore, unlike most adoptee memoirists, Carroll feels that the relationship with her birthmother made her life worse.

Memoirs' Variations and Goals

This book is about memoirs and not about therapy or statistics. People who write memoirs are not necessarily representative of their demographic group. But they may have insights about experiences they share with many others. Research on birthmothers shows that rather than the forgetting they have been promised, many have feelings of loss similar to those of our memoirists. Some adoptees who write may be like canaries in a coal mine, revealing problems that others have covered up or narrowly escaped. So might some adoptive parents, since they too can suffer from the irresponsibility of adoption agencies.

Still, in this book I discuss many memoirs in each category to emphasize that adoption experiences vary enormously and suggest reasons for some variations. For example, some adoptive parents who write memoirs want contact with birthparents, some do not because of what they know about how their child was treated, and some without such knowledge think contact would be threatening to their sense of full parenthood. Every birthmother who writes a memoir wants contact with her child, but some adoptee memoirists find that their birthmothers do not. Or one or both find the relationship too difficult to sustain. Nicole Chung, for example, discovers that her birthmother was abusive to her sister. In most of the chapters, I make the point about variations by comparing several memoirs in each of several categories, though the experiences and conclusions of birthmother memoirists have more similarities than the others. That chapter is shorter largely because fewer birthmothers have published memoirs.[27] But I have made a point of discussing a variety of experiences, including both Dusky's strained relationship with her suicidal daughter, and Ellerby's mainly harmonious outcome. No American birthfather, and only one from the UK, has published a memoir about relinquishment, although some birthfathers may have published memoirs that do not mention a child biologically theirs they did not raise.[28]

More than most memoirs, perhaps, adoption memoirs from all perspectives often have as their intended audience people who are or might be in a situation similar to those of the memoirist or might be dealing with others in that situation. Readers might be asking themselves, "Should I adopt?" or "What will it be like if I have my child adopted?" or "Should I try to meet my birthparents?" or "Why does my child want to meet her birthparents, and how would that affect our relationship?" A few memoirists in each category are explicit about addressing such a reader. This group includes adoptive parents Knobler, Reid, Wolff, Trimberger, and David Marin, but also birthmothers Dusky and Moorman and adoptee Kay. Many of these books would also be helpful to a reader asking, "What should I do about the difficulties my adopted child is having?" Or "Should I try an open adoption?" Or "Why is my birthparent (or my birthchild) finding our relationship difficult?"

But trying to help individual readers is not the only stance that the memoirists in this book take. Thomas Couser discusses the connection of memoirs with civil rights movements.[29] Adoptee memoirs in the United States, especially, may allude to and contribute to the movement for open records; birthmother memoirs to that and also to a movement of their own for better treatment; memoirs of transracial adoptees to antiracism movements; Green's, among those I discuss here, to the movement for gay civil rights; Savarese's, especially, to the disability rights movement, though the memoirs of Michael Dorris and Ann Loux are relevant to it also.

Some adoptee memoirs, such as those by McKinley, Hopgood, and John, are variants on the coming-of-age plot. Couser sees the portrayal of unhappy childhoods as "survivor testimony" (148), but memoirs by adoptees of childhood unhappiness are very often also attempts to educate prospective adoptive parents about how to raise their children better, expressing sympathy for their own parents who did the best they could, not having enough preparation. They might fall in his category of filial narratives, analyzing adoptive parents or birthparents or both (154). A few, especially those by Kay and Hopgood, are in part tributes to their adoptive parents. But memoirs from all positions in relation to adoption are also attempts to make sense of its role in their own lives.[30]

When Melosh wrote her summary of adoption memoirs, the memoir boom was underway, and the number of memoirs published and read has continued to grow since then. As Couser writes, this is a genre very close to the storytelling that everyone does in the course of their lives (26), and therefore widely accessible to both readers and writers. I hope that my inclusion of many recent memoirs will help expand people's awareness of the range of adoption experience. It is worth noting that even with this boom some important memoirs still have to be self-published. It is not a coincidence that memoirs by a pioneering adoptee (Jean Paton), a militant first mother (Dusky prefers this term), and two Black men, Jaiya John and Craig Hickman (the latter further minoritized by being gay), fall into this category. I also want to expand the canon to include memoirs of adoption from one white family to another, in which the main issue is class, not race—those by Harding and Jakiela. Perhaps I find these books particularly moving not only because of being in a white same-race adoption myself but also because I, like these memoirists and unlike most I discuss, am writing after the death of my adoptive parents and identify with that aspect of their explorations.

However, transracial adoption memoirs are especially compelling partly because through the lens of a single family, they dramatize the racial divisions of our world. My previous adoption writing emphasized the themes of adoptee search and reunion, but reading transracial adoption memoirs has illuminated for me the injuries of childhood experiences of bias and bigotry. Reading them has made me realize again how fortunate I have been to escape dealing with racial prejudice against me. While I was uncomfortable that my adoption was a secret, many adoptees are uncomfortable that their adoption is all too visible. Regardless of our relative visibility, all adoptees share experiences of loss and of being in a nonnormative family, and many of us have shared the experience of parents finding adoption a difficult topic to talk about and of complications in relationships with recovered birth family members. And while reading memoirs by adoptive parents and birthmothers, I have also had moments of identification with them from my own experience of parenthood, moments when I felt that I was learning from them more of what parenthood was about.

These memoirs showed me again what Elaine Scarry calls "the capacity of literature to exercise and reinforce our recognition that there are other points of view in the world, and to make this recognition a powerful mental habit."[31] Given the isolation that many adoptees and birthparents and adoptive parents feel, I would like this book to promote a sorely needed dialogue among our different perspectives as well as helping others understand and benefit from the viewpoints and experiences of the memoirists discussed here. As I show in *Reading Adoption*, fiction about adoption has often presented either the adoptive parents or the birthparents as uniquely important, though when analyzed in depth the treatment may be more complex. In this book I find that most adoptees' memoirs show both sets of parents as important.

Language

A few words about language issues. For centuries the tradition was to use *natural* to refer to children born out of wedlock and their parents. *Real* and *true* have also sometimes been used to refer to the parents who bore and begot children. But many adoptees and adoptive parents object to this usage, and many dictionaries also define *mother* in relation to ongoing care rather than to childbirth. A few memoirists treated here, most notably Harding, still use *natural*; this usage may have continued longer in England.

In 1976, Lee Campbell was the first person to use the one word *birthmother*, on the model of *grandmother* and *godmother*, to identify herself as she was trying to organize a group she called Concerned United Birthparents.[32] Many women who have surrendered children have followed her in calling themselves birthmothers, and so have many social workers and adoption agencies, though they often write it as two words instead of one. However, some believe that term denies a woman's continuing concern for the child and prefer *first mother* or *original mother*. These words are factually accurate and I use them occasionally, but I believe the use of the word by early activists Lee Campbell and Carole Anderson refutes the objection to *birthmother*. Furthermore, as *adoptive mother* does not imply that a woman's concern for a child ends with the finalization of adoption, so *birthmother* does not imply that it ends at birth. I prefer the one-word form to the two-word because this is what Lee Campbell used. Much of the time I use the term that the memoirist is using. Often it is just *mother*, and it is clear from the context which way the relationship began. I also write "birthfather" and "birthparent" as one word each, since Campbell did. The analogy with godfather and grandfather, etc., works for them, and they describe relationships more basic than those of other family members; however, in direct quotations I follow the authors' usage.[33]

And about the name of the memoirist as writer and character in their book: In the first and fourth chapters I refer to the memoirist as writer and as character by the same name. With the adoptee memoirists, when discussing them as children and young people in their memoirs, I sometimes refer to them with the first name they had at the time. If this leads to some inconsistency, that may reflect the sense of multiple identity many adoptees experience.

My Own Story

Let me locate myself briefly before the detailed treatment of other life stories begins. In some ways my experience was like those of many other adoptees at the time, though better than some, beginning with my birthmother's month with me before I was moved to my adoptive home. My new parents didn't have much, if any, counseling—it was 1945. They presented it positively—they had chosen me, and they would be able to take better care of me. (I didn't know or know of any single mothers so I assumed this was true.) But they didn't know not to tell me I shouldn't talk about adoption because other people wouldn't understand.

Like adoptive parents discussed by some memoirists in this book, they were not carefully vetted. My adoptive father may have already been on his way to the alcoholism that killed him at fifty-seven. But he was or had been the partner of the doctor who looked after the pregnant women in Cleveland's Florence Crittenton Home. He knew—as I found out in a thank-you letter my father wrote to that doctor, which his daughter had saved—that he did not know how to be a father, and no one helped him. On the other hand, my adoptive mother was warm, affectionate, open-minded, and education-oriented, although—or rather because—she herself had left school around fourteen for work to help her family, returning in her fifties. A more-than-good-enough mother.

Timid and in a conservative framework though she was, nevertheless my birthmother welcomed meeting me, introduced me to the seven sons born after her marriage, two of them still in high school, and encouraged me to visit again across the miles of four states. She got to the point where she would tell our story to a salesperson if I took her out to buy shoes. It was not an easy relationship for a while since we were very different, but we worked at it because it was important to both of us.

My birthfather didn't want contact with me at that time or later, but I will be forever grateful to him for sending me, without comment, a newspaper article about him with his picture. He was the one I looked like. He had a successful life and professional partnership with the woman he married a few years after he returned from the war in Europe. I eventually found her self-published late-in-life memoir while googling and discovered the names of their children. Thus, I was able to learn when he had died and then discreetly contact their son in time to meet him before the pandemic.

My birthparents met across the Jewish-Christian divide during World War II, she a naïve WAVE (member of Women Accepted for Volunteer Emergency Service) at twenty-six, he a streetwise eighteen-year-old who joined the army after his mother died, both away from their respective homes in small-town Wisconsin and Brooklyn. From what I know, they could never have been happy together, as each of them seems to have been in their marriages. They became pillars of their disparate communities. Possibly I was placed with an interfaith Protestant/Catholic couple partly because I was conceived in another kind of interfaith match and would not have fit with most agencies.

My experiences have led me to warm feelings for both adoptive mothers and birthmothers. Also, I remember, from years before my marriage, the time when getting pregnant seemed like a disaster to avoid and, from a few years after my marriage, before infertility treatments worked, the time when we started investigating adoption for ourselves (before I started seriously researching it beyond search issues).

Finding and contacting the early adoptee memoirists made a big difference to me. Jean Paton and Betty Jean Lifton both gave me guidance in my search for ancestry and later for the literary history of adoption, in person as well as in their books and letters. In reading their memoirs and the later ones in this book, I felt like I was discovering still another family, brave heroes who persisted against difficulties much greater than mine. The birthmother and adoptive parent memoirists helped me understand some of what my own mothers faced, and more about other dimensions of parenting. In these memoirs I have found moving portrayals of grief, anger, courage, persistence, joy, learning, and forgiveness. I hope my account of them will help readers understand the complexity of emotions that people may feel in their involvement with adoption and see the complexity of the social justice issues adoption can pose. And I hope that my readers will seek out these memoirs to live through their whole stories and to consider how adoption policies and practices might be changed for the better.

1

The Women Who Couldn't Forget

Jean Thompson, Lorraine Dusky, Carol Schaefer, Jan Waldron,
Margaret Moorman, Janet Mason Ellerby, Amy Seek

Birthmothers' narratives are the clearest and most unified voice against the win-win-win narrative of adoption. They remember lonely childbirths, the loss of children they were forbidden from ever seeing again, and the deceptive promise that they could forget their child and go on with their lives. In *God and Jetfire*, Amy Seek recalls that she thought that being a birthmother in an open adoption would be easy and found that it was not.[1] Every memoirist found that relinquishing a child is painful. As Jan Waldron writes in the preface to her memoir, *Giving Away Simone*, "One family's luck is another's loss."[2]

Not many birthmothers have published memoirs, compared to adoptees and adoptive parents, for a number of reasons. As adoption has functioned in the United States most of the time in the twentieth century, and often still in the twenty-first, birthparents are supposed to disappear. Adoption has been something to hide, with hidden further behind it problems such as infertility and illegitimacy, not supposed to intrude on the public image of the adoptive family.

Margaret Homans and Kate Livingston, the latter from her own experience, have discussed in detail further reasons for birthmothers' silences: The position of mother without child, especially, does not fit into our culture's narrative, does not give a place to speak.[3] Even the question of which word to use for this identity is contested. But women in this position share an experience impossible to forget: bearing a child and relinquishing it drastically changes a woman's life for close to a year, at least—a change that need not happen for a man who begets a child—and many would say that this change has lifetime effects. First mothers (a term some of them prefer) often write that they had little choice about what would happen to their child, that decisions and laws affecting them were made without their participation, but recently more have been demanding to have their voices heard—some through political activism, some through memoirs, and some in both ways. And the increasing interest in genetics may provide another reason for some to listen to them.

Possibilities for birthparents have apparently increased in recent years. Adoption now is often more visible and committing a child to it called praiseworthy. Many state laws still assume that birthparents will want to remain hidden, but most adoptions now have some degree of openness in that the adopting parents and the birthmother or possibly both birthparents have met.[4] In an increasing but still minority practice, the birthmother and even her family may have a continuing and regular role in the adoptive family's life. However, these changes, as Seek shows, do not negate the pain of loss.

Birthmothers' memoirs, which have contributed to new adoption practices, provide windows into very different lives from those in stereotypes. The first three in the United States that could be so called were published in 1967, 1979, and 1991; more followed afterward. And Ann Fessler's *The Girls Who Went Away* (2006) gave voice to many from the more than one hundred women she interviewed who could flesh out statistics and suggest that much in these memoirs is representative.[5]

"So which are you? An angel? Or a slut?" This is the question asked at a retreat for birthmothers Seek describes (167). As the discussion leader says, people think that they are either promiscuous or bravely self-sacrificing. Neither word would be used about a man who gave up rights to his child. Neither is the simple truth about the writers of these memoirs. Two of them got pregnant in their first sexual experience, all but one in a relationship of a year or more. They are human, not angels. They had little sex education.[6] Doctors generally treat them badly, seeming to punish them. Economics or their parents or both pressure their relinquishment.[7] Except for Seek, they receive little or no counseling or education about pregnancy and childbirth.[8] If they are told anything about what the aftermath of giving up their child will be, it is the false message that they will forget. Social workers and adoption agencies seldom forward information between them and the adoptive family, even if asked for, and more often give false information. Like Seek, these young women have no idea what they are getting into. In all these ways, most of these memoirists are typical of the women Fessler interviewed.

Many agencies now try to make adoption look easier to pregnant single women, by offering them the opportunity to choose from many possible adoptive parents and to keep some measure of contact with their adopted-out child if they wish (though the agreement on contact may easily be dissolved by adoptive parents). However, Seek's memoir shows that even a relatively privileged woman who has chosen adoptive parents in an open adoption that remains open still may not expect the pain she will experience.[9]

Pioneering Birthmother Memoirs

Reading these memoirs showed me that I was not the only person whose conception and adoption were occasioned partly by the social upheaval of the Second World War, with some couples meeting away from their home community and some of them and others breaking up as men went off to war. Premarital sex increased, but sex education and access to contraceptives did not. And on the other hand, return from military duty would mean a desire for domesticity, sometimes helped by the GI Bill, and desire to adopt by infertile couples. Though the increase in adoption began in 1945, the earliest first-person narrative of relinquishment did not appear until the late 1960s. Apparently it took the increasing openness of that decade for anyone to put her story into print.[10] The first book classified as a birthmother memoir by libraries, *The House of Tomorrow*, was published under a pseudonym—this shows how much stigma birthmothers felt in 1967, and the absence of other such memoirs until 1979, when Lorraine Dusky self-published one to great controversy, confirms that the stigma continued.[11] *House of Tomorrow* is in large part a detailed journal of life in a Salvation Army home for unwed mothers, presented as written by a college student pregnant by a man separated from his wife. Her situation is easier than that of many single pregnant teenagers because, while her parents are on a year's sabbatical in Europe, she has a motherly and knowledgeable older friend, Dorothy, who gives her kindly advice. The book gives a picture of a range of women under supervision without any help from psychologists. They can't tell each other their real names, and she sees lots of their other lies and feels humiliated about her own, but the picture is not entirely negative.[12]

They occasionally feel solidarity (Thompson 164) and try to help each other. The narrator is exhilarated after she experiences the "miracle of giving birth" (165). Under the laws of California (a state she has moved to because illegitimacy would not be on the birth certificate), she has been allowed to meet the adoptive parents recommended to her by one of Dorothy's friends, who just happens to live in California also. Because her son is sick, he stays in the home longer, and she sees him a number of times and after a week holds him and feeds him. She insists that he should go directly to the parents she has met and not to a foster home, and while she feels sad about giving him up, she believes, "They have everything to offer him—I have nothing" (171). There is an epilogue in which we find that six years later she is married and has children of her own, and she heard from Dorothy when the boy was one that he was "absolutely perfect" (179). Thompson presents her narrator as at peace, and uses an epigraph from the mystic Rumi, who describes children as "the sons and daughters of Life's longing for itself."

The experience narrated in this probably somewhat fictionalized memoir (the sympathetic and experienced Dorothy's convenient replacement of the parents seems too good to be true) is much easier than that in any later memoir, with no clear hint that the narrator is affected by painful memories or secrets.[13] Probably she is showing self-control by not discussing them— she makes a point of emphasizing in the epilogue the importance of "self-discipline and will power." But even she, for all her sugar-coating, writes that homes for unwed mothers should have more (that is, some) attention to their residents' psychological growth and well-being and that a birthmother (a word not yet in use) should be able to meet the adoptive parents and learn at least a little about the child.

Lorraine Dusky's *Birthmark* (1979), the first memoir of relinquishment published under the author's name, is very different. Dusky's situation is like Thompson's in that she is a college student pregnant by a married man in the 1960s, but otherwise her experience is worlds apart. I discuss her later memoir, *hole in my heart* (2015), in more detail later, but to mention a few of the conditions contrasting to those in *House* that appear in *Birthmark*, her childbirth is very painful, there is no possibility of meeting the adoptive parents, and she continually wonders what has happened to her child. She reads about adoptees "who were trying to change the laws so they could locate their natural parents,"[14] interviews Florence Fisher, the leader of Adoptees' Liberty Movement Association (ALMA), who will be discussed in the next chapter, and becomes part of the open records movement. She records testimony from a court hearing that suggests children are damaged by adoption, and questions the assumption that adoption always provides a better life. This book was widely reviewed, but often quite hostilely, as she discusses in her later memoir.

The taboo against birthmothers' writing about their experience was apparently so strong that I have not found another such memoir published (at least by a press rather than self-published) until 1991. That year, Carol Schaefer published another book about a pregnancy in the 1960s, *The Other Mother*, which shares something with each of the previous books.[15] Like Thompson, she spends part of her pregnancy in a home for unwed mothers—this one is called Seton House and is run by nuns—which does not give them any psychological help and requires lying and pseudonyms. She tells the stories of others she met there, and recalls the birth as a miracle (70). But like Dusky, she cannot forget her child, is not allowed to learn anything about his adoptive parents, discovers lies from the adoption agency, and through ALMA connects with adoptees and others seeking greater openness in adoption. These contacts eventually help her meet her son when he is about twenty, after she has formed a bond with his adoptive mother, which will continue. She cites some research about adoptees' psychological difficulties, which do not seem to have affected him, and emphasizes the need for adoptees and their "other mothers" to reconnect, but she does not explicitly challenge adoption as an institution in the way Dusky does. However, she implies criticism when she recalls a college psychology class about Harlow's and Bowlby's work on the impact of separating children from their mothers (Schaefer 123–24), and she protests the analysis of unwed mothers in her abnormal psychology text-book (135).[16] Hers is the first birthmother memoir to have been made into a television movie, for NBC in 1995.

It is also a distinctive memoir in its appreciation of the unseen and even the mystical. Unlike any other of these memoirists, Schaefer recounts talk-ing to her child before birth and even playing a game in which she patted him through her own body in response to his movements (48). Much later, when his adoptive mother tells her that he was moved from his first adoptive home to another when he was eight months old, she remembers feeling special concern for him then, and this seems a vindication of their continuing con-nection. She has faith in her ability to send him messages about her love at a distance. She recounts help from a tarot reader (215) and a clairvoyant (257) during her search; she also emphasizes that in spite of the many ways in which she is alienated from the Catholicism of her youth and family, she still be-lieves in the Blessed Mother and, when she prays at a statue in Paris's Sacre Coeur, has a comforting vision of her son (214).

Militant and Ambivalent Activists

Most of this chapter discusses later memoirs from Dusky and three other birthmothers, who all gave up their children in the 1960s, as well as that of Amy Seek, who around 2001 looked for and found adoptive parents who maintained an adoption so open that she could be treated like a close family friend, not a secret.[17] They narrate their various paths through many unex-pected difficulties, telling their stories in the hope of counteracting the dom-inant view of birthmothers' experiences and changing laws to promote more openness.

Memoirists Lorraine Dusky, Margaret Moorman, Janet Mason Ellerby, and Jan Waldron are all very consciously writing against images of the birth-mother. Dusky, in *hole in my heart*, protests the very word, not as much in use when she wrote *Birthmark*, and they all reject the euphemistic language that calls what they did "making an adoption plan."[18] Dusky writes that such language "totally obfuscates the emotional crisis that precedes any relinquishment" (1), a crisis that Moorman (*Waiting to Forget*, 1996), making the same point, refers to as "desperation" (44).[19] They all describe painful, solitary, unprepared experiences of pregnancy and birth, and the aftermath of giving up their children. They were treated poorly by doctors, nurses, and other professionals. All emphasize that they could not simply go on with their lives as if nothing had happened, as they were told they should.[20] They want to know what happened to their children, they are concerned about them, and their traumatic experiences of shame, mistreatment, and forced separation affect their later lives in many ways. Their writing is part of a mission to educate so that others will understand the consequences of adoption and to open records so that birthmothers and their adopted-out children can be in contact more easily.[21]

Though *Roe v. Wade* had legalized abortion, these writers knew that many women, especially those from Catholic or evangelical Protestant families, found abortion difficult to undertake. The legal change did not remove adoption from consideration by every woman with an unwanted pregnancy. The prediction of later regret was used against abortion, but these writers want it to be considered by those considering adoption. (Indeed, in Sisson's follow-up to the 2020 Turnaway Study, women who relinquished children after they were denied an abortion had more regret than those who had abortions or those who raised their children.)[22]

Three of these memoirists are professional writers, already published authors when they begin to write about their experiences of relinquishment and its aftermath. They write different kinds of memoir. Dusky is an investigative journalist, Moorman more a meditative memoirist (her first book was about her sister's mental illness), and Ellerby an academic in the field of literature, who contextualizes her own story with changes in American culture in *Following the Tambourine Man* (2007) and has more recently written *Embroidering the Scarlet A*, a study of how birthmothers and single mothers have been treated in American literature and film. Waldron's *Giving Away Simone*, close to Moorman's as meditative nonfiction, was her first book; since then she has published two children's books and a book that analyzes issues in men's lives, including those in her family.

Dusky's 2015 memoir covers the events in her 1979 one and carries the story through the years of her relationship with her adopted-out daughter and after, as she continues her activism.[23] Ellerby also tells the story of her relationship with her daughter, much smoother than Dusky's. Moorman ends her memoir when she receives a letter from her son, with a picture, describing his life and family but not encouraging further contact soon. Waldron takes her narrative from the history of abandoning mothers in her family through her reunion with her eleven-year-old daughter and their struggle in the fifteen years after to build a relationship.

Moorman and Dusky contextualize their own stories with much research about adoption, including concern with adoptees as well as with birthmothers. Both have medical information they wanted to convey to their children and could not because of uncooperative adoption agencies.[24] Moorman's fears about inherited mental illness appear to be unjustified, but Dusky feels hers about the effects of birth control pills she took have been confirmed by her daughter's disabilities. Dusky is emphatic about the problems that adoption causes, while Moorman's tone is more ambivalent and questioning.

Moorman begins her story as a happy mother of a four-year old. She has recently realized, however, that she is unusually reluctant to leave her daughter, and that this probably has something to do with the loss of her son to adoption over twenty years previously.[25]

Much of her story is confusion and denial. As a fifteen-year-old, depressed because of her father's death and her mother's absorption in her sister's needs, she gets pregnant the first time she has sex with her boyfriend, Dan. She is confused about the rhythm method, and a condom machine he expects to use has disappeared. She sees a doctor when her period is late and he throws her out when she asks about an abortion. Until she is more than three months along, she hides the pregnancy from her mother; then they try to hide it from the rest of the world. Dan would like to marry her, but they are both vague about planning.

When Dan leaves for basic training for the Navy (his father, opposed to their marriage, is a Navy man), Moorman writes, initiating a metaphor that she will frequently use, "If I had been anxious and frightened before, I now perfected the shell of numbness that had already begun to cover the soft, unprotected core of my being" (41). So, she lets the adoption proceed.

The Florence Crittenton Home for Unwed Mothers in DC (Moorman's family lives in Arlington, Virginia) looks too grim, so she gets a room with Mrs. Blake, who takes in student-teacher interns, and hides there from the outside world. Indicative of the problems in her family of origin, she finds it the "happiest, best-run home I have known" (55), with pleasant group dinners and a resident grandmother and cat, in addition to Mrs. Blake. Her English tutor, Mrs. Maurice, gives her a copy of *Childbirth without Fear*, recommendations for college in New England, and the message that she is "an intelligent, valuable person who deserved respect" (66). But she believes that she is giving her child the worst possible start in life and has an "overwhelming sense of loneliness" (63). Her doctor talks to her mother, not to her; no one is with her during childbirth; and she is forbidden and afraid to see her baby.

Back in her mother's house, Moorman says "I was a mollusk. For me, the shell was everything" (83). Babysitting for a neighbor, she starts to wonder if she could have taken care of her own child after all. "It was the only moment when simple grief broke through my protective shell" (92). (This becomes a "great wall the size of China's" on page 96.) She fiddles with waist buttons on her sweater when a neighbor visits and can't smile when trying out for cheerleading. After tolerating Dan for a while, she breaks up with him.

Through college, a year off doing office work, a marriage to a man who thought her past didn't matter, a move to Seattle, a breakup, and a move to New York, it seems she can't get things right. She sees several therapists for years without telling them about the pregnancy and relinquishment, but the therapy in New York seems to work partly because she then gets a job "in the company of smart, funny, and talented people" (105).

In this milieu, Moorman meets and marries a compatible man, Harvey. She wants a child, though she is forty, and has a pregnancy she enjoys. Her daughter seems "considerate" (116) even before birth, and she has little conscious thought of the earlier loss. But when she has trouble leaving her daughter at nursery school, she faces the fact that this has something to do with her missing son.

She reverses her denial, first telling her story to her psychiatrist. Then she buys a whole shelf of books about adoption and begins trying to contact other birthmothers, through Concerned United Birthparents in Iowa, a search and support group in New York, and eventually Manhattan Birthmothers Group, which she finds the most helpful. She recognizes many of her own experiences in *The Other Mother* (Moorman 153). Meanwhile she tries several times to get more information about her son through her adoption agency and the hospital.

Eventually the agency gives her information, including the fact that he is in the military like his grandfather and at least temporarily his father. Belatedly, the agency sends her son a letter from her, and finally, he responds. He doesn't want to meet her now because he thinks it would cause his mother to worry, but she describes his letter as "generous, open, informative" and says that it would make a happy ending for a birthmother in a sentimental novel that was too good to be true (213). His letter writing style and details about where he studied and now lives all sound familiar. And she says of the picture he has sent, "He looks like me. He looks very much like me." Moorman is convinced that he has grown up as a "treasured child," now an "appreciative, affectionate son" (214). She is as euphoric as after her daughter's birth, and when that euphoria wears off, she seems able to put the past behind her and look forward to the present and future with gratitude.

Some readers and writers, such as Dusky, would not find this ending enough to be grateful for, as it provides no more hope for future contact than Thompson's. But Moorman now has a happy marriage, daughter, and writing career, and she has been reassured about her son's life experiences and character. Her acceptance of his concern about his mother's feelings is the culmination of her many strenuous attempts to see other people's points of view throughout the book—for example, she thinks so many stories are made up about birthparents' deaths because adoptive parents find it hard to believe that people give up children for any other reason and think it will reassure their children that they were not unwanted (Moorman 149).

By the end of the book, Moorman has become something of an activist for open records and other reforms. She summarizes: "I see my story as a plea for family planning, for reproductive responsibility. I agree with those who say that giving away a child is an act that carries consequences that are inescapable for most birth mothers" (209), and therefore, the standards for achieving "informed consent" to this act ought to be higher.[26]

She includes in her memoir much that she learns during her search. From answers to an ad she places, she learns that many birthmothers had experiences like hers of intense separation anxiety with children that they raised. She discovers that some found community in Florence Crittenton Homes and some were miserable there. She learns that she was one of the 70 percent of unwed white women who relinquished their children for adoption in the years between 1945 and 1965, while in Denmark 93 percent of such mothers raised their children themselves (46, quoting Isaac). *The Adoption Triangle* gives her for the first time the feeling that, in relation to adoption, she "was someone whose existence mattered" (131), and so she has a right to information from her adoption agency (which she calls Winnicott after the psychologist who was famous for studying the impact of separation on infant development).[27] She also feels pride as she reads Linda Cannon Burgess's *The Art of Adoption* and finds the "message of the importance of genetic heritage" (136).

Joining others interested in meeting after being separated by adoption is not always affirming for her, however. At meetings of support groups mostly attended by adoptees, she says, "It stopped me in my tracks to see how separately we members of the triad carried our individual sorrows and how blind we were to one another's pain" (155). She learns of adoptees' experiences of shame, humiliation, anxiety, and anger about rejection. But she also writes critically of some views. At the adoptee support group meeting, she begins "to feel that some of the complaints I was hearing were not caused by adoption" (156). On the other hand, she is saddened to discover the condescension and exploitative attitude toward birthmothers in Dorothy Kalins's article "The Baby Hunt" (167).[28] Still, she seems forgiving to Kalins, because "the problem was not of rehabilitation but enlightenment: Kalins had never heard a conflicting point of view."

Several times she writes about whether she might have been able to keep her child. What she did was a choice, she acknowledges, but she comes to see more and more the social pressures in the United States at that time and her own lack of knowledge about the consequences of what she was doing. She feels that more available safe abortion is an improvement. However, Moorman says, "I can't force myself to think that adoption is *always* a mistake. But neither do I believe *absolutely* that adoption is the right route, even for a young pregnant girl with no resources. In other words, I can never be absolutely sure that the choice I made was the right one" (73).

Moorman's ambivalent language here is a contrast to Dusky's statements in *hole in my heart*: "I could never think, Yes, I did the right thing" (160) and even, "Giving up my child was the worst thing that I ever did" (200). Their self-presentations contrast in other ways as well: Moorman begins by implicitly reassuring the reader that she is now a mother by anyone's definition, enjoying seeing the resemblances her four-year-old has to other people in her family, Dusky begins with a critique of terms such as *birth mother*, insisting "I am a mother" (1), and then a prologue in which she says she always wonders about whether there is enough likeness between a mother and a child she sees to assure her that the child is not adopted.

Through much of her narrative, Dusky emphasizes her determination and the obstacles that she had to face in the 1960s. She fights her working-class father to attend college. Upon graduation, she is hired by a newspaper in Rochester, two states away from her home and school, and feels vulnerable as the first woman in its features department. Journalism is a male-dominated field, and her friendship with its unhappily married local star Patrick soon becomes "a cocktail of equal parts ecstasy and misery" (Dusky 27)—a doubly significant image since she often mentions them meeting for drinks. She thinks no doctor would give her a prescription for the pill.

Patrick insists on sex without a condom, her period is late, and she takes a pregnancy test. Her doctor, one of many irresponsible professionals these memoirs show, tells her the result is negative and gives her a prescription for birth control pills.[29] He twice refuses to test her after very light periods, and when he finally does, he tells her, "You are four months pregnant" (Dusky 30) and literally and figuratively washes his hands. She goes to Puerto Rico for an abortion, but the doctor there says she is too far along.

In denial that could be compared to Moorman's, Dusky takes a leave of absence, saying her father is dying, doesn't tell her parents about the pregnancy or leave from work, and hides in her apartment, telling only a social worker and one local friend. She strongly protests when the social worker tells her that she can never meet her child as an adult, but there is seemingly no alternative. She has no information about childbirth, gives birth alone, remembers nothing but the pain, and chooses not to see her baby (premature, in an incubator) when she has the chance.

Afterward, she returns to journalism, in Albany, still reminded of her daughter whenever she sees the yellow flower forsythia or a little blonde girl with hair like hers. In 1972, when she has moved to New York, adoptees' searches and ALMA, led by Florence Fisher, hit the *New York Times*. Excited,

Dusky breaks her silence and goes public. For the magazine *Cosmopolitan* she interviews a woman about finding the mother who gave her away. She goes to ALMA meetings regularly (at this point birthmothers and adoptees were working together rather than in separate groups, as they will do in 1993 when Moorman tries ALMA) and testifies in court for open records. She tells her mother and brothers about her pregnancy and relinquishment for the first time and finds that they accept her lovingly.

She does not find the same openness with the adoption agency who placed her baby. And her urgency to get information from them increases when she learns of the adverse effects of the DES hormone on women to whose mothers it had been given while they were pregnant. She is concerned about the hormones in the birth control pills that she took during the first four months of her pregnancy.[30] She asks researchers, who agree that anyone with such prebirth exposure ought to get regular checkups. She tries to get the adoption agency to send this information to her daughter's adoptive parents; the agency claims they have, but she later finds this is a lie.

Now published in *Cosmopolitan, Parents, Town and Country*, the *New York Times*, and elsewhere, Dusky writes *Birthmark* (1979). It gets noticed, but most reviews oppose her position, with *Newsday* calling her "a fearful specter that threatens the integrity of families." However, *Publishers Weekly* glows: "A poignant, candid record [that] should amount to a convincing argument to change laws that prevent adoptees and natural parents from knowledge of each other's lives" (Dusky 95).

Two years later, Dusky meets "Mr. Right" (101), Tony, who understands her story immediately. With his encouragement, Dusky decides not to wait the three years until her daughter is eighteen, pays a searcher, and receives contact information. Jane's adoptive mother shocks Dusky by telling her the girl is learning disabled. Jane has epilepsy and seizures, and they had tried to get in touch with Dusky earlier; however, the adoption agency wouldn't cooperate. Although Dusky gave the agency much information about herself and Jane's father and their family history, the adoptive family received almost none of it.

Still, Dusky is happy to learn from Jane that she wants to be a journalist, an ambition that reinforces her belief in genetic similarity. Dusky flies to visit her that week and discovers that they look alike and have similar taste in clothes. The hard part is learning about Jane's health. From the age of five she has had frequent seizures, often requiring hospitalization. So she wouldn't hurt her head if she fell down, she wore a hockey helmet to school and was frequently teased about it. Stress gave her more seizures, and she sometimes faked seizures so she could stay home. Eventually she was put on Depakote, which slows down brain activity, impairs concentration, and makes her gums swell and bleed. This is why she seems learning disabled. Dusky has no proof, but she thinks that the birth control pills that she took might be the cause of the seizures, and information she learns later about the high amount of estrogen in such pills at that time reinforces her belief.

They visit each other several times, mostly happily, but soon Dusky discovers in herself another medical problem that she thinks Jane might have inherited. She has long had extreme emotional disturbance in the week before her period is due, and in doing research for an article, she finds a doctor who prescribes progesterone to patients with this symptom. She takes it, and it works. Later, when she sees violent emotions in Jane, she recommends progesterone, but Jane resents the suggestion.

Jane stays with her for extended periods of time during several summers, and for years, they keep in touch. But Jane often disappears suddenly. During one disappearance Jane has a child she plans to give up for adoption. Jane marries and has another child, Britt, with whom she shares her relationship with Dusky, but Jane's husband leaves when the child is two, and suddenly Jane attempts suicide.

Jane has enough good days to plan a big family wedding with another man, and the relationship with Dusky also continues, though unstably. Jane takes college courses to get a better job, but Depakote affects her concentration and the demands at work are too much for her. Depakote also causes suicide attempts, and one of them succeeds.

After the funeral and the mourning, Dusky seeks out and finds Jane's adopted-out daughter, Sarah, though their relationship does not last. More successfully, she continues her adoption reform activism, which gives her a worldwide network. After the traumas of her relationship with Jane, she ends the book with a summary of her blessings, which include her new enjoyment of traditionally feminine skills such as baking and sewing, and her relationship with the daughter of her now dead college boyfriend, who is involved in the adoptee search movement and who she thinks of as her "alternate universe daughter" (273).

Moorman and Dusky have very different personae, Moorman's more gentle and Dusky's more assertive. Moorman is satisfied with a letter as a happy ending, deferring to the needs of the adoptive mother, while Dusky pursues contact and relationship, maintaining her own rights. But both want to educate people about the long-lasting pain after relinquishing a child in adoption. Both write of not having enough preparation for their decision, and the books are intended partly to warn anyone considering doing the same thing about what the consequences might be. They want to refute stereotypes of birthparents, and to change state laws that make it harder for adoptees and their original parents to have information about each other and to meet if they want. Moorman and Dusky both stress the importance of knowing genetic heritage, including family medical history, and are frustrated that adoption agencies often make this difficult. They both write about the misunderstandings they encounter in talking about adoption with others, Moorman especially in defending Cara Schmidt, the birthmother in the much-discussed De Boer/Schmidt case of 1993, also considered by Waldron, and Dusky in discussing the reactions to *Birthmark* (91–97) and during her complicated relationship with Jane (199–201).

However, Dusky is more opposed to adoption as an institution and emphatic that it is often harmful to adoptees as well as to their original mothers. She weighs in more than most birthmother memoirists on issues debated by adoptees, such as the relative influence of nature and nurture and the issue of whether adoptees feel unwanted. She frames her narration of her daughter's instability with statistics suggesting adoptees are overrepresented in psychiatric treatment (163–64); she thinks that because so much of personality is genetic, this overrepresentation often occurs because these children "are so different from their parents that their parents have difficulty dealing with their idiosyncrasies" (149n), and furthermore "being given up for adoption . . . is one hell of a whack to many an ego" (165). Some researchers have found adoptees are disproportionately at risk for suicide attempts; she notes that according to statistics, her own daughter's risk of that kind was also heightened by epilepsy, hereditary PMS, and sexual abuse in her adoptive family.

Although Moorman has worried about her son, her contact with him at the end of her memoir gives her no reason to believe he is troubled in anything like the way Jane was. Still, early in her search for understanding, she is affected by adoptee rights activist Florence Fisher's words that her files are full of pain (17). When, later, she reads an article saying that adoption is "a psychological burden to the adoptee" (72), she comes closest to criticizing adoption as an institution: "if birth mothers carry a lifelong ache, and if adoptees are similarly afflicted, then for whom is this adoption business designed?" But less militant than Dusky, she poses her critique as a question.

Moorman presents her view as changing somewhat during the course of the research behind the book. Near the beginning of that research, critiquing a *New Yorker* editorial idealizing adoption, she is looking for acknowledgment that "adoptive parents and adopted children are capable of the same range of human behaviors and feelings, positive and negative, as biological parents and children" (16). At a later point she is startled by the pain expressed by adoptees at a meeting of ALMA; near the end, she writes that she knows there is a difference involved in adoptive parenting, but she doesn't know what it is or what it means (159). She even identifies with adoptive parents who are reluctant to let their children go, since she feels that way with the daughter she is raising (169). But she does not always so identify. One of the few times that she feels "horror" in recounting the words of an adoptive parent is when having a second child to adopt from the same parents is called a "miracle"

(161), ignoring the "nightmare" (162) that she thinks the birthparents must have experienced.

Both memoirists recount the history of sealed birth certificates, the demographic trends in adoption, and other background material. Dusky is able to draw on recent research about open adoption, which shows it can be a step forward if the openness is maintained but that it often is not. She surveys recent work explaining the frequent deception and corruption involved in the invocation of an orphan crisis and summarizes, "Children are transferred from the poor to the wealthy" (197). Gabrielle Glaser's reference to the "adoption-industrial complex" (118) would resonate with her. So would Gretchen Sisson's research and analysis, discussed later in this chapter.

Women from Conventional and Unconventional Families

Janet Ellerby's and Jan Waldron's experiences of pregnancy and relinquishment are close in time to those of Moorman and Dusky, but their memoirs contextualize more with their very different family histories than with the adoption reform movement. Ellerby's family, privileged Republicans, have a history of denial: before she was born, her uncle shot his children, wife, and himself, and they removed all the family pictures in which he appeared and hardly ever mentioned him. Waldron's family think of themselves as unconventional free spirits, and the women in her line have a history of giving away their children.

At the heart of Ellerby's book is a story of pregnancy, birth, and relinquishment much like Moorman's, and a story of meeting again and continued relationship, which is, however, very different from either Dusky's or Waldron's. Like Moorman she gets pregnant in high school, in her first sexual encounter. Like both Moorman and Dusky, she doesn't know much about either pregnancy or birth control, practices denial, doesn't see a doctor to check on pregnancy until it is too late, and then goes into hiding. Her hiding is even more elaborate than Dusky's or Moorman's—as her parents demand, she travels across the country from California to stay with her aunt and go to high school in a wealthy Cleveland suburb, and at a later stage to the Florence Crittenton Home in Akron. Meanwhile she writes her best friend lies about her life, and her family mails postcards from other locations to back up her deceptions (Schaefer recounts a similar pretense, 17). In a parallel to Moorman's "shell" image, she writes, "I had a secret life and a secret self that I painstakingly hid. On the outside, I had become a much better student because I could concentrate now with a ferocity that had escaped me before" (8). In the Home, she had no schoolwork, only a one-hour class about childbirth, and apparently no counseling, sex education, or encouragement of open discussion with the other girls.

Because her child is born earlier than expected, she is accompanied to the hospital only by a cruel on-call nurse and a kinder taxi driver. The doctor, a substitute, doesn't know she is not going to raise the baby, and Ellerby is able to see her, though not allowed to hold her. (Schaefer's doctor also congratulated her as if she were going to keep the baby.) The separation is like a tear, an implosion, a knife, and she feels she must construct a new split self and sign her rights away.

After leaving, while Ellerby is suffering and hiding her "truer, grieving self" (131), nevertheless she makes friends, enjoys traveling in Europe, frequently seeks a fresh start in a new location, and marries four times, hoping that having another baby will remove the pain of losing the first.[31] It never does.

Returning to school, Ellerby gets a degree in education, and one of her teachers encourages her to go to graduate school in English. During this time she sees a TV movie about a teenager searching for her birthmother and begins trying to contact her daughter but discovers the records are sealed, and she can't find the name of the adoption agency. While teaching grade school and raising three children alone, she gets her PhD and writes a dissertation entitled "Repetition and Redemption." She is "fascinated by first-person narrators who harbored secret traumas that could not be healed unless they could tell the story that would assuage their pain" (199). An editor considering publishing her manuscript recommends that she add an autobiographical introduction, and she is so reluctant to tell her story that she never contacts him again.

She is quickly hired at the University of North Carolina at Wilmington, far from every place she has previously lived. The job brings her tenure and also a colleague so insightful and kind that she eventually marries him in a much more stable and honest way than she had married the others.

Helped as Dusky and Moorman also are by good marriages, she finally finds the daughter she named Sorrow (after an out-of-wedlock child in Thomas Hardy's novel *Tess of the d'Urbervilles*) thirty-five years before. It takes a searcher found through a friend of one of her adult daughters. Ellerby writes to her, and Merideth, as she now is named, calls; they talk.

Merideth sounds kind and warm and glad to hear from Ellerby though she has never tried to find her. Ellerby is struck not only by how much they look alike but also about how similar Merideth's experience has been to those of the children Ellerby raised herself. Merideth's parents also divorced when she was young; she also lost touch with her father, had several siblings, moved to a different state with family nearby, knew money was tight and got summer jobs, and had childhood memories of vacations on beaches by oceans and lakes. All went to large universities; Merideth majored in journalism like another of Ellerby's daughters and liked gardening, as did Ellerby's mother and her son, Todd. She is reassured that Merideth "grew up in a family where she was greatly loved, where she fit in seamlessly" (239). This is very different from the way Dusky sees Jane's family, made most vivid by the fact that they all complain that Jane walks with a heavy step, the same way Dusky walks.

The current sadness in Merideth's life is that her much-loved and loving adoptive mother died three years previously. In a sense Ellerby is now filling some of that mother's place, as that mother filled in for her—she supports Meredith through a miscarriage. But she knows that they are "not mother and daughter. Not in the way she had been with Anne and I was with my daughters," not sisters, not "just a friendship"; "we would have to create a hybrid, something entirely new" (253–54). This is a contrast with Dusky's insistence that she is Jane's mother, and perhaps a sign that limited expectations help make this relationship easier, though with Jane's illnesses there is no way her relationship with Dusky could have been easy.[32]

Even more is resolved as Ellerby writes about Merideth to her own parents, now in their late eighties, and they respond that they always wondered about her and were never sure that they did the right thing. They are now glad to know their other grandchild and great grandchildren. And she is present when Merideth has a child who survives; this seems like flipping the coin of her own loss of Merideth in childbirth to "the other gleaming side" (287). Like Moorman, who compares the letter from her son to a novel ending too good to be true (213), she thinks of her visit to Merideth's home as "the kind of day a fiction writer might allow herself to create for the best possible ending" (Ellerby 255). But her many years' loss of Merideth still weigh on her. She still has insomnia and nightmares about fearing the loss of a child, and that is the note on which the book ends, rejecting the bias in life-writing toward a happy ending.[33]

However, in those last pages she also describes looking at natural beauty and remembering happy moments to escape the return of sadness, and overall the book's tone is not one of defeat. More explicitly than the other memoirists discussed in this chapter, Ellerby contextualizes her life with references to the change in America between the 1960s and the 2000s. She locates herself as the child of privileged parents whose fallibility she first realizes at Kennedy's assassination. Ellerby tells us when she first met people of color teaching in the Job Corps program, and she links her parents' cover-up of her pregnancy to their earlier denial of her murderous uncle's existence. After portraying many examples of generational conflict, she eventually notes that her parents have finally become more permissive. Shocked as they were about her potential overnights with a man during college, they are now quite willing for an unmarried grandchild to sleep in the same room as a partner on a visit to them.

There is a hint of a similar transition in parents also in Schaefer. While her mother had earlier told her that if she and her boyfriend Chris married and kept her child, they would have to move to another state or else her father would lose his job (Schaefer 102), after she finds that child as an adult and Chris also wants to meet him, her mother says that "she had always believed Chris and I would have made it if we had gotten married" (202).[34] Was it her understanding then or her memory now faulty? In all of these memoirs social changes toward openness in the late twentieth century permit people to voice views that they earlier could not, and an implicit and sometimes explicit message is that reasons for sealing records of birth out of wedlock no longer hold.[35]

Waldron's story is different from any of the others in many ways, though like Moorman and Ellerby she got pregnant in high school. The women in her family have a history of giving away their children. Her own parents are less conventional than parents of other birthmothers—her mother makes a point of getting her contraceptives, but is more disturbed and less available. Waldron feels that her pregnancy is an attempt to literally get her mother back to take care of her. It doesn't work. A teenager, she tries to raise her child for close to three weeks, but panics and gives her to one of her high school teachers and his wife, who have told her they were interested in adoption. So, unlike the others she knows where her child is and theoretically could get in touch. For a year she constantly fights the impulse to call and reclaim or see her; afterward, using an image that would appear in the title of Dusky's much later book, "the hole left by her absence lapsed into a tolerable ache that for years made the day ahead feel slightly restless, as if I had forgotten something" (86). She contacts Rebecca eleven years later, after she bears and is raising two other children. The adoptive parents are glad to see her and to relinquish some of their time with their daughter, but, as with Dusky, tensions arise; she thinks children need more structure than they do, and they never work out in conversation what Waldron's relationship with Rebecca would involve, nor do Waldron and Rebecca. "We were trying to come up with answers, but we barely knew the questions, so we fudged, fibbed, and tested" (132). The pain and confusion appear in even more detail in Rebecca's own memoir, *Surviving the White Gaze*, which is discussed in the third chapter.

As Rebecca's title suggests, Waldron's situation is from the beginning more fraught because her daughter is half African American by birth. She does not deal with this nearly as much as Rebecca will when telling her own story.[36] Waldron just sketches some problems. The adoptive parents had told her they were interested in an "ethnic child" (60), but they have never sought help in dealing with Rebecca's hair—she does. She sees that it is hard for Rebecca to grow up in an all-white town, with neighbors who considered her "a mystery, an exotic (as in not indigenous) puzzle" (185). She can see Rebecca's hunger "to know the biological family whose stories could teach the experience of moving in black skin in this world" (186–87).

Racial difference is certainly part of why Waldron's reintegration with her daughter is so much more difficult than Ellerby's. She is the only birthmother to write about a strong sense of physical difference from her child. But also important is that the reunion takes place when her daughter is only eleven and far from being able to control a child's inevitable feelings of hurt. Aware that Rebecca feels rejected, she critiques "survival fantasies" (157) in which adoption and relinquishment are painless. Furthermore, she believes that any conflict between the two of them becomes more painful because they do not have the memory of happy childhood times to mitigate it. Without the medical problems and sad ending of Dusky's Jane, and with, at least at the beginning, a better relationship with the adoptive parents, their relationship has some of the same roller-coaster quality. Rebecca also feels torn between her birthmother and her adoptive parents, expresses a lot of resentment, and sometimes withdraws for a while.

But they write a multitude of letters (for example, at least eight from August 1989 alone) about their feelings for each other, and are determined to work things out. The letters, many included in the memoir, show much heartache on both sides. Eventually Waldron for the first time apologizes to her daughter, who is now twenty-two.

It seems, in Waldron's telling, that they have reached an equilibrium. Waldron recounts amicable meetings with the mother who abandoned her around the time of her pregnancy as well as with her birth grandmother, and muses on motherhood and adoption. She writes that she and Rebecca will never have "an easy second-nature pull. . . . That kind of tie can be found between the women who stay and the children they keep—*in both adoptive and birthbound families*" (211). (Notice her greater respect than Dusky's for adoptive families.) Waldron, like Moorman, is ambivalent about adoption: she believes that it gave her daughter parents who loved her, though she mourns her own loss of their early years together. Just meeting again is not enough to heal the wounds of relinquishment, she knows from her own experience, but on the other hand, she and Rebecca are mother and daughter because, she writes, "above all else that is what we want; we have lived the alternative, and it is unbearable" (210). Rebecca provides the afterword for the book, writing, "We have created, through love and our struggle, a language for our relationship that was and continues to be desperately needed" (235). Although their story is different from the others in that Waldron had tried to raise Rebecca and always knew where she was, it is similar in that in all these stories relinquishment is more painful than anticipated. In a succeeding chapter, we will see that *Surviving the White Gaze* tells an even more painful story in which the reconciliation does not last.

Open Adoption: A Modern Solution?

In *God and Jetfire*, Amy Seek portrays an entirely different world from that of the memoirists who relinquished children in the 1960s, but like the others, she still cannot escape grief and regret. When she gets pregnant, in the year 2000, she is an architecture student in college (an even more unusual choice for a woman than the journalism that Dusky pursued). Initially her circumstances are easier than those of the others. She tells her mother she is pregnant early on. Legally, she could have an abortion, because of the *Roe v. Wade* decision, though her mother discourages it; she goes to an appointment in an abortion clinic but feels uncomfortable and leaves. Although she rejects her boyfriend's offer to marry her, he stays with her and helps. She has a sympathetic counselor at Catholic Social Services who tells her about open adoption, including the fact that adoptive parents can close it, though she does not warn Seek about the grief that she might feel even if they do not.

Seek chooses a childbirth educator, Nina, to be a midwife and helper during pregnancy as well as doula. In her world things have changed; neither single pregnancy nor adoption has stigma. She does not have to hide; rather, she tells people that she is "doing adoption" (60) and finds "mothers everywhere . . . emerging to advise" her (70) about physical issues of pregnancy.

Before learning she is pregnant, Seek has decided to break up with her boyfriend, Jevn, because she feels she can't be herself with him. Nevertheless, he is interested in a relationship with the child and collaborates with her in picking the best possible adoptive parents from the many who send her "Dear Birth Parent" letters. They meet several couples who have made the cut after answering most of her 111 questions, but there is one whose idealism resonates most strongly with hers. Graduate students in theology, they don't have a lot of money, and she is reassured that her goal for her child in the adoption is not financial security. They charm her by answers that, she writes, "rearranged my map entirely so compellingly elaborating an answer that it was rezoned in my own mind" (89), and when she drives up and the man holds up his arm in the air greeting her and indicating where to park, she sees this as an "honest gesture that split the sky and freed me from my own formless and uncertain desires" (95). In effect she falls in love with this couple and the daughter they have previously adopted. She feels that "open adoption [is] perfectly suited to the modern world and the kind of hybrid solution I was looking for" (26) and that because she admires Paula and Erik so much, "with the right couple, open adoption would be *easy*" (59), not like abandonment. She is in denial, but with more illusion of being in control than the other memoirists. Most of them feel like they don't have a choice. She feels that she does. But her emotions will soon become more complicated.

She and Nina get the hospital to agree to more than a page of instructions about the procedures they will use in childbirth, and though she has a long labor, apparently the procedures are followed. When the child is born and she holds, nurses, and looks at him, she finds him "the only person who did not make me doubt myself" (118). Her life is now a blur of "rest, darkness, love, and waking to find the best things in life are true."

Childbirth has given her new feelings. A seventy-two-hour waiting period is mandated in her state and she wants to be a mother for all of the hours, and even more. She feels, "I'd become another kind of creature, and for all I knew my child was some new and necessary subsistence. . . . I couldn't tell anyone this, that I was rethinking the whole plan" (125).[37] Erik and Paula come in the early days after birth, she lets them take Jonathan, as they have named him, overnight and even back to North Carolina before she finally signs, more than a week after the birth. She wants to feel the pain of separation all at once (131), but in fact it lingers.

Open adoption can mean many things, at its minimum involving a meeting between both sets of parents and their exchanging contact information. It can be followed by an agreement to occasional letters and photographs, by annual or more frequent meetings, or even by taking vacations together and lifelong kinship-like relations. Gretchen Sisson includes interviews with some birthmothers for whom adoptive parental openness turned out to be minimal, others for whom it was a serious commitment, at least for a few years.[38]

In the period covered by *God and Jetfire*, Seek and the adoptive parents are unusually compatible and close. It seems she has the best possible experience of open adoption, with adoptive parents she admires who are not threatened by her; she is able to see her son frequently and they all meet and visit her parents. She becomes part of their family, and they become part of hers.

But when she is with her son, Seek is conscious of censoring her gestures and language, so that she won't seem to be usurping the position of mother that she has yielded to Paula. Although she talks about much with Erik and Paula, this she can't discuss—a paradoxical lack of openness in an open adoption. The worst is when she hears that he cries a lot, which he never did with her, and this makes her think that he is broken. But the crying ends in a few months. What persists is the conflict about whether she is a mother or not. And regret. Seek more and more feels that "there wasn't really anything out there better than loving a child" (293–94).

Like most of the other memoirists, Seek describes joining a group of people affected by adoption. She goes on a retreat of birthmothers, mentioned at the beginning of this chapter. She can't contribute to the criticisms of men's behavior that the others share, but she joins in their "paradoxical idea of motherhood: we were the best kind of mother because we gave our children away" (172), their discomfort in talking about their experience with anyone and their feeling that they are hiding their "desires, [their] regrets, and [their] grief."

Seek as narrator is idealistic, passionate, eloquent, and imaginative. She thinks of sitting outside in the evening during pregnancy as giving her son memories of the sunset. She sounds like a complicated person to live with intimately because she shares with us so much of her ambivalence: Jevn cares for her needs during pregnancy and childbirth with more commitment than many spouses, though she has rejected his marriage proposal, but she complains both that he is not more interested in her pregnant body, before birth, and that he does not like her to walk around naked, afterward. When they have a drink after she attends a talk about his new book, she "feels sad that [they] could talk casually, as if the past had no presence" (265). Much as she admires Paula and Erik, she also feels that "recognizing their generosity undermined my own. I was still, every moment, every day, giving them my son" (266).

Soon she is filled with regret. Volunteering at a crisis pregnancy center, she wants to say about adoption both "don't" and "do it" (202). She is not one to present a clear activist message, though she does give details that relate to themes adoption reform activists emphasize. More money would have allowed her to keep Jonathan; in the postbirth time while she still has rights to him, she checks on the cost of the campus daycare center and finds it daunting. Neither the first crisis pregnancy center nor the women's center where she could have had an abortion gives her counseling; the counseling that she receives from Catholic Social Services fails to prepare her for how difficult open adoption will be.[39]

She writes, "The hardest thing about it was that it had been my decision" (187). She has the landscape architecture career she wanted, but she also wants to build a relationship with Jonathan that will feel spontaneous even if it is not authorized by official motherhood, and to connect him with her parents. At the beginning of the book, she tells us that she achieves the first, though it takes nine or ten years: at the end, the next year, she helps him go up in a glider with her terminally ill father.

Connections

Most of the memoirists who have met their surrendered children find it important to connect them with their own parents. Besides Seek, this is especially important for Ellerby and Schaefer—an opportunity to discover their parents' own feelings of regret and their changed attitudes. But it also happens with Dusky, who recounts going to Mass with her mother, husband, and daughter, and arranged for her daughter to stay overnight with them.

While Waldron's own parents virtually abandoned her as a teenager, she takes Rebecca to see her great-grandmother, decrepit in a nursing home. The most important family connection that she makes besides her own is between Rebecca and her other children.

All the memoirists have some comments on their children's similarity to themselves, something adoptee memoirists also note. Seek writes of "long, skinny fingers extending from short narrow palms. . . . Hard and fast evidence of his birth and our connection" (242). When Moorman hears of her son's membership in a special "commando" unit of ROTC, she thinks he must be like his father's side and nothing like her, but when he writes and sends his picture, her impression is very different. Ellerby emphasizes how similar her surrendered daughter's growing up has been to those of the children she raised herself as well as how similar their appearances are. When Waldron is a single parent and Rebecca is fifteen to seventeen, they have a few idyllic years of companionship and feeling similar: "her laugh was mine, her humor familiar, we both loved to dance" (145), though in the third chapter we will see that these were not so idyllic for Rebecca. With Dusky, it is physical similarity, journalistic ambitions, and personal style; uniquely emphasized here, similarity with the daughter accompanies sharp contrast with the adoptive family. She and Jane, for example, often spontaneously pick similar clothing—both like fedoras—but she feels that Ann resents the kind of clothing presents she sends.

All these memoirists are in what Nicole Pietsch calls "*an ambiguous, intermediate place* of motherhood and not-motherhood."[40] Katherine Sieger, like Seek writing as a birthmother in an open adoption, describes feeling "like an outcast in a space you believe you have a right to inhabit."[41] All the memoirists have to deal with the question of how to be a mother to a child they did not raise. Dusky maintains that she is a mother without any qualification to the word; the others generally accept the name of birthmother. Ellerby emphasizes that she and her daughter have a new kind of relationship, with some elements of mother and daughter but some of friendship or aunt and niece. Of course, she is happy when Merideth tells her son, "I got to have two real mommies" (255).

But for Seek, precisely because she does see her son as a child, the issue is more troubling. She writes, "I couldn't deny my motherhood, and I couldn't claim it honestly" (174), and she is helpless and trembling when as a three-year-old he says, "Amy, pretend I'm your baby" (213). She feels awkward about giving maternal advice to Jonathan, but at the time she is writing her book, when he is twelve, Seek has no hesitation in referring to him as "my son."

As Seek observes, there is a structural problem in the relationship between mothers of two kinds. Much as she admires Paula, for a long time she feels discomfort, tension, artificiality, self-censoring when with Jonathan in

Paula's presence. The women can talk about it to some extent, and she can empathize when Paula tells her that "because she'd seen the strength of my bond with Jonathan, her motherhood could never be simple" (178). She writes, "Whatever the animal complexity of what we'd done, ethically and intellectually, we were solidly on the same side." When she hears that Jonathan and his sister compete about which of them loves Amy, she writes, "It was funny to think of love that way, as if one person's love could inch over and threaten someone else's . . . the very conception of love we had to overcome" (214).

Moorman feels love for her son's adoptive parents and gives up her quest to meet him, after seeing a letter in which they describe him and his younger sister as "considerate and interesting people . . . nice people" (203). Ellerby has no desire to compete with Merideth's memory of the mother who gave her unlimited "support, love, and encouragement" (242).

However, Dusky, with such a troubled daughter, deals with a live and present adoptive mother and has much more difficulty. The relationship begins well, when that mother, Ann, is glad to hear from her, and Dusky feels relief that her daughter has loving parents. But at the reunion, she has an experience similar to Seek's, of having to restrain her affectionate gestures, and so does her daughter: "I am watching myself holding her, hugging her, but not so long that her father will think it inappropriate . . . she would tell me that she had choreographed her reactions to me so she wouldn't hurt her father's feelings, or her mother's, who would certainly get a detailed report" (122). When she first meets Ann, she feels she is being "inspected like a side of beef" (123). Still, the two bond to some extent over anger at the agency's failure to pass on Dusky's medical information, Ann tells Dusky that Jane wanted to find her, and, by the end of the weekend, Ann gives Dusky a big hug.

But as time goes by, visiting them or communicating with them from afar, she repeatedly feels judged as an outsider. Theirs is the most vivid case in these birthmother memoirs, and perhaps in all the memoirs discussed in this book, of "adversarial motherhood."[42] It seems they come together only at the big ritual occasions of Jane's marriage and death.

Moorman, while writing her memoir, places an ad to survey birthmothers on "how relinquishing a child affected their parenting of subsequent children" (173), and she finds that, of the dozen who answered, only two were at peace with their decision, and they both had lives "permeated by religious faith," one Sufi, one Christian (176–77). Some spirituality or religious ritual is important in each of the memoirs, though it does not permeate them. The memoirists generally have negative memories of the role of religion in shaming them or controlling their sexuality, but that is not the last word. Moorman ends her memoir, in the aftermath of the letter from her son, by saying, "The prayer of thanks that I have wanted to say for years. Thank you, God, for all your blessings. Thank you for the daughter. Thank you for the son"

(214). Seek is baptized when her son is six months old, though she says the only thing she is certain of about God is that she thinks of Him all the time.

Schaefer has replaced Christian religion with an interest in Jungian, Taoist, and other spiritualities based in mysticism and reincarnation, but she still believes in the power of the Blessed Mother. The usually nonreligious Dusky, when she takes Jane to meet her mother, goes to Mass with her family at her old parish and finds that her "heart repeats: *Thank you God.* Thank you for giving me my daughter" (137). Later, after Jane is dead and she finds unexpected rapport with her college boyfriend's daughter, she writes of letting in "mystical convergences" (263).

While some adoptees' memoirs also end with gratitude and something that could be described as a ritual, there is more explicit religious language in these than in most of the adoptees' memoirs that I have read. Possibly it is because the birthmothers are older, brought up in a more religious time, but possibly it is a counterbalance to, relief from, the guilt or shame or exclusion that these writers feel from parental and/or social/church reactions to their pregnancy and from their broken relationship with their child. That break was overwhelmingly pressured rather than a free choice (in Seek's case, the pressure came mainly from the demands of her program as an architecture student) but several, even Dusky, seem to rejoice in somewhat religious terms in their restored relation. Ellerby, who stopped going to church when a couple driving her from Sunday services to the Florence Crittenton Home were cold to her, implies some irony when she associates her daughter's meeting her family with the "reconciliation of all penitents" on Maundy Thursday (272) as well as with Easter and when, in describing their celebration of Thanksgiving with her own parents, she alludes to the parable of the Prodigal Son: "we did not slay a fatted calf, but we celebrated Merideth's homecoming in no less a ceremonial matter" (279). Close to the end, however, she writes of her presence at the birth of Merideth's son, "I do not believe that there is a god who hears my particular prayers and decides whether to intervene or not. But I do believe in the sacredness of people and am deeply aware of intricate and holy mysteries, patterns in which I have played a small part" (287). For whatever reason, Waldron, with the least religious background, is the only one who, making her own ritual, describes the scene when she "first told Rebecca [she] was sorry": "I looked at my grown-up girl and wanted to tell her for the first time how much I hurt for her. Like a case of violent hiccups, the spoken words triggered an unstoppable rush of 'I'm sorrys.' . . . My daughter, silent, wet-eyed, placed her hand on a rueful mother's arm, and said, 'I know'" (197). While there are still conflicts afterward, Waldron writes, that then they "began to know each other for the first time" and she felt she could grieve Rebecca's pain without knowing whether relinquishing her was the wrong choice. (In the third chapter, we see how large the conflicts afterward remain.)

Dusky, on the other hand, who knows relinquishment was the wrong choice but could not imagine facing her parents, let alone supporting herself, as a single parent, feels rejected when she calls her daughter to apologize after they have been in touch for years, and after an hour of conversation, there is no follow-up. Just two paragraphs later, she describes going to a Christmas Mass with her husband's relatives and feeling the absence of peace in her heart as she makes the ritual handshake of peace to her neighbors. An exact contrast with the earlier Mass with her family.

Moorman, Dusky, Ellerby, and Waldron all felt at the time that, given parental shame or absence, unavailability of abortion when they discovered or acknowledged that they were pregnant, and the impossibility of marriage, they had no choice except relinquishment, though later most of them look back on it as a choice. Seek, by contrast, with *Roe v. Wade* in force, is conscious of making a choice for open adoption and thinks that it will solve her dilemma. But for all these memoirists (Thompson's difference here is one reason why her book seems somewhat fictionalized) relinquishing a child is painful in itself and has long-lasting and unanticipated painful consequences. None of the memoirists receives adequate counseling. These memoirs are, as Florence Fisher describes her files to Moorman, full of pain. The pain is made worse, for all but Seek and Waldron, by the lack of cooperation of adoption agencies and, for all but Seek, by the erasure or secrecy of original birth records. Legislators who keep the records closed insist that they are protecting birthmothers, but these birthmothers certainly did not want their identity to be perpetually hidden from their children.[43] As Dusky and Waldron write most explicitly and some of the others suggest occasionally, there are many things wrong with our system of adoption. It is thought of much too easily as a panacea. Waldron writes, "We dance around the reality of adoption as if we were dodging hot coals or thunderbolts, dedicated to constructing fables in order to tolerate the searing complexities" (224). Sisson's conclusion years later, after interviewing many birthmothers, is "adoption transfers babies from those with less social privilege to those with more" (*Relinquished* 215).

But these books are not only stories of pain. They are stories of purpose. Margaret Homans discusses the difficulty birthmothers have in fitting their stories into the traditional narratives of epic quests (276–77, 283). In one sense, Moorman's is the most traditional because it ends when she makes contact with the son she is seeking, but as Homans points out, the movement in her story has been halting and sporadic, not typically epic. However, I would argue that these memoirs are all stories of women on quests that are indeed brave and heroic, though innovative rather than traditional. Their quests are not just to find their lost children but also to build a relationship with them, if possible, and in either case, to build a life that comes to terms with past losses but still savors the present and its possibilities.

Are these women unusual? They have enough talent, persistence, and connections to get a book published, and they have a story they yearn to tell. And they are gripping storytellers. Are their stories representative? In the next two chapters, memoirists Lori Jakiela, Florence Fisher, and Betty Jean Lifton and film narrator Avery Klein-Cloud tell of birthmothers who either didn't want to meet at all or were in contact only reluctantly. In her edited collection *Adoption and Mothering*, Frances Latchford points to a significant minority of birthmothers who "did [not] or do not understand their relinquishments to be coerced" (78).[44] But Emily Hipchen, Sarah Saffian, Jeanette Winterson, Jaiya John, Jane Jeong Trenka, and Deann Borshay Liem, at least, find mothers with stories of loss and longing similar to those told in this chapter. Many researchers have concluded that such feelings are much more common than rejection of their returning adult children.

Ann Fessler found that many, like our memoirists, frequently wondered about their children, and when they knew that their children were adults, put their names in a reunion registry if they knew about it. Some sought them out, and some were found, and Fessler writes that, of those who have been reunited, "most all expressed great relief at knowing their child. They felt the reunion was the beginning of their healing process" (247).[45] It could be argued that those willing to be interviewed by Fessler were those more open to reunion, since they were willing to talk with her. Nevertheless, statistics from various sources, including contact preference forms submitted in states where original birth certificates may become available to adoptees, also indicate that the vast majority of birthparents, between 93 percent and 99 percent, are open to contact.[46]

When given a chance to redact their names in states that opened original birth certificates to adult adoptees, only 0.5 percent of mothers who had relinquished their children, one out of every two thousand, chose to keep their anonymity (Glaser 326).

Margaret Homans and Janet Ellerby have recently examined some fictional representations of birthmothers and have found them mostly bound up in stereotypes or traditions of silence and punishment. However, one documented case of an artist learning from birthmothers is Rodrigo Garcia's film *Mother and Child*, discussed by Ellerby in her book *Embroidering the Scarlet A*. Karen, in this film, is still haunted by the loss of her child thirty-seven years previously, and she has developed a protective distance from people somewhat like the "shell" that both Ellerby and Moorman discuss. Like them, she eventually develops a relationship with a man with whom she can be honest, and this helps her search for her adopted-away daughter. Because the adoption agency disastrously misfiles her letter with medical information (something not so far from the obstacles many of these memoirists find in communicating with agencies), her daughter dies in childbirth, but like Dusky, she finds consolation in a surviving granddaughter. Ellerby quotes from Sarah Burns the information that in making the movie Garcia drew on "memoirs and stories about young unmarried women who were forced to relinquish their children."[47]

These memoirs, Fessler's book, Sisson's research, and other sources, show that birthmothers have repeatedly been pressured, deceived, denied important information, mistreated, and indeed corruptly exploited by crisis pregnancy centers, maternity homes, orphanages, adoption agencies, and medical personnel. And these are white American middle-class women.[48] The treatment of poor women and women of color, whose children have been too often been inequitably removed by Child Protective Services in the United States or trafficked or kidnapped or threatened by draconian family limitation policies in other countries, has been even worse.[49] Such women have rarely if ever had the leisure, education or connections to write and publish a memoir, though sometimes others have told their stories, as Kay Ann Johnson and Xinran have done for birthmothers of China.[50] In the chapter on adoptive parents' memoirs, we will see that none is able to tell much of the story of their child's first parents, though a few try hard to imagine it.

However, for white American women, even though the experiences of Waldron and Seek show that an open adoption still has serious difficulties, the fact that an open adoption such as Seek's is increasingly possible is a step forward.[51] Kate Livingston, herself having arranged such an adoption, has articulated a philosophical basis for seeing birthparents in an open adoption as part of the family, providing a context of origins so the child can have "multiple sources of family identity" as well as remaining involved even though secondary to the adoptive parents.[52] She draws on the formulation of political theorist Mary Lyndon Shanley that "the identity of the child is constructed neither exclusively by the original family nor exclusively by the adoptive family, but by the child's knowledge of or contact with both of these families."[53] This formulation of identity is close to what we see in most of the adopted memoirists discussed in the next two chapters, who as adults have moved from closed to open adoption. Still, just as we will see some adult adoptees finding their relationships with birthparents difficult to maintain, many birthmothers who were happy in open adoptions for a few years find them less open and less satisfying as time goes by (*Relinquished* 180–81)—even, as Sisson quotes Livingston from an interview, "profoundly . . . disempowering" (234).

2

Same-Race Identities

Seeking Ancestry, Exploring Relationships

*Jean Paton, Florence Fisher, Betty Jean Lifton, Sarah Saffian,
Jean Strauss, A. M. Homes, Emily Hipchen, Craig Hickman,
Elyse Schein, Paula Bernstein, Jeanette Winterson, Jeremy Harding,
Lori Jakiela*

What is it like to be an adopted child, teenager, adult? Until the last quarter of the twentieth century, very few adoptees wrote about their lives. Psychologists, adoptive parents, and social workers gave their views. Novelists and playwrights imagined the experience. A few of them were adoptees who turned it into fiction. But firsthand reports were rare. Jean Paton, the earliest adoptee writer I discuss, quite accurately had a strong sense of how unprecedented was her attempt to collect them and place her own experience among them. While the situation is different today, nevertheless conference and media panels discussing adoption often are made up of adoptive parents and professionals only. Important voices are missing, not only those of adoptees, but also those of birthparents. The current picture leaves too much out.

As with birthmothers, there are oversimplified public images of adoptees. Considering their usual legal position in a closed adoption, they might be seen as "innocents who must be protected from being found" or on the other hand "ingrates willing to torment their adoptive mothers and fathers" by searching.[1] In some communities, they are called lucky; in others, they are stigmatized.

But adoptees' memoirs vary more than birthmothers' memoirs in the emotions they reveal and the self-images that they have. Paton believed there was a special kind of discomfort shared by adopted people. Some of the memoirists quoted in this chapter have a similar feeling, but a few make a point of saying that they did not experience it. Considering details in these memoirs and those in the next chapter, we often find other experiences besides relinquishment and adoption that would contribute to a sense of instability as well as evidence of prejudice against some in their early environment. Whether adoptees are always wounded, as Nancy Verrier has argued in *The Primal Wound*, seems an open question, unless we invalidate some memoirists' reports of their own experience.[2] Still, almost every adoptee who writes a memoir, at some point, or perhaps many points, expresses a sense of injustice, at least about being denied information relevant to their own history, perhaps by their parents but most often by adoption agencies, orphanages, or state laws. In addition, many of these writers, like the birthmothers whose memoirs we have discussed, experience negligence or bad judgment by professionals involved with adoption. *Identical Strangers* is coauthored by twins separated as part of an experiment dealing with the influence of environment on a genetic tendency to mental illness. Another adoptee, Homes, is given to a mother clinically depressed because of the death of her son. A social worker who places a child with the violently punitive and repressive Wintersons later refers to them simply as "not what one would call modern."[3]

Searches and New Relationships

The first memoirs by adoptees helped create a movement criticizing adoption practices and eventually opened up possibilities for change. These memoirs stress what the authors think adoptees have in common—a practice like that of the early texts of many social movements, such as feminism or civil rights. Similarities frequently mentioned by early adoptee memoirists include fear that there is something wrong with them, feeling different from their adoptive parents, and curiosity about their birthparents. The first three U.S. adoptees to write book-length memoirs, Jean Paton, Florence Fisher, and Betty Jean Lifton, stress these emotions. They also include parts of other adoptees' stories and references to literary adoptees, all contributing to the idea of similarity of experience. None of the adoptive parents, in these earlier memoirs, wants to talk about adoption or help them search; their adoption is a carefully kept secret, something that would have been impossible if it had been transracial. If adoptees meet their birthmothers, the meeting makes a big change in their lives, but the most likely problem is the birthmother's continuing desire for secrecy.

As in other social movements, differences in experience emerge later. Some adoptee memoirists come from families more open about adoption. Several feel very similar to their adoptive parents. Some discover many other problems in their relationship with birthparents besides (or instead of) the desire for secrecy. In a few memoirs, birth family members, at least initially, are more active seekers than the adoptee. And while the first published adoptee memoirists were all white, adoptees of color are now writing memoirs about more complex experiences. Most of them are discussed in the next chapter, but this one considers a memoir by Craig Hickman, an African American man.

Jean Paton's *Orphan Voyage* (1968) might be called the first adoption memoir published in the United States, though only a small portion of the book is a traditional memoir about her individual experience. Paton stresses from the beginning that adopted people have not written or spoken publicly as adoptees. She writes, "No one else has ever really understood what being adopted had meant to them, or even attempted to find out."[4] Before writing her own story she published *The Adopted Break Silence*, a collection of adoptees' answers to a questionnaire she had sent those who responded to a personal ad she placed in the *Saturday Review* in 1953 (the closest thing to an internet search then possible). In *Orphan Voyage* she surrounds her narration of her own search with the results of her interviews with adopted people in her home state of Michigan. She locates her birthmother's sister, visits her after much preparation, and finds her welcoming. "You are Emma's girl, aren't you?" her aunt asks, assuring her that "[her] mother would very much want to see [her]" (86). They meet the next day, her mother tearful, and their relationship develops stability over time, with her photo displayed in her mother's house so friends can see it. Of the difference in her own life after meeting her birthmother for the first time, she writes, "All I now had to do was to learn to live without inhibited curiosity and an imagined mother" (121). A friend says, "You've changed! You never used to laugh at yourself."

Paton was adopted at five months of age, sent to a foster home two years later when her first adoptive father died of liver cancer, and, after about eight months, was adopted a second time by a more lasting home. She first discovered that she was adopted from the taunt of a neighbor girl at twelve. Though she was bright and an omnivorous reader, because of her emotional conflicts she took eight years to graduate from college.[5] These details are not in her memoir, which essentially begins when, as a social worker in her midforties, she decides to research the lifelong impact of adoption. *Orphan Voyage* developed out of the newsletters that she sent to many adoptees with whom she was in regular contact, who, like her, wanted to be part of a community. Thus, in the late 1950s some adopted people in the United States had their own national network for the first time. After Paton describes her own reunion, she discusses the experiences of other adoptees and meditates on their philosophical and even theological issues.

In *Orphan Voyage*, she speaks of the condition of adopted persons as uprootedness and exile. She writes that when an adopted person realizes what adoption means and "is barred from contact with his natural parents . . . he will be variously afraid; his fear will sometimes be transformed into a protective rigidity, and sometimes will combine with the frustration of the situation to provoke a condition of resentment" (107–8). She feels that one of the sad results of the bar to meeting between adopted people and their "natural parents" is that this prohibition prevents forgiveness.

Orphan Voyage was written in the 1950s and circulated in mimeographed form for years until its publication in 1968 with an epilogue. Thus Paton, born in 1907, does not show the influence of social changes, especially with regard to sexual behavior, that in the previous chapter several birthmother memoirists observed, writing in the late twentieth century or the twenty-first. She believes that illegitimacy is and ought to be a source of revulsion (29) and that it always will be. The word *birthmother* had not yet been invented; instead, she writes often of "natural parents" and "natural mothers" or often simply refers to them as mother or father. Skeptical about adoption, she uses the term *orphan* to describe herself and other adoptees. It is surprising to find her writing of the "vengeance which young adopted people feel toward their natural parents" (88). Few if any other memoirists recount such feelings toward unknown kin.

Florence Fisher's *The Search for Anna Fisher* (1973) is a more conventional memoir in its focus on the memoirist, but she too cites other adoptees' experiences as important frames for her own. Like Paton, though almost twenty years later, she placed a personal ad in a newspaper seeking contact with other adoptees.[6] She quotes some of the many letters adoptees sent her after she placed that ad. And each of her chapters has as an epigraph a quotation from an anonymous adoptee whose situation is similar to hers, at best curious and at worst feeling exiled.

The feeling that "some dark secret surrounded her birth" (Fisher 24) strikes her when the kindergarten registrar asks to see her birth certificate and her mother orders her out of the room. Two years later she finds a Photostat with her parents' names and the name "Anna Fisher." She becomes obsessed with looking for similarities to herself in family photographs. Meanwhile her unhappily married mother tries to keep little Florence from having friends, to the point of attempting suicide—and later attacks fourteen-year-old Florence with a coat hanger to keep her from an all-girl overnight.

She marries to get away from her family, is frightened thinking about what unknown genetic traits her child might inherit, and then is delighted that he looks just like her. Finally she gets her mother to a psychiatrist, who prescribes shock treatment. The treatment calms her mother, but just when they finally have a good, close relationship, her mother loses her power of movement. After six weeks in the hospital, her mother dies of a brain tumor.

A cousin-in-law confirms Florence's fear that she was adopted. Her father, other relatives, the doctor who delivered her, the hospital where she was born, and the lawyer who drew up the adoption agreement all refuse to give her information, but the Bureau of Vital Statistics supplies her birthparents' names and occupations, with an address in Brooklyn. (She discovers that her birthmother's name is also Florence, and so she concludes that in giving her that name, according to Orthodox Jewish tradition, her adoptive mother has declared her birthmother dead.) She goes, in vain, to every apartment at that address for information, and then makes hundreds of phone calls to people named Fisher or Cohen (the other parental name on her birth certificate). She tries the courts and learns about the law sealing adoption records. Constantly she is told that her curiosity is not justified. She persists, feeling that the knowledge is her right. Eventually someone at the hospital gives her her grandparents' names when she says her mother is trying to locate them. She tries the Cohens and Fishers in the microfilms of old New York telephone directories, gets help from the lawyer of the now dead obstetrician who delivered her, and learns about all the public records available in the New York Public Library.

After seeing her mother's birth certificate, parents' marriage certificate, grandparents' death certificates, and mother's phone number (learned from the old-age home mentioned on her grandmother's death certificate), Fisher (the family name she takes) has a long and warm phone conversation with her birthmother under the pretense of being a cousin. They arrange to meet, and she says, "I have never known nor will I ever feel again a wave of happiness such as I did the moment I first saw my mother" (201). But confronted with the documents, her mother says three times, "I'm not the person you're looking for," asks about her life, and flees but also drops her wallet, an act Fisher sees as a sign of ambivalence (208). After Fisher sends the wallet, a letter, and a diary of her search back by personal messenger, they meet once more and talk for three hours, discovering many similarities, with a reconciliation that makes Fisher feel "inside me, that great void was filled. . . . The evening had been like looking in a mirror—and seeing a reflection for the first time" (223–24).

Months later her mother calls her, and many more phone calls and a long lunch follow. But a public controversy about a contentious adoption has broken out in the interim—the case of Baby Lenore, whose original mother changes her mind when the child has been with another family for five days. Fisher has now read more about adoption (including *Orphan Voyage*), has started trying to influence legislators to open closed adoption records and has been interviewed at length in print. She has received thousands of responses, mostly supportive but some hostile, and has started an organization, Adoptees' Liberty Movement Association, which some birthmothers discussed in the previous chapter joined. When she is about to appear on television, her mother, still keeping their connection a secret, wants Fisher to use a pseudonym, but she can't relinquish her hard-won name or her leadership of the community forming around her. Adoption began as a personal issue that she thought of only in response to her own missing connections and history—now, seeing that it is an issue for many other people, she gives up a personal relationship with her mother that would demand that she hide.

But there is more personal happiness in searching for her after all. By contrast to the resistance she encountered in looking for her mother, she finds that a funeral director in her father's town in New Jersey is willing to call its twenty-one Fishers and place an ad for her. Very soon she is having a three-hour phone conversation with her father, who says, "This is the most wonderful moment of my life!" (Fisher 256). She visits him in California, where he gives a loving parental welcome, trying to make up for all that she had missed as a child, even Disneyland.

Like Paton, Lifton, and many of the other adoptees and birthparents who write memoirs, Fisher protests against the professionals who deny her information. Through ALMA, she starts a registry through which adoptees and birthparents can escape legal barriers and contact each other.[7] Wayne Carp and Jill Deans have seen Fisher as having a rights-based approach in her search for her parents and history rather than a need-based approach, and it is true that she, as part of ALMA, filed a suit for open records based on constitutional rights and argues during the memoir that it is her right to know her history.[8] But Fisher often writes about *wanting, needing* connections. When she finds a "huge hole" instead of the building on the address on her mother's marriage certificate, and says, "This time I really had gone back to my roots" (161–62), this follows up her earlier reference to "great emptiness" (67) that she thinks might be filled if the doctor who delivered her would answer her questions and anticipates her later feeling that talking with her mother has filled the "great void" inside her. In the prologue to her book, she quotes the statement of the American Academy of Pediatrics Council on Child Health that "the adopted child retains the need for seeking his ancestry for a long time" (14).[9] Feeling that she needs to know her roots (17, 89) to know herself, she writes of having "an emptiness, a longing in [her] heart that only they [her natural parents] could fill" (90). This is a counterpart to the image of a "hole in my heart" in Dusky's later book.

Adoptees in the Memoir Boom

Since Paton and Fisher published their books, memoirs have become more popular than ever. Many other adoptees' memoirs narrate meeting one or both of their birthparents. Barbara Melosh writes in her 2002 book *Strangers and Kin* that most memoirs by adoptees "affirm the credo of the search movement: reunion heals the losses of the past" (249), "drop the curtain soon after reunion, and seldom venture onto the territory of bad reunions" (252). The only memoirs she describes as stories of bad reunions are by men she identifies as "at the margins of the search movement" (253), and Melosh argues that adoptees' memoirs, especially those of female adoptees under the influence of that movement, have marked what happens after the initial meeting as "unsaid and unspeakable" (253). Though newspaper articles, folklore, and classical comedies also find convenient endings in reunions, Melosh misses both that the early memoirs—those of Paton, Fisher, and, as we will see, Betty Jean Lifton and to some degree Jean Strauss—to a large extent *construct* the movement and that many memoirs *do* continue after reunion (often showing that reunion is not enough in itself to heal wounds) or, like Fisher's, show one newly found relationship that fails and another that promises to continue. The main early exception is *An Adopted Woman*, by Katrina Maxtone-Graham (1983), which gives a blow-by-blow account of all the rejections the author received in her search until her final victory and then apparently idyllic relationship with her birthmother.[10]

Twice Born (1975), Betty Jean Lifton's memoir, the most influential for the movement, extends well past reunion and explores the difficulties of her relationship with her birthmother. Emily Hipchen and Jill Deans, just a year later than Melosh, declare, "adoption life writing . . . often builds toward disappointment."[11] Looking at *Twice Born* along with more recent memoirs by adopted people, I find a complicated picture, in which reunion, though important, is not enough. Rather than memoirs of search and reunion, these are mostly memoirs of search, meeting, and aftermath. There are many other similarities among these books, and even in some areas of apparent contrasts, resemblances appear beneath the surface. Later in this chapter, I discuss search memoirs by two other adoptees, Lori Jakiela, who never meets a birthparent except in that her birthmother sends her mostly hostile emails, and Jeremy Harding, who ends his memoir shortly after one meeting; both focus more than the other ten memoirs by same-race adoptees here on their relationships with their adoptive parents.

Lifton's *Twice Born* discusses how being adopted affected her early life, adolescence, and young womanhood as well as the circumstances that led her to search for her parents.[12] Her birthmother is willing to talk to her on the phone but keeps their relationship secret; by the time she looks for her birthfather, he is dead, but she learns more about him from relatives and his friends. While telling this story Lifton provides historical, literary, psychological, and cross-cultural perspectives on adoption. This book is the best-selling adoption memoir ever in the United States, and in 2006, the third edition was released in paperback. Previously, Lifton had written children's books, two about folk-tale animals and one about Hiroshima survivors; four of her later books are also about adoption (two of them for children).

The other memoirs of growing up adopted and meetings with birthparents I discuss here were all published at least twenty years later than *Twice*

Born's first publication and tell stories that are very different in some ways. In Sarah Saffian's *Ithaka* (1998), birthparents are the seekers. Saffian's adoptive mother died when she was six years old. Her father soon remarried. The family seems very stable when, at twenty-three, she is contacted by her birthparents, who have married and had other children. Saffian is not ready for a face-to-face meeting; they exchange letters over several years, but eventually, they do meet and continue their relationship. *Ithaka* includes the birthparents' letters as well as Saffian's and also her narrative of her struggle to come to terms with this new family, thus giving us two sides of the story.

Jean Strauss's *Beneath a Tall Tree* (2001), like all these except Saffian's, emphasizes the search for information. The book begins with her relinquishment for adoption and then narrates memories of her childhood, including her father's death, and later, her mother's, as well as her own marriage and children.[13] Its basic structure, however, is her quest to draw a family tree, which becomes more and more inclusive as the book proceeds and Strauss finds her birthmother and then her birthmother's birthmother. Eventually she includes her adoptive family as well. A previous book by Strauss, *Birthright*, tells something about her search and reunion as part of a guide for others.

Emily Hipchen's *Coming Apart Together* (2005) emphasizes the difficulty of knowing the truth about the past. Raised in a troubled adoptive family and always suffering from stress-related vomiting, Hipchen tells how an extreme incident motivated her to sign up with the state adoption registry for medical information, hoping that she could use this for more purposes.[14] Her birthparents, who have married and had other children, contact her, and they meet. Much of this book recounts her attempts to find out about their lives before her, and to imagine their stories from the details she is told. One of the most important themes is how the love that she finds in the father she did not know earlier contrasts with her experience of the tyrannical and violent father she grew up with.

Craig Hickman's *Fumbling toward Divinity: The Adoption Scriptures* (2005) is unusual in many ways. Black authors such as Maya Angelou have written about being raised by grandparents, but Hickman was formally adopted by unrelated Black people. Mostly, he writes of himself in the third person, except in the letters to family members he includes, and in poems, and in one early reconstruction of his thoughts after he meets his birthmother. Appendices include not only the records of his relinquishment, his time in foster care, and the deaths of Black gay men important to him (mostly from AIDS) but also poems to his (adoptive) parents, one, identified as "a song of adolescence," that recall beatings and complaints from his father and words that are "piercing, sharp needles" (363) from his mother.[15]

When he meets his birthmother, he wails "three decades and three years of tears" (55). She, his birthfather, and other relatives welcome him, and she visits him and his husband and stays for months. Eventually, he tells her off for being homophobic, dishonest, rigid, and controlling. After a year without contact, he sees her and most of his birth family at the wedding of his favorite uncle's daughter and pointedly does not invite her to visit. Most of the memoir is set in a world of Black people, except for his white Dutch husband and an apparently integrated group of gay friends, and explicit racism occurs mainly in his memories of not belonging, being accused of plagiarism at Harvard, and the hostility of boys in a car with a Confederate flag decal while he was traveling in Wyoming. The danger that Hickman writes about most often, within his own family and occasionally from strangers, is homophobia, since he is sexually active with other boys and, later, men, from an early age. Trying to explain himself, he writes to one of his birth sisters, "Imagine believing that who you are, your very essence, is the result of evil" (277). In context this applies to both gayness and illegitimacy, since several in her family believe the first is punishment to his mother for the second.

A. M. Homes begins her memoir, *The Mistress's Daughter* (2007), with the night when her parents tell her that her birthmother is interested in contact, just at the point when she, already a critically acclaimed novelist, is about to publish a novel about an adoptee whose psychiatrist is a birthmother, *In the Country of Mothers* (1993). Homes has many phone conversations with her birthmother, eventually meets her, and finds her very difficult.[16] She also meets her even more difficult birthfather, who insists on a DNA test, meets her only in hotel lobbies, and asks her to call him only in his car. After her birthmother dies, she regrets her earlier lack of sympathy for the troubled woman. She becomes obsessed with tracing her birth genealogy on both sides, and eventually with her adoptive genealogy as well. She attempts to join the DAR since her birthfather's ancestry should justify her claim, but he won't provide her with an acknowledgment or test results to prove it. One chapter imagines the questions she would ask him in a deposition and outs him, using both his name and his photograph. The book ends with memories of her beloved adoptive grandmother, recently dead at ninety-nine, and her triumph of having given birth, as a single woman of forty-one, to a daughter in whom she sees many resemblances to her grandmother.

In *Identical Strangers*, by Elyse Schein and Paula Bernstein (2007), the family members who meet again and collaborate in writing their stories are twins adopted separately. They eventually find a photo of their birthmother and learn something about her life, but she has died long ago, and their birthfather is unknown. As they narrate this search, the authors also write their changing thoughts about whether identity and family come more from nature or nurture and find out more about why their adoption agency, Louise Wise, separated them. At first they are struck by their similarities, but many of their habits and life styles differ, and their relationship goes through changes a bit like what sometimes happens between adoptees and birthparents, one wanting more relationship than the other.[17]

Why Be Happy When You Could be Normal (2011), by the well-known English novelist Jeanette Winterson, is, to my knowledge, the only memoir by an adoptee mentioned in the *New York Times'* 2019 list of the best fifty memoirs of the previous fifty years. Winterson's adoptive parents, portrayed in a softened form in her widely read novel *Oranges Are Not the Only Fruit*, are more difficult than any of the others—her depressed adoptive mother often refuses her daughter food and locks her either out of the house or in a coal-hole, and her quiet adoptive father might beat her under his wife's instruction. She never feels they love her and refers to her adoptive mother only as "Mrs. Winterson" throughout. Extremely devout Pentecostals, they tell her not to mix with other children at school. Any manifestation of adolescent sexual interest would have been off limits with them, but Winterson's night with a girlfriend leads not just to private punishment but to a public exorcism at her church and an end to the relationship.

Though Winterson does wonder about her birthmother, the main emphasis in the memoir is less on search for ancestry than on her early and long-continued mistreatment and a search for a way out of her family and the psychic wounds inflicted on her during her childhood and adolescence—part of that way out is attending Oxford. After portraying the failure of an attempt to reconcile with her mother during a college vacation, the memoir skips ahead twenty-five years in which she graduates, becomes a successful novelist, and adapts *Oranges* for television. Disappointed that the wide publicity of her story has not brought contact with her birthmother, she discovers some of her adoption papers, has a painful breakup with her partner, attempts to take her own life, decides to write herself out of madness, and begins her search. She meets her birthmother, a mixed experience, but she is hopeful.

Openness or Silence? Growing Up Feeling Different or Similar?

A few of these adoptees make a point of their experiences' differences from that of the best-known narratives. While we see in the next chapter that several transracial adoptees vividly remember parents' distinct reluctance to discuss adoption, and there is similar reluctance in the memoirs of Lifton and Fisher, there is less such silence in the later memoirs of this chapter. The two writers with the best long-standing relationships with their adoptive parents, Saffian and Strauss, recall early open and positive talks about adoption. Although Strauss feels her grandparents didn't accept her for a while and didn't want to discuss the third-grade family tree project with her parents, she remembers her mother sometimes talking with her, as a child, about the woman who gave birth to her. In her early teenage years, when her mother's surgery makes her anxious and she asks her, barely home from the hospital, for information about her origins, her mother gets the adoption file and something she describes as "a baby dress. A gift from your mother" (*Beneath* 71).

There are other problems in her childhood—especially her difficult brother, who is also adopted and turns out to be mentally ill. Still, her childhood memories include victories over adversity, such as when she earns her grandfather's acceptance by her success at fishing, or when she holds and soothes her mother after her father's death. Unlike the other writers, she talks about childhood times with friends and her enjoyment of athletic activities. Her serious pursuit of her birthmother begins not because of a personal crisis but because of the self-revelation from her screenwriting professor that a child of his was adopted out.

Saffian also recalls asking a parent a question and getting an immediate, frank answer. At seven, in the first year after her mother's death, she finds her father's datebook for the year she was born and discovers that she didn't come home from the hospital for two months. She asks her father about the delay, and she says, "Even when I was young, he took me seriously, was attentive to my questions and straightforward in his answers" (4). After explaining that she couldn't come home because she had jaundice, he told her about her adoption. "Mommy and I tried to have you on our own, but we weren't able to. . . . So we adopted you, which means that someone else gave you to us to be our daughter." By contrast with Lifton's mother's insistence that they had insisted on a legitimate child, Saffian's father says that they wanted a girl and birthparents who were college graduates or at least in college. Although Saffian uses some language of commodification in discussing her reaction to this—"I did have the sense of being carefully selected, deliberately ordered"— she writes, "The message that I was supremely wanted overrode any potential feelings of being unwanted by my original set of parents" (5).

Hickman, similarly, says that his parents "told us that we were lucky because they chose us. No way would we ever have to wonder whether or not we were wanted because they picked us out" (156). He also remembers his mother saying to him and his sister, also adopted, "Someday you will wanna find your birth mothers. Surely, I say to you, you will wanna know where you came from. If you decide to find them, I'll support you" (115). She believed that any woman, "in her right mind and true heart" (184), would want to see the child of her womb again. Still, he wonders why his birthmother "made the [choice] she made" and "always wanted to know who I really looked like" (155, 156).

Separated twin Paula Bernstein remembers a matter-of-fact approach to adoption, with her brother and her best friend also being adopted. It did, however, involve fantasy as well as fact. Her parents told her that when they took her home from foster care at five months, she "still weighed less than ten pounds" (Schein and Bernstein 20), and she loved to romanticize the "heart-wrenching tale of a pathetic orphan and the parents who rescued her from certain death, . . . so incongruous with my comfortable suburban upbring-ing" (21). She treasured "the lime-green hardcover book my parents gave me, the touching story of *The Chosen Baby*" (182). She was "proud to be adopted" (182) and a few years before her narrative begins, wrote an article for *Redbook*, "Why I Don't Want to Search for My Birth Mother" (30). It was her sister, Elyse Schein, who initiated the search.

It is tempting to connect the openness in discussing adoption that Strauss and Saffian experienced with their parents to the absence in their memoirs of a feeling of difference from their adoptive family that is present in so many other memoirs. Strauss never mentions feeling different from her parents. Saffian writes at length that she did not. She emphasizes her happiness with her father and her stepmother, whom she calls Mom, whom she first grew to know and love as a babysitter. More than any of the other writers discussed in this chapter, she discusses the similarities she feels with her adoptive parents. (This theme recurs in memoirs discussed later in this chapter by Lori Jakiela, and Jeremy Harding, though in more strained relationships with emphasis on less comfortable and more abstract likenesses of attitude.) She includes both her stepmother and her dead mother, but the similarities with her father get the most emphasis: "precise speech patterns, animated facial expressions and physical gestures" (Saffian 84); "his posture, his carriage, his gait, the way clothes hung on his frame, which mine happened to resemble" (185), "taste for savory foods . . . myopia, . . . unusually sensitive feet" (276). Her father used to say "Unfortunately, you have inherited the Saffian stom-ach," and she recalls, "I had always been comforted by these comments and didn't feel them a charade, knowing no other benefactor for my physique or delicate constitution" (185). She is even used to thinking of herself, in rela-tion to her father, as a "[c]hip off the old block" (225).

Most of these adoptees, however, write that they grew up with a strong sense of difference, as did Fisher and Paton. Some of their complaints might be made by children raised by biological parents, but the knowledge of the existence of another set of parents gives additional force. Lifton calls herself a "changeling" and wonders if it is because she is adopted that her feelings don't seem adequate to her mother (31). Homes is frustrated because she is athletic and her parents are "entirely unathletic," (18) and remembers as a child crying over and over again, "I want my mom" and getting the response, "I'm right here. . . . I'm your mother. I'm all the mother you've got" (38). Hip-chen wishes for a mother who would be "not so short-tempered, not so dif-ficult to understand, not so other-than-me" (40) as her adoptive mother is. On the other hand, Winterson believes that dealing with her difficult mother, whom she portrays as violent, punitive, and close-minded, as well as ignorance about her beginnings, has led her to creativity. "Adopted children are self-invented because we have to be. . . . To avoid the narrow mesh of Mrs. Winterson's story I had to be able to tell my own" (5). Without suggesting anything wrong with her relationship with her adoptive parents, Bernstein also has a sense of difference and is proud to think of herself as "my own invention" (4, 47).

Lifton and Hipchen have adoptive parents who are bothered by their daughter's birth out of wedlock. Lifton's mother claims that the parents were married; the Hipchens are cruelly suspicious: unbelievably, they think their daughter is pregnant at twelve when her second period is late. Several of the writers feel that their adoptive parents are uncomfortable discussing their birthparents or want to forget about them, fearing, as Lifton thinks her parents might, "bad blood" (31); in general they associate their adoptive parents with emotional control. Winterson's mother never controls her own emotions, however, and Winterson thinks she remembers seeing a "terrible argument" between her and another woman. Asking "Was that my mum?" provokes a blow that "knocks [her] back" (12).

Developing Identity

Most adoptees mention fantasies about their birthparents. Hipchen remembers thinking that her "imagined mother" would "welcome [her] as a part of her body she'd been missing all these years" (40). Lifton imagines ghostly birthparents hovering over her, both loving and frightening (24); Saffian imagines fairy-tale parents as a child and Marie Osmond and John Travolta when she is a teenager (6). In her early thirties, when Homes hears that her birthmother wants contact, she has hopes of finding "a goddess, the queen of queens, the CEO, the CFO, and the COO. Movie-star beautiful, incredibly competent, she can take care of anyone and anything" (8–9). Bernstein at seven imagines that she might be the daughter of Sonny and Cher and at nine identifies with Little Orphan Annie, singing along with the song about imaginary birthparents in *Annie* (22). Schein, on the other hand, has fantasies about her adoptive mother, who died when she was six. "When I jumped rope better than the other girls in my Long Island neighborhood, I knew it was because my mother was with me" (3).

Several memoirists discuss how they developed a sense of identity and belonging through their reading. Lifton identified her birthparents with Romeo and Juliet and thinks of the narrator of Sherwood Anderson's *Winesburg, Ohio* as she treasures her wish to move to a new atmosphere (22, 26). Homes as a child devours biographies and reads again and again books about two people who were sent away by their families—Eleanor Roosevelt and Babe

Ruth—and claims she combined them into a mythical Eleanor Babe who both started UNICEF and had a mean curveball (234–35). Winterson also finds a sense of agency through reading and eventually through writing. Even her mother's religious obsession presented so devastatingly familiarizes her with the eloquent words of the King James Bible. "I got a sense early on that the power of a text is not time-bound" (27). Hickman's memoir is full of reimagined biblical quotations and other religious imagery, for example, "And so she brought forth her firstborn son, and wrapped him in her arms, and named him Joseph, and gave him up for adoption because there was no room for him in the White [his birthmother's family name] house" (186). Making the point more explicit, he writes, "My life is a metaphor for Christ's. Christ's life is a metaphor for mine" (272).

For some, identity and belonging become explicitly political in relation to adoption. Lifton finds a crucial turning point as she attends an early meeting of ALMA, which Florence Fisher was then forming. While she is ambivalent about Fisher, the meeting makes her feel as if she has now "found her true brothers and sisters" (165), and she comes to understand more of the pain of women who have lost children to adoption. And at this point she learns of Jean Paton, Orphan Voyage, and her Museum of Orphan Literature, which contains "all those thousands of volumes of poetry, prose, plays, and nonfiction that have some connection with people like me" (170). And she draws many into the adoption reform movement and mentors them.

For others, finding a community of adoptees is more complicated. Strauss begins her search because of her screenwriting teacher's revelation about his feelings as a birthfather. Her initial experience with other adoptees is quite different from Lifton's. She attends a national adoption conference for the launching of her book *Birthright* and experiences enough obvious rejections that she concludes, "when one writes a book about something so personal and complex, others who have gone through the same experience, but with different perspectives, can feel mis-portrayed, if not betrayed" (*Beneath* 156). Still, after publishing these books, she has continued to work for adoptees' rights, largely through documentary filmmaking. Saffian describes attending meetings of search/support groups and feeling uncomfortable about the prescriptive group leaders and the "extreme expression of emotion" (124). She does, however, gain some perspective on the problem of being found unexpectedly by hearing another adoptee talk about being rejected by her birthmother (125). Homes connects her situation with adoptees' general lack of rights. For Schein and Bernstein, the important people in similar situations are twins, both adopted and nonadopted. The book reports much research on hereditary similarities and environmentally caused differences among twins, and the memoirists report conversations with a few others separated by Louise Wise Services.

Most of the memoirs explicitly confront the sealed adoption records, concealing adoptees' original names and the names of their original parents, that prevail, to some degree, in most states of the United States.[18] This important theme in Lifton's book is also dramatized when Strauss begins her search and when Homes wants to prove she is eligible for the DAR. Even Saffian, whose birthparents have sought her out, can't get her records from the adoption agency, the Bureau of Vital Statistics, or the hospital where she was born. The search is shorter for Winterson, once she starts, because the records in England have been open for adult adoptees since 1975, but she still has some bureaucratic hassles and fears publicity because, as a well-known novelist, she is a celebrity.

Apart from this unusual privacy issue, most of these adoptees don't seem to have had the sense of secrecy around adoption that loomed over both Lifton and me, coming from earlier generations. However, it was still important in Homes's family. When Homes was in her twenties, her parents told her that she had been picked up at the hospital by their next-door neighbor, who had disguised herself so as not to be recognized. For Bernstein and Schein, the important missing records are not only those of their birth but also those that document the experiment that involved separating them from each other, at a time when most adoption agencies were keeping twins together.[19] They suspect, and find evidence during their interviews, that the agency separated them to find out about the influence of different child-rearing practices on children whose birthparents were diagnosed with schizophrenia. This distressingly seems like puppetry comparable to *The Truman Show* (103), and they consider suing Louise Wise Services; however, their lawyer quotes a price tag of over $150,000 to argue their case and says they wouldn't convince a jury they had suffered enough (146).

Mirroring and Other Resemblances

Long before these memoirs, George Eliot portrayed, in the title character of her novel *Daniel Deronda*, an adoptee who feels a lack when looking in the mirror. Daniel's "own face in the glass had during many years been associated for him with thoughts of someone whom he must be like—one about whose character and lot he continually wondered, and never dared to ask."[20] Fisher's comparison of her first meeting with her birthmother to "seeing a reflection for the first time" (224), quoted earlier, is a common theme in adoptees' memoirs. The issue of mirroring is even more fraught for Bernstein and Schein. Upon first meeting, Schein thinks "We are strangers who inhabit the same body" (52), and later, "Sharing my face with Paula feels eerie" (81). Their differences are relatively small. At their first meeting Bernstein observes, with somewhat more distance: "Thinner lips, more angular face. Her complexion is more olive, but her neck flushes red when she gets excited just like mine" (51). When they finally see their birthmother's high school yearbook picture, at first she thinks it looks foreign, but then it comes into focus as a model for both: "She's got the same thick, coarse, wavy hair. The same mischievous glint in her almond-shaped eyes. The same high forehead and oval face" (247).

Many adoptee memoirists write about fulfilling their desire to see some-one whose appearance resembles theirs. Hickman writes to his birthmoth-er, "I found you to see whom I look like, to see how it happened, to see where I came from, to see who you are, to see why" (267), and begins his book with "the first time he sees her face" (3). He then retells his life story up to the time when he meets her again, and the story switches to her point of view as he imagines her noting that they have the same "protruding bottom lip . . . car-amel-colored skin with the reddish tint" (54). However, this similarity is not enough to create a good relationship. Nor is similarity enough for Homes, who writes of an unexpected resemblance she sees in her extremely difficult birthfather, "That's my ass walking away. His blue sport coat covers it half-way, but I can see it broken into section, subsection, departments, of ass, high and low just like mine. . . . This is the first time I have seen anyone else in my body" (51). And likeness is not always comfortable. Hipchen, delighted when, a few days after their first meeting, her birthfather extends his long arms and says, "These are pitchers' arms. . . . These are your arms" (29), at a later cel-ebration, when a photo of her with her siblings is projected on a succession of monitors, is for at least a moment unnerved by all the similar faces (106).

Genetics does not always produce obvious likeness in appearance. The two writers in this section with the best relationship with their adoptive par-ents, Strauss and Saffian, both see little physical similarity with their birth-parents. It is only near the end of her long-delayed visit that Saffian thinks, "We all have the same eyes" (289). We might assume that this reluctance to see similarity comes from their better relationship with their adoptive fam-ilies. But Lifton too, as critical of her adoptive mother as any of these writers except Winterson and Fisher, says of her birthmother, "I sat and looked at the woman across from me and knew I would not have recognized her as my mother had we passed each other on the street" (121).

Many of these writers find they have other things in common with their birthparents than appearance.[21] They may be as trivial as, for Homes and her birthmother, both keeping money in a jeans pocket (102). But talking on the phone with her, Homes thinks, "Things I know about myself, things that ex-ist without language, my hardware, my mental firing patterns—parts of me that are fundamentally, inexorably me are being echoed on the other end, confirmed as a DNA match" (26). Some similarities can be problematic. She hears that her birth grandfather died young of a heart attack because "he liked rich food" and then feels a pain in her chest, thinking "the things I enjoy most are dangerous" (27). When Strauss discovers that she and her birthmother are both anxious about flying, both hyperventilate when they are anxious, and both worry a lot, she refuses to acknowledge the likeness at the time but notes it in the memoir as an example of her denial (141–42). Saffian, similarly, says that her emotional birthfather "revealed a side of herself she didn't want to acknowledge" (176). She feels especially linked, uncomfortably, by the fact that he was also adopted and writes, "When he looked lost in his cab driver's license photo, I saw my own feelings laid bare" (176)—paradoxically, since she has so much emphasized that she did not feel loss from being adopted.

Still, finding resemblances is one of the ways people "do" family; in a biologically made family, this practice is frequent in welcoming a new baby. And sometimes instead of a clear temperamental likeness the connection is a compromise. After identifying her wild bootlegger father as a figurative "Black Sheep" and her timid mother as a "White Sheep," Lifton comes to see herself as the "Gray Sheep" who keeps her "volatile emotions controlled" (208).[22] In contrast to Saffian, Strauss improves her difficult relationship with her birthmother as she empathizes with her birthmother's year and a half in an orphanage, and their bond is finally cemented when together they find her birth grandmother. When she meets her birthmother, Winterson focuses less on physical similarity than on a similarity of temperament: "yes, we are alike. The optimism, the self-reliance. The ease we both have in our bodies" (216). What Winterson wants is love, much more than physical mirroring, as Homans writes (290).

The narrative by the separated twins shows additional complications to resemblance. Schein is initially struck by the similarity in talents and interests between her and her sister Bernstein: both are writers, and she is a filmmaker while Bernstein is a film critic. Her Spartan life style as a single woman by contrast to Bernstein's greater domesticity with a husband and two children leads to some tensions, but Bernstein in the last paragraph before the epilogue writes, "In each other, we recognize a kindred spirit" (266)— something of a contrast to her earlier reluctance to search and insistence on the importance of nurture over nature. More fraught is the issue of their possible temperamental similarity to their birthmother, who from her first year of college to her early death was frequently in mental institutions and was diagnosed as schizophrenic. Though they are apparently leading happy lives now, both had had emotional difficulties, including an eating disorder, during college. Elyse Schein grew up with a not-quite-compatible stepmother and a schizophrenic brother, has facial scars from a severe sulfa allergy and decided wrinkles between her eyebrows, and as she tells it, once faked a suicide attempt to get attention from her parents. Paula Bernstein was diagnosed with clinical depression in her early twenties and prescribed Prozac, which gave her the energy to quit her job and become a successful film writer. Dealing with the focal issue of nurture versus nature, her psychiatrist says, "Perhaps you were both predisposed toward depression, but Elyse attributed her depression to outside factors, whereas you felt confused because there was no obvious reason for you to be depressed" (95). Their depressions could be considered a result of postnatal history as well as inheritance, since they experienced separation from both their mother and each other and then from their foster parents. Indeed, other experiences at Louise Wise might well have contributed to their depression, since Samuel Karelitz, a pediatrician on its board, experimented with reactions to pain using babies confined there, easy subjects to take advantage of since no parents had the legal right to object.[23]

Reunion's Aftermath

Contrary to the suggestion that reunion with birth family in itself is healing, every writer who describes how they try to integrate birthparents into their life finds it difficult, and the twins find their relationship complicated as well. With Lifton and with Homes, in relation to her father, the problem is largely the birthparent's wish for secrecy. But Strauss, Saffian, and Homes (in relation to her mother) find expressions of intimacy that they feel are premature or inappropriate (e.g., asking Homes to adopt *her*). Saffian and Strauss, who have both lost their beloved adoptive mothers, are sensitive to anything that seems to disparage that relationship. Hickman is bothered not only by his birthmother's homophobia but also by the fact that she blames his gayness partly on his adoptive mother's not being strict and prayerful enough. Bernstein sometimes feels that Schein, who is single and not close to her family, is too needy. Hipchen says of her birthparents, "They have hurt me deeply, frustrated me over and over; I have disappointed and shocked them profoundly, repeatedly" (205). In the last chapter of her memoir, Winterson writes, "Whatever adoption is, it isn't an instant family—not with the adoptive parents, and not with the rediscovered parents (227). I have read a lot of overwhelmingly emotional accounts of reunion. None of that is my experience. . . . I can't be the daughter she wants" (229). Two of her meetings with her birthmother are friendly, but during the third she shouts in anger, "At least Mrs. Winterson was there. Where were you?" In spite of all her suffering with her adoptive family, she does not want to return to her biological one (229)—still, she has to stop thinking of herself as an orphan. Around fifty years old when she meets her mother, she has more of an accumulated identity to reconstruct than the younger memoirists most of this chapter has dealt with. Though both her origins and her early experience are working-class, something she emphasizes, her current life is very different. She has a successful career and a literary network including a mentor, the detective fiction writer, Ruth Rendell (then still alive), and a loving partner.

Most of these memoirists find that meeting their birthparents, or even learning about them, requires a drastic change in their worldview. Hipchen speaks of the inadequacy of the mental structures she has built (127), Homes speaks of a "shift in the architecture of the precarious frame" of her life (10); and Saffian of the "shell of self-sufficiency . . . slowly cracking" (59–60) and having her "fantasy heritage whisked out from under me, like in the old magic trick, only I wasn't left intact as the place setting is supposed to be after the tablecloth has been yanked away" (15). The shell image, which she later refers to as a "functioning outer façade" (211), also appears in birthmother memoirs discussed in the preceding chapter, a sign of how difficult adoption issues can be to acknowledge on all sides. The three adoptee memoirists just quoted were all surprised by being contacted by one or both birthparents, and so had less time to prepare for this shift, but Lifton also writes of moving mental furniture when the reality of her birthmother replaces the fantasies that she has built around her (139).[24] The theme of being numb, and emerging out of numbness, whether temporary or long standing, appears in Lifton, Homes, Saffian, and Strauss. Strauss feels numb when she first meets her birthmother. Homes finds herself emerging from numbness as she identifies with the ancestors she is learning about on the web—"the looking, the digging awakens numb spots, labyrinths in my own experience, in my ability to process" (150).

Saffian emphasizes the related image of the contrast between being open and being closed, as she begins and ends with a chapter titled "Aperture," notes the power in her birthfather Adam's self-description as open-hearted, and realizes how inadequate are her words to her birthparents about achieving closure. "It is still always easier, simpler, to be loved by one set of parents, by one family" (305). Part of her opening up is acknowledging that some parts of her identity are inherited. Bernstein, similarly, learns that she is not totally her own invention, and that hereditary ties are important to her as well as constructed ties—in fact, this opposition is not a dichotomous one because, like all reunited family members, she and Schein have to work on constructing their relationship.

All these memoirists are interested in a larger network of relationships, not just in their birthparents. Hipchen, Saffian, Homes, Winterson, Strauss, Hickman, and, of course, Schein and Bernstein all meet full or half siblings, in some cases people to whom they can relate much more easily than their parents. Hickman's first and most beloved contact in his birth family is his mother's brother, who wanted to raise him and considers him the son he never had. Schein and Bernstein enjoy meeting each other's adoptive parents, and Schein likes being an aunt to Bernstein's children. Homes is permitted to meet only one half brother, under very strained conditions, but she is fascinated by what she can learn of both her birthmother and her birthfather's ancestry, as is Lifton, who must deal with similar secrecy; in the afterword to Lifton's third edition, we find that she eventually does meet her half brother (271).

Close to the end of their memoirs, many of these writers emphasize a family they have constructed and suggest that their search and reunion experiences have prepared them for it. Hipchen, now married, says she has learned how to love from the acceptance she received from her birthfather. Homes, now a single mother, and Strauss see their biological connection ongoing in children, and value that relationship more than their relationship with their parents. Among the last events Lifton places in her narrative is discussing her adoption and reunion with her children. Hickman affirms his relationship with his chosen family of gay friends, who support him even in the rare times of problems in his relationship with his husband. One of them says, "You can't choose your relatives, but you *can* choose your family. Why? Because your family is the people you connect with right here . . . in your *heart*. It might include your relatives; it might not" (306–7).

All the writers present themselves as taking some control and making choices, although what they can do is of course responsive to their own particular situation. For most, the basic choice is deciding to search, but Saffian takes control by insisting on a long period of letter writing before meeting; Hipchen, by signing up with an adoption reunion registry; and Homes, by choosing when she would meet with her birthmother, going to her funeral and her apartment after her death, and outing her birthparents by name in her memoir. (Most adoptees who write memoirs use pseudonyms for living birthparents who want to keep their identities secret.) Schein decides to search and her sister, Bernstein, to meet her when contacted, and the two of them together look for records and confront psychologists and social workers. After meeting Peter Neubauer, the psychiatrist who oversaw the whole study involving research on separated twins and triplets, Schein writes, "We have faced the monster in the closet. . . . It feels like a huge victory—as if we've taken back a piece of our lives that had been toyed with and locked away forever" (226).

All of them seem to grow, and several to gain in empathy for difficult parents of both kinds, over the course of the narratives they present. The renewed relationship with adoptive parents that most show by the end of their memoirs might reassure adoptive parents whose children want to search.[25] Most emphatically, Hickman says to his adoptive mother, "You're the only mother I've ever had, the only mother I'll ever have, and the only mother I've ever wanted" (297). Writing about her to a birth sister, he says they have developed a more mature relationship "because we have to challenge ourselves to be *different* in our relationship with each other, and that challenge is constant" (270). Hipchen shows compassion as, midbook, she narrates her adoptive father's death from a mysterious virus. Homes feels more belonging in her adoptive family, and sees the centerpiece of her family life in the table she has inherited from her grandmother; Strauss realizes that she can put her adoptive family into the family tree that she has been building as she finds her birth genealogy. Even Winterson writes that "Mrs. Winterson . . . was . . . absolutely right for someone like me who, like her, could never have accepted a scaled-down life" (207). Most seem to agree with Lifton's conclusion that "she who raises the child is the mother" (219), though as we see in a few pages, Homes insists on using that word in the same sentence to apply to both mothers without any qualification, to emphasize the paradox. Bernstein's relation to her adoptive parents appears unshaken, and Schein has gained more family through her meeting with her twin. But one of the ways that Bernstein's perspective about adoption has changed is that she has more empathy for birthmothers. Speaking of her family, she says, "As comfortable as we are in our relationship, our gain resulted from others' losses" (243). Schein has also gained this empathy. She refers to reading Ann Fessler's *The Girls Who Went Away* for more understanding and decides to speak of Leda as "our mother" rather than birthmother (244).

In general, writers with worse relationships with their adoptive parents, including Fisher, Lifton, and Winterson, understandably express worse feelings about themselves related to adoption than others do. Hipchen says she grew up believing that people would leave her (136). Homes calls herself "an amalgam . . . glued together, something slightly broken" (38), "adapted, . . . amputated and sewn back together again" (54) early in her book. When rejected by her birthfather, she says that she would need a "national monthlong festival, a public parade celebrating my existence" (70) to convince her that she is welcome on the planet, and even then she might not believe it; however, we come to see that her feelings change.

Strauss recalls an early feeling of difference in her community, having a last name (Sacconaghi) that was Italian but sounded Japanese and was accompanied by blonde hair that didn't fit with either ethnicity, but she doesn't make generalizations as global as do Homes or Hipchen. Presumably it was evident that she was saner than her schizophrenic brother. However, in *Birthright* (1994), Strauss writes of healing as the goal of search and reunion, even as she reports her anger at a psychologist who claims that complete healing was impossible for adoptees. While her relationship with her adoptive parents is better than that of most of the other adoptees, in both books she discusses the difficulties she had with her birthmother in the early years of their relationship. These may be the greatest signs that she did feel rejection. In *Birth-*

right she says, "I never really had a problem with being adopted, never really felt conscious pain or loss, until I began writing the first draft of this book"[26] (340). Strauss seems more practical and less introspective than the others; it is characteristic that both *Birthright* and her earlier *The Great Adoptee Search Book* (1990) are focused on helping other adoptees—first with their search and then with their reunion—much more directly than is the case with most other memoirists with their first books about adoption. While she writes in *Birthright* that it is important for adoptees to "give [themselves] permission to deal with adoption losses" (329), she also decides to "focus on the benefits of being an adoptee—not just the love and experiences I share with all my families, but also the gifts that come from working through the losses" (341). She includes the wisdom and compassion that come from suffering, the empowerment from surviving trauma, and—what rings truest to me about the persona that she has shown—the ability to adapt (341).[27]

How about Saffian, apparently so happy with her adoptive family? As she works out her confusion at how to relate to the Leyders, as she calls her birthparents, she admits feelings she hadn't acknowledged before: "feelings about being abandoned by the woman who had given birth to me, and then being abandoned a second time by the woman who had adopted me [in her death]" (200). She comes to this realization at the end of a chapter titled "Chimera," a choice she never explains. According to the *American Heritage Dictionary*, in biology, a chimera is "an organism, especially a plant, containing tissues from at least two genetically distinct parents" but in Greek mythology, surely known to someone who named her book *Ithaka*, it is "a firebreathing monster represented with the head of a lion, the body of a goat, and the tail of a serpent."[28] This ambiguous title is the closest she comes to Homes's image of adoptees as "amalgams." However, this image of herself, heading a chapter in which she is for the first time bothered by other people asking about her heredity, is a point of transition. She has been emphatic about not wanting to give up her identity as Sarah Saffian, not seeing her previous self as a pretense (121), in the way an adoption counselor encouraged her to see it. She articulates what she has received from each of her three mothers, saying that "the realness of each woman's motherhood didn't diminish the realness of the others'" (188). She finally comes up with a formulation that permits her to accept the complexity of her life, without seeing herself as monstrous: "just as one can have many children, one can, in varying degrees, also have many parents, many families—and even many selves, or discrete but complementary parts that make up the whole" (302).

For Bernstein and Schein, the issues are even more complicated. In addition to seeing themselves as influenced by heredity as well by the family in which they were raised, they must come to terms with the facts that adoption for each of them followed a double loss, of twin as well as original mother, and that this was caused by specific people, some of whom they have met. Both speak of the discovery of the separated sister as explaining feelings they have always had: as if a buried memory sometimes emerged, when she felt depressed Schein used to say, "I feel like I've lost a twin" (16). And for both, the sense of contingency, that they might have had a completely different life, has a special force, though others write of it as well. Bernstein fluctuates about the notion of fate: at one point, she sobs at thinking that agency workers, not fate, led to her rather than someone else being "Paula Bernstein" (34). At another point, she says with more certainty, "Life works out the way it was meant to be" (47), a view stated more often, as we will see, by adoptive parents. Schein is also ambivalent. "It's unfair that I should have to choose between this life and the hypothetical life I might have had if we were raised together" (144).

Some adoptees portray their childhood as happy, while others do not; for some, feeling abandoned or damaged or exiled is an important part of their history while for others such feelings seldom emerge.[29] In spite of the differences in the emotional tone of their childhood memories—Strauss emphasizes happiness and Homes unhappiness—there is a convergence between the way that Strauss and Homes write about their familial identities near the end of their books. Strauss writes, "My grandmother forces me to see how I have held my adoptive family in one hand, like a ball of blue clay, and my birth family in another, like a ball of red, interpreting them as unrelated parts of myself. But they are not separate. They are the same. They belong together. Grandma reshapes my view of my family. She helps me make purple" (*Beneath* 201). Early in her book, when Homes describes herself as something "glued together," she says, "I am not my adopted mother's child, I am not Ellen's child" (38). But at the end she says, "I am my mother's child and I am my mother's child, I am my father's child and I am my father's child, and if that line is a little too much like Gertrude Stein, then I might be a little bit her child too" (238).

Homes's change in attitude here is striking. She writes, "I grew up convinced that every family was better than mine" (78). Therapy helps her hypothesize that, because her nine-year-old brother had died only six months before she was adopted, her mother had been afraid of losing her too and therefore afraid to attach. "I grew up with the sensation of being kept at a distance . . . I feared that there was something about me, some defect of birth that made me repulsive, unlovable" (6). She believes she "grew up doused in grief" (10) and writes of sometimes feeling "relieved by the fact that I am not *of* my parents . . . followed by . . . the pain of how alone I feel" (7–8). Unlike Saffian, she feels uncomfortable with the image of herself as having been "ordered" like "merchandise . . . like cake from a bakery" (15). But as she searches in the archives, along with many other people, for distant relatives, she feels "the hum of identification, a sense of wholeness and well-being" (149). She feels both highs and lows, imagines the lives of many different people she finds with names from her birth family and eventually starts learning more about the relations in her adoptive family as well. She realizes that she and her adoptive family have shared "the experience of growing up within a narrative that, while it is not [her] own biologically, is now [hers] socially and culturally" (160). She spent childhood weekends in museums, eventually tells us that her adoptive parents were "the guidance counselor and the left-wing artist" (155), and now, though she never mentions it in her memoir, in addition to fiction she writes art criticism and artists' catalogs.[30] Near the end of the book, she credits her adopted mother's mother with contributing to her becoming a writer and to her determination to become a mother herself (225).

Homes is a bohemian though acclaimed novelist, and Strauss has been the president's wife at a number of colleges; however, they converge not only in becoming comfortable about being connected to both adopted and birth family but also in feeling more part of American history as they search for more information about their ancestors. Homes, surfing the web, is fascinated by the stories that she finds of American immigrants who may not be related to her either biologically or by adoption (180–81). And Strauss, having traced an ancestor in a Civil War battle and others in royalty many generations before, concludes, "I am related to everybody" (*Beneath* 259). By contrast to her earlier feeling of alienation, Homes notes parallels between her experience and those of others. As she looks at all the people searching for their genealogy in the New York City Municipal Archives, she realizes that "the quest to answer the question *Who am I?* is not unique to the adoptee" (152).

Discussions of adoption often include the stock question: "Nature or nurture, which is more important?" Many of these memoirs (and recent science) suggest that the only possible answer is "Both." Surely in some circumstances adoptees act in a way determined by neither, but more information may make their behavior look different. When Winterson discovers that her mother had expected to adopt a boy, to the point of buying baby boy's clothes, she writes, "I thought my life was all about sexual choice and feminism, and . . . it turns out I began as a boy" (202). Mrs. Winterson was prepared to raise a boy, and that preparation, Winterson now believes, affected the kind of nurture in their early mother-child interactions. Analogously, geneticists now talk of hereditary qualities appearing because of environment that promotes them; thus, the identical twin memoirists may have inherited a tendency to depression from their birthmother, and their losses may have facilitated its emergence: nevertheless, for whatever reasons, they have resilience she did not have.

Ethnicity is often mentioned by adoptees in closed adoptions as something they need to know, but for none of the same-race adoptee memoirists just discussed does ethnicity seem important in their summing up, though several have discovered in their birth family ethnicity and religious traditions not part of their adoptive family. Later in this chapter, however, considering two other memoirs, we find that the birthmother's Irishness is mentioned more frequently—perhaps because it blends with the working-class identity more salient in those memoirs than in any discussed here so far, except perhaps Winterson's. In the next chapter, we read of adoptees who in their conclusions feel that putting their parents of different races and ethnicities together, if only through a private ritual with photographs, is very important.

Can we draw any further conclusions from these memoirs, unscientifically small sample though they are? Together with the memoirs of birthmothers, many of them show unethical behavior by professionals and pain resulting from sealed records and shame about adoption. A few describe adoptive parents biased against them and their heredity (something that emerges as a larger problem in the next chapter, where the issue is race). But the memoirs also show that reunion is not the end of the story, because coming to terms with birth family is not simple. One might speculate that those who write memoirs are likely to be among those for whom identity is most complicated, because they are likely to be introspective. Or perhaps the complications of their lives as adoptees contributed to their introspective nature, and these writers have better verbal tools than many to deal with such complications. The experiences of these adoptees have parallels in the lives of many who do not write memoirs: Lifton observes about the adoptees she has treated and/or surveyed in *Journey of the Adopted Self*: "they thought that just the sight of the birth mother or father, or a member of the birth family, would render them whole. Instead, they may feel more fragmented than before."[31] However, contrasts among the memoirs show that adopted people's experiences of both their adoptive families and their birth families vary enormously, as do the way they (we) formulate their (our) relation to each and often to the several parts of each. There is no easy formula. Nevertheless, Homes, who was found by her birthmother and recounts the worst relationships with birthparents of any in this group, speaks for virtually all these writers when she ends her book by saying, "I couldn't not know" (239).[32]

Is adoption in itself traumatic? Winterson conveys a stronger sense of believing that adoption is inherently damaging than most other memoirists, apart from Lifton, who compares "A-doption disease" to "A-bomb disease" (*Twice Born* 156). Winterson writes, "Adoption is outside. You act out what it feels like to be the one who doesn't belong. And you act it out by trying to do to others what has been done to you" (7). Using the image of the primal wound made famous by Nancy Verrier in her book by that name and adding a more literary ancestry from Odysseus onward, she writes near the end, "My mother had to sever some part of herself to let me go. I have felt the wound ever since" (220). Some readers might speculate that the wound looms larger for Winterson than for many American adoptees because the UK has a stronger sense of the importance of biological ancestry, which has also led to opening birth records to adult adoptees as a national policy. However, we will see later that British male adoptee Jeremy Harding has no feeling that there is a wound in adoption itself, and a number of these memoirs suggest that for many adoptees the early trauma is as likely to be from neglect in an orphanage or hospital as from having been relinquished.

Winterson's sense of being wounded must have been heightened by the sheer terror of her early home life. If the Winterson household had been different enough that a child could have been born to them, but the same in most other respects, that child too might have felt wounded. But victimization is not Winterson's final emphasis. She cites many examples of wounds in literature and tradition and finds a sort of consolation in "the nearness of the wound to the gift" (221). Like many other adoptee memoirists, she writes of some kind of forgiveness near the end. The last two sentences, following a description of difficulties with her birthmother, whom she calls Ann, and Ann's fraught relationship with her own mother, are, "The possibility of love. I have no idea what happens next" (230).

As confronting isolation is a frequent experience of adoptees in these memoirs, so is connecting with others, whether linking to the past, sharing experiences, or hoping that other people can benefit from their story. Not all adoptees can come to terms with their lives as much as these memoirists seem to have. There appears to be a higher risk of mental health problems during adolescence for adoptees than for other teenagers (some have argued that this statistic means that their parents have more trust in professionals and thus are more likely to seek help for them; there was such an attempt in the Homes and Hipchen households, but not apparently in the even more difficult households of Fisher and Winterson).[33]

Theoretically, modern adoption is supposed to be for "the best interest of the child," but children seldom have the opportunity to communicate their feelings publicly during childhood. Thus the reactions of adoptees to their experience have a special authority in analyzing the costs and benefits of various adoption practices. These individual stories tell us about institutional problems such as negligence, bad judgment, and systematic deception.[34] They sometimes tell us about parental and social prejudices and shame about adoption—see especially memoirs by Fisher, Winterson, and Hipchen—which are further testimony to institutional failures. But the memoirs of transracial adoptees, discussed in the next chapter will give the most sense of previously untold painful experiences. Homes, for example, had difficulties as an athletic child of unathletic parents, including a depressed and withdrawn mother, and Winterson had more because of her mother's fanaticism and punitiveness; however, unlike transracial adoptees, they did not live in a world in which many people and institutions were tilted against them because of their appearance.

As we consider memoirs of birthparents and adoptive parents elsewhere in this volume, some of the stories will speak to each other across chapters, explaining to people with different relations to adoption what an experience feels like from another point of view. Bernstein's insight "our gain resulted from others' losses" (243) echoes Jan Waldron's words "one family's luck is another's loss,"[35] and this insight has reverberations in other chapters. The story of *Identical Strangers*, with its picture of psychologists and agencies playing calmly and callously with other people's lives, anticipates a theme that we see very often in this book—intermediaries in adoption withholding information, telling lies, and failing to offer sorely needed counseling. This becomes even more explicit in the documentary film *Three Identical Strangers*,[36] which reveals that Louise Wise placed one triplet out of three in a family where the agency already knew the father's authoritarian way of child-rearing. That one committed suicide as an adult.

Reconsidering Adoptive Parents While Searching

Frequently the author of a memoir or autobiography makes only their own character complex and memorable. Apart from Strauss's and Saffian's, adoptive parents figure in most of the memoirs just discussed chiefly in relation to the problems they present for the memoirist. These problems loom especially large in Winterson's, but none of those memoirs attempts to explore formative influences in those parents' lives, and only Saffian gives much attention to temperamental or attitudinal similarities between the memoirist and her adoptive parents. Two memoirs are different in both ways, and they give a fuller picture of how adoptive parents can be both difficult and loving, instead of, like most of the ones discussed earlier, narrating the complexities of a relationship with birthparents after reunion. Jeremy Harding writes, in his memoir *Mother Country*, "It's one of the axioms of adoption that when you go looking for people you don't know, you begin to discover the people you imagined you knew" (42).[37] This may be an axiom, but it is rarely documented as thoroughly as Harding does. And in Lori Jakiela's memoir *Belief is its own kind of truth, Maybe* (her capitalization preference), a discovery about her adoptive father's childhood experience and how it may have motivated her adoption is climactically placed. Both memoirs are full of speculations about which of their author's qualities come from nature and which from nurture. Both sometimes feel different from their adoptive parents and sometimes feel similar in uncomfortable ways.

These two search memoirs, one by a London-born man who lives in France and one by a woman born and living near Pittsburgh, both portray and analyze strained relationships (though not so bad as Winterson's) with less educated adoptive parents by people who have become professional writers well-known in their respective worlds. Harding's previous books include *The Fate of Africa* and *The Uninvited: Refugees at the Rich Man's Gate*, which won the Martha Gellhorn award for journalism in 2002.[38] Jakiela wrote two previous memoirs: *Miss New York Has Everything* and *The Bridge to Take When Things Get Serious*.[39] She won the City of Asylum Pittsburgh Prize in 2015, and that year *Belief* won the William Saroyan International Prize. The outcomes of their birth family searches are strikingly different. But both, like most of the memoirists just discussed, reject for themselves the idea of finding identity in birth origin alone.

During the time he covers in his memoir, Harding knows too little about his birthmother to speculate about similarities to her and finds few in what he learns about his siblings; Jakiela learns mainly about screaming and paranoia in her birthmother's current behavior. Unlike the memoirists discussed in the earlier section of this chapter, neither recalls (or includes recalling) much fantasizing about heredity in their childhood, except that Jakiela expected her original family might have been interested in words, as she is.

While in both cases the adoptions are same-race between white people, and thus the adoptees do not have to deal with racism directed at them, both provide material for analysis of class and class mobility. Both searchers discover that their adoption, in a more focused way than usual, was aimed at improving their adoptive parents' lives—impressing a rich relative or distracting from trauma. They also find the importance of various kinds of shame: Harding learns that his adoptive mother broke off the close connection that she had had with his birthmother because she was trying to rise in class. Jakiela imagines the humiliation her birthmother experienced as she tries to understand the resistance her birthmother has to reunion. She also discovers her adoptive father's early sexual trauma and how this shaped his personality. Both writers, however, conjure images of their (now deceased) adoptive parents as they conclude their memoirs.

In many ways Harding's experience as narrated is easier than Jakiela's. This begins with the contrast between the social worker he deals with, who he says "talked generously and practically" (8), as he takes advantage of the UK's 1975 law allowing adopted people to see their original birth certificate, and the Catholic Charities counselor Jakiela sees, in an office that "smells like antiseptic and rubber gloves."[40] Jakiela deals not only with restrictive Pennsylvania law, Catholic Charities, and a birthmother who says she refuses contact and won't give information but also with a counselor who laughs hysterically after passing that message on. Still, Jakiela's story is leavened not only by her own humor but also by her warm descriptions of day-to-day life with her beloved husband and children.

Both Harding and Jakiela, more than the adoptee memoirists discussed earlier, explicitly discuss their choices of adoption terminology, a discussion that helps foreground their interest in their adoptive parents. Jakiela, from a working-class background, where *real mother* is a term often used by contrast to *adopted mother* (for example by a policeman on 124), opens her memoir by writing, "When my real mother dies, I go looking for another one. The Catholic Charities counselor's word for this other mother I want after decades to find is biological" (13). Soon after she refers to "My mother, the mother who raised me" and says that "biological" makes her think of "warfare" (14). The phrase "the mother who raised me" continues until page 95 and resurfaces once at the end. The other one is almost always *birth mother—birthmother* in the Catholic Charities reports she quotes and builds on later.

Harding, by contrast, explicitly rejects that term. He also says he "wouldn't really want to say 'my mother' about either, even though I do" (5). Sometimes he calls them "Mother One" and "Mother Two," but most often they are Margaret and Maureen, respectively. Otherwise, he uses *natural mother*. Many adoption professionals have discarded that term because they think it implies that adoption is unnatural.[41] For the intellectual Harding, however, the antithesis "cultural" is more relevant: "Adoption is one of the modest triumphs of human culture" (xvii). However, he breaks down this opposition by continuing, "Another [triumph of culture] is the fact that a mother may feel something like love for her biological children throughout her life, whether they are insistently present or torn away from her by circumstance at an early stage." Retrospectively, Margaret comes to exemplify this—close to the end she becomes "my first mother, also my last" (177), while Jakiela's birthmother makes no such transformation.

The ancestry search story in *Mother Country* begins with Harding contemplating his original birth certificate, which lists Margaret Walsh as his mother. The UK's Children Act of 1975 and Adoption Act of 1976 has allowed him to see this, with the aid of a social worker. He is in his fifties, his adoptive mother, Maureen, is in the throes of dementia after years of partly alcohol-related confusion, his adoptive father, Colin, dead; so, he assumes, is Margaret. He explores the addresses listed on the certificate and begins the adoptive family search as well, interviewing Colin's sister Rosemary and old friend Boris, who tells him that Colin was able to get family money after he produced a child (adoption unacknowledged). Harding goes to the Family Records Center to find marriage and birth records and then to the Kensington Public Library for voting records. The name Privett appears at an address near one of his childhood houses, and he remembers that someone named Privett had been mentioned by Rosemary as an intermediary in the adoption. When he visits Peter Privett, he discovers that Peter's now dead wife, Lillian, had once been a close friend of Maureen, but Maureen had totally broken with her after adopting a little boy—Harding himself. This break was motivated partly by the desire to keep the adoption a secret from the aunt who would provide money and partly by Colin's desire to solidify Maureen's rise in class by removing her from her previous working-class friends. Harding tries to find out more by visiting John Webb, a friend of the Privetts who knew Maureen, and who he thinks might be his father, but Webb avoids any acknowledgment.

Harding hires a professional tracer and starts calling people living near or perhaps related to some of the many Margaret Walshes he finds in the records. Eventually one calls back and identifies herself as his cousin and Margaret as a lively seventy-year-old. The three meet for a very long lunch and talk, so successful that near the end Margaret says, "We were all nervous . . . and now we're none of us nervous" (177). The relationships are clearly to be continued. Other adoption memoirs, as we have seen, show that such a meeting is the beginning of another story. A postbook interview published in the *Guardian* presents it as a happy one.[42]

Jakiela's birth family connection story begins in a Catholic Charities office with a counselor interviewing her, first in person and then by a questionnaire asking, for example, "What is your expected outcome?" (17). She returns home to find an email saying, "I am your sister" (29); however, the timing is coincidental, and the email is the result of gossip. The emails, from someone with the username Blonde4Eva, continue, and their semiliteracy dismays the verbal Jakiela. The counselor tells her not to answer. In a few days, she calls to say that the birthmother refused any kind of contact and swore and screamed at her as no one else ever has. About a week later, Jakiela finds many angry 3:00 A.M. and thereabouts phone messages from her sister on her voicemail.

Sometime later, she gets an email from her brother. He has read her first memoir, which mentions her birth name and her birthmother's name, told her long ago by her parents. He is more rational and welcoming, and they talk, first on the phone, then in person, and then with spouses and the other sister. Not long after, she receives more angry social media messages from her birthmother, oddly beginning, "I will pray for you" (215). She names the birthfather, also hostilely, calling him "the Jew" (219). Hate-filled messages from her birthmother and the first birth sister continue, while her brother and her second sister warmly accept her as part of the family.

After recounting the first contact with her brother, Jakiela inserts a fictional interlude, a reconstruction of the early pregnancy of her birthmother, whom she calls Marie. She imagines Marie hiding out in her older sister's closet, humiliated by the family members who knew and by their priest. Then she provides another imagined memory—this one a picture of Marie's father's violence, lack of love, and paranoia—then a third of the appearance, deceptions, and smooth dancing of the man who got her pregnant, and a fourth of her time in the home for unwed mothers, mocked by a multitude of statues of the Virgin Mary and repelled by her new baby's clubfeet, which remind her of her father's leg injury. The reconstructions come in part from Jakiela's official record, in part from what her siblings have told her; they are her attempt to understand her birthmother's rejection of her as a reaction to shame and other suffering.

Jakiela continues to be obsessed by this rejection and the hostile messages, hoping that their tone will change and she will get at least a family medical history. Concern with them becomes as obsessive for her as concern for her children usually is—she later identifies her mood as grieving. Looking for her "birth mother's buried softness" (239), she examines the records again and finds it. In the last reconstruction, Marie returns to the orphanage about a year later, touches the child's belly, asks if the child seems happy, and asks twice if the child will have the necessary surgeries. Jakiela writes her a long email thanking her for a good life and saying that it was the right thing to give her up to a "woman who loved her and who [she] loved" (247). The first response she receives is the most civilized that her birthmother has ever sent: "I've thought of you often. It's just too much after all these years. What's done is done." But the second response says that she wishes she'd had an abortion. After this, Jakiela finally asks her husband to send a message to stop the emails, and they do stop. In the epilogue, she tells us that her relationship with her brother, and to a lesser extent the sister they had drinks with, continues, and even Blonde4Eva sends her a nonhostile message that she has a new job and is happy.

These summaries of the development of birth family connections in these two memoirs leave out much of the books, for both are filled with vivid memories and thoughtful analyses of adoptive parents. Both memoirists are trying to make sense of the meanings of adoption and family, but Harding evokes more visually his family home and routines and London's various geographies as well as the subtleties and large patterns of class relationships and Irish immigration history. Jakiela, by contrast, recounts more of the vicissitudes of child-rearing and partial parallels to her life in the life of other adopted and/or working-class friends and family members.

Class and Shame

The search in *Mother Country* reveals a story of class scorn and class shame, while the narrative in *Belief* tells two stories in which class shame and disadvantage and sexual shame are combined. Harding remembers being a contented child until, like many British upper-class children, he went to boarding school at seven, and when home on vacations gradually realized the oddness of his parents. His mother had told him before school began that he was adopted (for a few years thereafter he thought all children were), that she and he were both orphans, and that her grandmother had taken her to Egypt, returned with her to a very big house, and given her rides in a horse-drawn carriage—all these adventures, he discovered as a teenager, were fantasy.

Maureen loved the musicals *Oliver* and *My Fair Lady*. This affection takes on special meaning during Harding's ancestry search as he discovers that she grew up in working-class poverty, though marriage raised her out of it and her first husband even paid for her to have elocution lessons like those portrayed in *My Fair Lady* (106). Colin, her second husband, "was fiercely opposed to any social arrangement that might keep disadvantaged people alive too long and put a burden on more fortunate families like ourselves" (16). Hating working-class people in general and wanting to keep away from them as much as possible, he barred her from seeing her early friends, one of whom, it turns out, was Margaret Walsh. Maureen's memory of their friendship may have affected the sympathetic way she described his first mother to young Jeremy—as a "little girl" he came to think of as frail (55). In his youth, Harding saw his parents, formerly sociable, as exclusionary and lonely, living on the river, "moat-people" (8); when they visited other parts of London, it was important to avoid public housing projects, which, even if well-constructed, Colin detested (14).

As memoirist, Harding gives almost without comment the monologue in which Colin's old friend Boris reveals the mercenary motive for the adoption, letting the reader imagine his feelings, to which Boris is clearly insensitive. When Harding tries to get more information, Boris is scornful and changes the subject to Colin's bridge game, and deflected feelings emerge: "I felt unusually, pathetically eager to defend my father and perhaps inflict pain on Boris's poodle" (51). Maureen had continued to be friendly to working people and temporarily enjoyed becoming a flower seller (more connections with *My Fair Lady*), but Colin stopped this job and stopped such interactions as much as he could. On another visit trying to get more information, after telling Maureen's former friend John Webb about the end of her work in the flower trade, Harding pauses his narration and writes, "I suddenly felt very blue about Maureen, sad about her life" (107).

Though the economic and cultural deprivation of Jakiela's birth family was worse than what she grew up with, her birthmother and her adoptive parents are all working-class people. Her parents were, she writes, "too old to qualify for a healthy white baby girl" (111), but were given her because she had two clubbed feet, which required many operations. Although she knows this now, they always presented adopting her as their choice, and growing up, she often felt good about it. They told her her original name and that of her birthmother, but there were times when suspicion of her origins emerged. At the dinner table when she uses new words she had learned by secretly reading the dictionary, her mother would say, "I don't know where you came from" (34). Later she says, "You probably get your smart mouth from *her*" (119).

Jakiela's mother is not as unequivocally suspicious of her ancestry as are parents in the memoirs of Winterson, Fisher, and Hipchen, whose father believes that she is "genetically incapable of love" (169); sometimes she encourages Jakiela's search for her birth family, expressing the wish that children and adoptive families could be better matched in personality. But at other times she is hostile to them, whether because of a sense of moral superiority to a presumably unwed mother or because of fearing competition for her daughter's love with another family or indeed the outside world. She would say, "I want what's mine to stay mine" (35), and "She'll get ideas" is an ominous prediction to her. Many of these attitudes can be associated with anxiety about a child leaving a class, ethnic, or religious group.[43]

The idea that Jakiela had inherited her interest in words is immediately deflated when email contact with her birth family begins. Her new brother's first email is more articulate and formal than those from others in the family, but when he calls, his voice "is a distinct working-class accent [she's] heard all [her] life and tried to escape" (137), though somewhat softer. They can some days later find a commonality in singing Irish songs, but he admits to envy at her growing up without "the deadbeat piano playing father, his mother, her troubles" (183). Her birthmother writes angrily, unaware of how strongly Jakiela feels about her working-class identity, "Your ancestors were hard working and proud individuals and you just beat that down" (222). But all she knows about Jakiela, besides her desire for contact, probably, is that Jakiela has published a book that reveals her name and therefore the history that she has been trying to keep secret. As with the other mother, it seems, it is partly the interest in words that marks Jakiela as different.

Thus Jakiela draws on an environment not totally foreign to her as well as on the Catholic Charities files, when she imagines the humiliation of her birthmother in her vignettes about Marie. Hit herself in childhood with a wooden spoon by her mother and a belt by her father (*Belief* 102), she can easily imagine that Marie's even more violent father "would beat this child out of her if he knew" and that "sometimes Marie becomes her father and beats her own head" (145). Jakiela's adoptive father, a millworker, mistrusted people in general and much preferred dogs (*Miss New York* 34–36); she hypothesizes the same of Marie's father (*Belief* 152, 156). Jakiela has apparently been told that he had one wooden leg—and since he worked in construction, which in her imagined vignette he calls "the danger business" (*Belief* 153), typically in a building eight stories up, it probably replaced one lost in a work accident.

The conversion of class shame into depression and generalized anger is not uncommon.[44] Jakiela sees much of her birthmother's shame as coming from Catholic tradition, writing of "the old-world Irish Catholic horror I was born into" (80) and imagining the many images of the Virgin Mary in the Rosalia Foundling and Maternity Home as meant to say "This is what a good mother looks like. . . . You can pray to us for salvation because we are what you'll never be" (173; I use her spelling though public records call it Roselia). She writes, "Marie grew up in the church with her parents and their parents and so on. She knew cruel" (173). She thinks of the church-run Irish Magdalene homes, which exploited unwed mothers and mistreated many of their children (45), when Blonde4Eva writes that her mother, a child of immigrants from Ireland, was "very proud Irish. . . . Catholic" (48). Jakiela still ambivalently identifies as Catholic, in contrast to her "born-again Christian" in-laws, but writes of the "American Catholic [implied from the phrase in the same sentence, quoted earlier, horror] I was raised in and thought bad enough" (80–81), and remembers her pastor Father Ackerman's advice that parents should make their children grateful by using "their hands for beatings, so children would feel that physical connection" (115).

The Irishness of the birthmothers is emphasized in both memoirs, though with the significant difference that for Harding, who doesn't interview anyone Irish until he hears from his cousin near the end of his search, Irishness apparently has no special associations with religion or beating or shame. But indeed there would have been contrasts between the experience of midcentury Irish immigrants to London and that of earlier Irish immigrants to the United States and their children. Since the 1930s, many more Irish people have immigrated to England, especially women to London, than to the United States, and among their communities in London they probably felt less embattled.[45]

Looking through various records for Margaret Walsh, Harding sees many Irish names and notices the areas of London where they are found. Their listed occupations give him a social history of the change from immigrants to "first-generation exiles" (126), and he tries to envision the lives of those in the "tough immigrant drama." He finds "Irishness" attractive but more relevant to understanding Margaret than himself. Later, when his cousin Mary asks him about Irishness, he thinks of Irish writers, Irish songs, and the Irish rugby player Mick Doyle (174–75). He learns that Margaret has been able to keep another son, who was born before she got married, so somehow she has become able to deal differently with the associated social stigma. In *Mother Country*, apart from the assumed pressure to have Harding adopted, the element of shame appears much more in his adoptive family than in what he would call his natural one. This may be partly because the meeting with Margaret and Mary occurs so late in the narrative and few details of their lives appear. There are traumas in their world—giving up the baby was hard, Margaret did not want to talk to the social worker afterward (34), the father is not to be mentioned—but she has moved beyond them.

The second story of sexual shame that occurs in *Belief* is one that Jakiela discovered not during her search for her birthmother but more than five years earlier. It is, however, relevant to her adoption, and she includes it in this book, close to the end, as part of the lead-in to her father's death—the revelation occurred about a month before, as if he wanted to make sure she knew while he still could tell her. He tells the story as if he were a child—he was nine or ten in the time he thinks back to: "He touched my peepee" (269). It was his soon-to-be brother-in-law, Whitey. Jakiela's mother has known about this incident for a long time, it turns out. Jakiela's father had a beautiful voice as a child and sang in the church choir. Whitey was in a band and so had an excuse to listen to his singing, alone. Afterward, the boy cried for a long time. No one noticed. He told no one. He stopped singing. His submission to Whitey and his failure to tell may have resulted in part from the deference to authority emphasized by overlapping Catholic and working-class cultures (Kelly and Kelly 262; Wilkins and Pace 391). Her mother tells her, "I think that's why he's always been so miserable. . . . We thought maybe adopting you would help . . . I think it helped, having you" (Jakiela, *Belief* 271).

Depression is indeed frequent among child abuse survivors, so with that shame combined with his class shame, it is remarkable that he was able to feel and express love for his daughter as much as he did (Kagan 47). Depressed for a different reason than loss of a child, he attached to her closely as Homes feels her mother could not. Just as Harding does not react explicitly to the news that he was adopted to help his parents' finances, Jakiela never comments directly on the revelation that she was adopted as therapy for her father. (Her mother had unsuccessfully tried for years to persuade him to get real therapy.) Any possible anger on her own behalf is far outweighed by compassion for her father and anger at Whitey and at his sister, who has always refused to acknowledge the abuse. The story is relevant to this book not just because of the light it sheds on the reason for her adoption and the psychology of her father but also because of the connection she makes between her father and her birthmother: "Because of the terrible things that happened to my father, he called people cockroaches. I think of my birth mother like that, a hard shell, refusing to die, scaring everyone she crawls past" (234). She is like a cockroach but at the same time like Jakiela's beloved father in that she has been mistreated. As Jakiela writes earlier, "Cruelty is a bandage" (88).

Changing Interpretations of Identity, Ancestry, and Family

Harding and Jakiela both narrate changes in their ideas about their identity related to adoption and the events of their search. Harding has for much of his life thought of himself as "a free spirit" by contrast to his "marooned" parents (8). He feels "impartial" by contrast to "most other people . . . condemned to peer at the world across the obscurity of the breeding hutch" (154). He has rejected the maxim "blood is thicker than water" (5) and identified with water; his childhood home was on the river. But as, in his quest for information, he meets John Webb, who had known both his adoptive mother and his birthmother and who he wishfully thinks might be his father, he realizes that he would like to know his ancestry and escape from the fluidity of water. Bernstein, as we saw earlier in this chapter, experiences a similar change of attitudes, and others, such as Saffian and Strauss, also come to feel more connection with their ancestry.

The issue of possible hereditary similarities in appearance comes up briefly for Harding when with Webb, and at the end with regard to his cousin, though not his mother. More importantly, he sees in himself similarities to his adoptive parents—ways he has been influenced by Colin, and in some cases by Maureen, that he regrets. He is not as impartial as he thinks. As he walks through a public housing project near where Margaret used to live, he realizes that he shares some of his parents' anxiety about such projects (88–89), thus some of their attitudes toward class. He compares himself to Colin in letting Maureen down by not showing her affection—"a pair of undemonstrative men" (80). When he interviews someone who lived in Margaret's neighborhood long ago and can't identify her class, he feels he'd "begun falling aimlessly, or gently rotating in zero gravity, with the familiar markers of class and social identity turning gently about me like luminous debris in the aftermath of a space-probe disaster" (146). And when he finally meets Margaret, he feels "robbed of the words for . . . difference or affinity by social group and background; wealth and poverty" (176). While he had earlier critiqued Colin for his "them and us" attitude, it is clear that he shared some of it, even if with different divisions, but now he feels that he is getting beyond that, ready to picnic with Margaret over "the battle lines of the British class system" (176). He suddenly sees his worldly success as a sign of limitation: "I'd been able to pile up wealth, incapable of functioning in the world without the thought that it was there to fall back on" (175). By the same token, he realizes that Margaret's large family, and her closeness to them, constitute another kind of abundance. Harding's growth in appreciation of working-class people might be compared to the move away from internalized racism that transracial adoptees' memoirs often narrate. His feeling that their picnic on the battle lines is a celebration of transcendence of the class system is perhaps the British analogue to the mixed-race—majority Black—celebrations that conclude the memoirs of adoptee Jaiya John and adoptive father J. Douglas Bates, discussed in later chapters.

Through most of Harding's memoir, he describes how what he learns makes him more sympathetic to Maureen and more critical of Colin for cutting Maureen off from her friends and her flower-selling. However, he evokes a farewell image of each that recalls his affection for them in early childhood.

He imagines Colin in his gardening clothes, off on the boat over the Thames to do the shopping. "We both like the river" (141). He sees that if he had just met them briefly, "they'd have seemed bracingly eccentric" (172). His last image of Maureen is of her quickly reaching out to save his two-year-old son from falling into the water, showing her motherliness—the image of the falling boy is one he had applied to himself earlier in the memoir, in analyzing the photograph of his christening party. Calling up these images is a kind of personal ritual of tribute to them.

Jakiela remembers having often said and felt that adoption was not an issue for her and even having felt good about being wanted and chosen. However, unlike Saffian, who makes a similar claim, she includes many memories of times in which it was an issue, such as vignettes of how both she and her African American adoptee cousin looked and felt out of place when some family photographs were taken (*Belief* 110–11, 114, 119–20, 121). She often felt sad about not identifying with any of the ethnicities in her adoptive or her birth family. "Until I married and had children, I was single, solitary, someone who most days wanted to take up no space at all" (47). In *Miss New York Has Everything*, which includes a narrative of her time as an airline stewardess, she feels bad about the fact that the ethnicity people are most likely to attribute to her, from her appearance, is German (162–69). When her birthmother refuses contact, Jakiela realizes even more fully how much she felt deprived by being adopted. With a desire that Hipchen, among these memoirists has most explicitly recalled, she had really wanted "to know something that looked and moved and laughed and loved and was sad like me" (99).

When she does feel that she may have similarities to either one of her adoptive parents or her birthmother, usually the likenesses are painful. Hearing about her birthmother's screaming at the social worker, she thinks, "I've found my roots, the map of what I was born with" (94). None of the other adoptee memoirists discussed except Harding worry about similarities to their adoptive parents, but Jakiela does. "For decades," she writes, "I've tried not to be like my father" (265). Thinking both of his suspicion of the world and her mother's worries and fear of loss, she writes, "There is so much of my parents in me I barely believe in blood" (77). But similarity to her birthmother may feel even worse. When she neglects her children because she is obsessed by her birthmother's rejection, she thinks, "I am a terrible mother. Like the birth mother before me, and so on and so on. And this time my mother, my real mother, a good mother, is not here to tell me otherwise" (236–37). She does not conclude with this attitude, however. She resolves "If paranoia and cruelty run like cancer in my birth mother's bloodline, I am hoping something else will show up to provide balance and grace" (240), looks at the Catholic Charities report again, and finds the memory of her birthmother's final visit and touch. Here is the hidden kindness that she had hoped to find in her blood-line, as a sign of her own possibilities, even if her birthmother can no longer extend kindness to her.

Jakiela's memoir many times recounts with annoyance people telling her that she was lucky and should be grateful—experiences recounted by many adoptees, though more often, among memoirists, by those adopted transracially. But toward the end she accepts these words. In escaping her birthmother she *was* lucky and more like her birthfather. "We were both, my father and I, lucky. We made it over the wall" (220, she has just referred to her father as "a German and a Jew" so implicitly crossing the Berlin Wall is made an image of their escapes). She tells her birthmother she is grateful to her for giving her up to a mother who would love her, and she recalls with gratitude her last days with each of her adoptive parents. In the last chapter before the epilogue, she writes about her daughter's perfect pitch, a tie to her father's early singing, and her daughter's hope that the last caterpillar in her daughter's science experiment will transform into a butterfly. Can she and her children keep the good things in their family history and leave behind the bitterness?

The contrast in what each memoir includes and excludes clearly relates to gender and perhaps to some extent to nation. It is striking, in comparison to Jakiela's and other adoption memoirs by women, that Harding says very little about looking for similarities to himself in his children—just "I'd had only a few years practice in the arts of physical comparison based on kinship" (105); this may be a matter of British reticence or perhaps related to a wish not to violate their privacy or a sense that it is too far from the main concerns of the book. Meanwhile, although class is important in Jakiela's memoir, Harding is much more explicit about its influence, as British writers often are.

Jakiela is living with and taking primary responsibility for her children during the time recounted here. Harding apparently is mostly not; his wife and three children are in France, where he usually lives (Kellaway). He says in his preface that he thinks of this book as in part for his children and particularly to "show that people were joined up, and separated, in all sorts of ways" (xix). But they do not figure much in the book. Jakiela, unlike Harding, frequently discusses similarities between herself and her children as well as recounting her care for them in crises; Harding, instead of showing himself preoccupied with his children, mentions two occasions on which he intended to buy Christmas presents for his children and bought other things instead and has them with him only on two visits with family members.

The image of maternal care, however, is important to both of them: Harding repeats the phrase "good care" found in the social worker's report on his condition in his adoptive family, and almost the last image he evokes of his mother is of her instinctive reaching out to keep his two-year-old son from falling. But this iconic memory of her does not have the same two-sided personal meaning for him that it would for Jakiela. When Jakiela recalls her adoptive mother's account of her anxiety that the social worker would find her unfit, she identifies with this anxiety (73–74). As her mother is dying, she says, "You were a good mother," and her mother responds, "You're a good mother" (246).

Belief includes so many examples of her mother's close-mindedness and Jakiela's feelings of discomfort when growing up that the mutual praise here may seem remarkable. Sounding like Mrs. Winterson, whose similar question gives Winterson's memoir its title, Mrs. Jakiela even asks her teenager, "Why can't you be normal?" (96). But immediately after remembering those words, Jakiela recalls that her mother would write in notes for her lunchbox and recite, at bedtime during her childhood as well as much later before going into surgery, "Not blood of my blood or flesh of my flesh, but heart of my heart" (97). Rather than giving an explicit narrative of a moment when her attitude toward her mother changes, Jakiela places early in the memoir, before many of the unhappy memories, a time when her one-year-old son won't stop crying, her grocery bag breaks, spilling milk all over the car, and her mother takes over and praises her for being a good mother, "a gift, a mantra, a promise" (27)—is it the first time for this praise? It is clearly a time when she needs it. And another sign of how important her maternal role is to her is that her memoir proper ends with her daughter's singing lessons and butterflies in transition. Several other adoptee memoirists—Strauss, Lifton, Homes, and most of the transracial adoptees discussed in the next chapter—place scenes with their children at or very close to the end, but Jakiela is the only one whose children figure so much all the way through.

Harding wrote a new introduction for the 2010 American paperback edition 2, in which he explains that he had the legal right to see his original birth certificate while his American counterpart might not, depending on state of residence. Crediting Wayne Carp's scholarship,[46] he gives a history of adoption secrecy in the United States, argues that sealed birth records are outdated, and suggests skepticism about the resulting American industry of "intermediary programs" and parent-child registers (Harding ix–xiv). Jakiela's story reinforces such skepticism. Since Pennsylvania was then a closed-record state, Jakiela had to go through Catholic Charities to get her birth certificate. While her parents had long ago told her her birth name and her mother's, she does get more material from her Catholic Charities file. However, for a long time she feels locked into allowing their social worker, whom she does not like, to be the intermediary in any contact. Obviously her birthmother does not like this social worker either. By contrast, Harding's adoption counselor makes good suggestions for research. He consults family friends and relatives, the Family Records Office, the voting rolls, the street directory. Theoretically Jakiela could have, for example, gone to a records office to try to locate her birthmother's married name by looking up years of marriage records, but that probably looked like an impossible task. And she does have those children to take care of. Harding explicitly says that he chose his title as an analogy to "Indian country" (xxi), suggesting, as does his memoir work's origin in a BBC series called "Another Country," which became a *Granta* issue, that the world of mothers is foreign to him.

Putting these two memoirs together suggests something of the great range of results that a search for birthparents might produce, with Jakiela's awful mother being even worse than Homes's father, the worst birthparent in the earlier section of this chapter. It is ironic, considering the traditional belief that class barriers are stronger in England than the United States, that the Irish immigrant to London, Harding's birthmother, has had a happier life, and thus one more open to reunion, than the daughter of Irish immigrants to the United States, Jakiela's birthmother, though there is much evidence that the United States has become increasingly economically stratified, with a theoretically possible happy poverty difficult to find. The memoirs also suggest a great range of contrast in personalities that adoptees might have. Jakiela portrays here a life very lonely before her marriage, full of shame and self-doubt. None of her adoptee friends or relatives speaks of a good relationship with either adoptive parents or birthparents. Apparently they are all working class and poor. Her depression could be seen as caused by growing up in an atmosphere of economic and educational deprivation, as Jonathan Turner (193) and Jerome Kagan (188) would see it. But not surprisingly, she seems drawn to Nancy Verrier's theory that separation from a mother to be adopted produces a "primal wound" (218), though she does not commit to it. Harding mourns the loss of his easy relationship with his parents in early childhood, but they had the resources to get him to excellent boarding schools and Cambridge University (Kellaway), and he has managed to turn his sense of not being "what anyone had in mind" (154) into an advantage. When his memoir becomes introspective, it is to suggest that his search is shaking up a self-confidence that might even have been excessive. In his introduction to the U.S. edition, it is clear that he prefers the "civil rights" argument for openness about birth records to anything that depends on the idea of adoptees as necessarily wounded (xiii–xiv).

These contrasts are easy to attribute to the contrast between the experience of a man raised in a privileged atmosphere and that of a woman from a family with less money and little educational guidance in her youth. But it is also relevant that Jakiela was in the Rosalia orphanage for close to a year—perhaps longer than many other children because her clubfeet made her less "adoptable"—and that year probably did have the experience basic to the primal wound theory, as she explains it, of "scream[ing] and scream[ing] for mothers who never come" (218), in addition to much lonely time spent in the hospital because of operations for her legs, while Harding was in Maureen's care by the time he was eleven days old. (According to Verrier's theory, however, he still would have missed his first mother.)

Margaret Homans shows that many adoptees' memoirs involve creating fictions about their origins.[47] Jakiela creates such fictions in the vignettes in which she imagines her birthmother under the name Marie, not to pretend that she has found the identity of a birthmother, as is often all that can be achieved because of closed records, but to help understand and forgive her. Crucially, she says, "I choose to believe in my birth mother's underground tenderness and mercy" (245). For Harding, by contrast, fictionality is mainly associated with the stories that Maureen made up for him about her adventures with her grandmother as well as with her identification with Eliza in *My Fair Lady*. He analyzes her story of adopting him as a class fable, notes that her favorite books are about families getting separated and then reunited again, suggesting that she wanted to believe this could happen, and calls her "terrific . . . with make-believe" (102)—his discovery about her previous life shows the falsity of most of what she told him about himself and herself. When his cousin contacts him, the investigative journalist says, "I've no way of knowing if any of this is true," and includes her answer, "It's all true" (163).

Jakiela's title, *Belief is its own kind of truth, Maybe* (lowercase her preference, with *Maybe* stressing ambivalence), indicates from the start that she has more tolerance of fiction. For her, all family life, indeed all life, involves wishful thinking. She quotes her mother as saying, "People believe what they need to believe" (182) and takes her title from her earlier comment about her mother's pride in the survival of her dogwood tree, based on the belief that they are difficult to grow (58), as well as in her parents' inventing "a movie version of their meeting" (182), a fantasy like Maureen's stories about her childhood. She acknowledges that her own beliefs may often not have objective grounds and does not feel objectivity is always necessary: "I believe a lot of things because it's better to believe them than to believe their opposites. . . . [My parents] loved me enough to make me believe I was beautiful. The truth is, I have one of those faces people don't remember" (199–200).

Now she thinks of her relationship with her husband and children as depending to a large extent on stories, sometimes true ones. As she anticipates retelling the story of the hospital room where the doctor discovered that her daughter had stuffed a toy reindeer's nose up her nose, she thinks, "This story will become one of our favorites. . . .We will tell them the way old ladies at church tick off prayers on rosary beads, which is how I think of family now, the most sacred thing" (255). But she emphasizes the distinction between the way most people depend on their parents' stories about their lives and the way she as an adoptee, "to sketch in the details of what was lost to [her]," has had to ask many other people, documents, and "[her] imagination" (289).

In Harding's memoir, just a few points suggest some appreciation of wishful thinking and family fictions. He remembers that when Maureen picked him up after his graduation, she asked him about his studies with just the word and tone a duchess might use—"for a moment there you were the real thing" (184). And at the very end, after having discovered that her father was a "wine and spirits merchant's carman," when he thinks he has found the "genealogy" (using that word for the first time) of her stories of riding in her grandmother's carriage, he likes to imagine that her father "would have let her up on the dray when she was a little girl. Once or twice, surely, by way of a treat" (189).

Both of these memoirs, like most by adoptees, turn away from the idea of finding identity in birth origin alone and toward something more complex. John McLeod writes of "adoptive being," which treats "bio-genetic" and adoptive modes of kinship as "concomitant instances of 'being with.'"[48] But these authors, like many adoptees (such as Winterson claiming Ruth Rendell as one of her mothers and Homes claiming Gertrude Stein), have achievements and loyalties determined by neither adoptive nor genetic parents. Strained as her relationships with her adoptive parents often have been, in the course of her memoir Jakiela realizes that her birthparents provide very little material through which to construct her identity. She has tried the genetic roots fantasy and found it unlivable—she is related to her birthmother's life primarily as someone who has escaped it. She has also escaped some of the limitations of her adoptive parents' lives; she can honor what they gave her and put her efforts into the family she and her husband have created and into her writing while trying to maintain relationships with her birth family and her working-class loyalties. The hope for her daughter's caterpillar's metamorphosis into a butterfly is significantly placed at the end of the memoir proper, while the last page of the epilogue is about the town of Braddock, where her mother was a nurse and her father a steel mill worker and where they are buried, a tribute comparable to Harding's summoning up images of his parents at their best as he takes leave of them.

Harding has a less self-doubting personal and professional identity. He never mentions in this book whether he used his sense of being an outsider in writing a thoroughly researched and grippingly written book on refugees (*The Uninvited: Refugees at the Rich Man's Gate*).[49] He began his memoir assuming his birthmother was dead and wanting to write a brief tribute to her, knowing her life must have been difficult; he briefly thinks of what sort of life he might have had if she had kept him, based on the lives of his brothers: "I'd have been the father of five children (4.3 to be exact) conceived with two partners. I'd have left school at an early age" (175). None of them sound like they "hold with the idea of roots," he writes, adding, "This much we had in common" (174). Clearly he, like Jakiela, and like Winterson, also dealing with class difference, prefers his current life to that one—but at the same time, meeting Margaret provides him with new relationships entirely different from those he already has, structured as they are by class and professional expectations, and he values this opportunity.

Harding and Jakiela both go through a process of reconstructing themselves in the time portrayed in their memoirs, in which they revise what they think about their relationships to all of their parents, not choosing an identity based exclusively on either birth or adoption or both. Though John McLeod's book about adoption narratives I quoted a few pages earlier is about transcultural adoptee experience and theirs is transcultural only in the Irish ancestry of their mothers and therefore much less visible, his conclusions about the multiplicity possible in adoptive being apply to them as well. While one recent summary says that the typical adoption memoir "valorizes origins and troubles the primacy of social construction,"[50] many adoption memoirs also emphasize, as another summary says, "the construction of families out of something other than sheer biology" (Hipchen and Deans 166). Many memoirists conclude with the acknowledgment that both their adoptive and their birth families and ancestries have contributed to their identities (Saffian 302; Homes 238; Strauss, *Beneath* 201; see some in the next chapter also). However, few other adoptees, apart from Winterson, put as much stress as Harding and Jakiela on the details of their adoptive family life.

Part of the reason for this difference in stress may be that these two memoirs are written soon after adoptive parents' deaths; death sometimes makes it easier for adoptees who have worried about hurting their parents earlier to search. While in some memoirs adoptive parents figure primarily in terms of their perceived lack of understanding, Jakiela and Harding move beyond this point, and both end their books paying tribute to three-dimensional people whom they love and miss. Perhaps the reason for this contrast is not just that their adoptive parents are dead but that the memoirists are older and have their own experiences of parenthood, more than most of the others.

When she is about to describe her first meeting with her brother and sister by birth, Jakiela writes, "We are all the stars of our own movies, the only ones worthy of a close-up . . . I never considered them in their own close-ups" (193–94). But she does make special efforts to give each of her adoptive parents, and even the birthmother who does not want to meet her, several close-ups. Harding gives vivid pictures of the happy times he had with his parents as a young child and mourns his mother's later descent into alcoholism and dementia and his father's into increasing exclusion, class prejudice, and futile search for more money.

There are many reasons for the greater focus on adoptive parents in these memoirs. Not only was Harding so moved by what he discovered about Maureen that he wanted to write about her, but also, because Margaret is still alive, he is trying to respect her privacy—referring to her at his last mention not by her married name but as "the former Miss Walsh" (177). Jakiela begins her narrative by writing, "When my real mother dies, I go looking for another one" (13), mocking the idea of the adoptive mother as a substitute by framing her search for her birthmother as a search for a replacement for her dead adoptive mother. In her epilogue she says, "I've never met my birth mother. I could, but I don't need or want to anymore" (290). Even if her birthmother could relate to her with less hatred, her dead mother is irreplaceable.

Harding's final discussion of his ancestry search story breaks down the distinction between adoptive and blood relationship: "The process that Margaret and I had begun turned into a second adoption. . . . What mattered was to want to engage with another person, and to continue believing this was a good thing to do" (176).[51] With her birthmother, Jakiela can no longer believe that it is a good thing to do. However, of her brother, she writes, "That I met him is its own miracle" (221). Writing in the epilogue of what now seem to her like a normal relationship, she says of him, as she says of no one else, "We'll high-five each other when we say or hear something true" (289).[52] But the last sentence of her epilogue is an ambiguous tribute to the job-creating but air-polluting steel works of Braddock, a tribute that resonates with what she has said about her parents' love of her, the title, her continued working-class solidarity, and the power of wishful thinking: "People who are born here find it beautiful" (291).

I spend so much space on these two memoirs for several reasons. First is their vivid picture of mixed feelings about adoptive parents, evoking both painful and happy memories resolved in acceptance, forgiveness, and love. Next, and closely related, is their explicit discussion of class. Few other memoirists represented here write of it in as much detail. Hipchen briefly notes a class gap between her birthparents, who met because his athletic ability got him a scholarship to a prep school. Winterson tells about her adoptive father's work as a road mender and coal shoveler and her birthmother's work as a machinist (16) and writes, "I didn't want to be in the teeming mass of the working class" (17). Jakiela still identifies with that class; Harding doesn't, but he is glad to picnic on the battle lines of the class system.

Some contrasts between these two memoirs may call attention to the fact that, apart from Homes, most of the recent writers who feel that adoption (or more accurately, being relinquished for adoption) is in itself damaging—Jakiela, Winterson, Hipchen—grew up under the influence of a religious culture that emphasized shame. This was a more general attitude in the earlier memoirists, Lifton, Fisher, and Paton, but Pentecostal and some Catholic traditions as presented in these memoirs preserve old attitudes.

Jakiela's conjecture about the impact of her year in the orphanage plus later time in the hospital because of surgery on her legs invites a closer look at the instability in the early lives of so many of these memoirists, particularly the ones most uncomfortable about adoption. Lifton is put in an orphanage at five months, visited by her birthmother until she is two, and then put in a foster home for four months until her adoptive parents take her (89). At three days, Homes is given to her adoptive parents, who are grieving the loss of another child six months previously. Hipchen is in a Catholic orphanage for three months, all but the first few weeks without her birthmother. Jakiela spends much of her early years in a hospital because of operations on her feet. Hickman is in a white foster home for a year and a half, perhaps in the hope the brace would fix his bowed legs. The records of home visits included as an appendix in "Documents of His Genesis" describe him as "exceedingly happy" and frequently smiling (337). But his adoptive mother asks his birthmother, "Why do you think Craig cried so much?" (171). In the previous chapter, Seek observes a similar change in her son's behavior after his adoption. Regardless of whatever problems might result from the first separation, about which psychologists disagree, many of these experiences of temporary stay in hospital, orphanage, or foster home may also provide material for a lifelong sense of instability and loneliness. Christine Ward Gailey writes of "the range of traumas kids may experience in birth or foster homes [before adoption], which may turn children into survivors akin to refugees."[53] I return to the point about early experience at the end of the next chapter, with more examples to compare.

The narratives of Harding and Jakiela reveal another issue that rarely emerges elsewhere in this book: extrinsic motivation for adoption. An intrinsic motive would be adopting because you like children or want to help a child. While motives are often mixed, these memoirs place unusual emphasis on the extrinsic part: in Harding's, pleasing a relative in order to inherit money, and in Jakiela's, helping a spouse who is depressed because he was sexually molested as a child. Other extrinsic motivations might be wanting general social approval or the approval of a church, which, we see in *The Language of Blood*, Jane Jeong Trenka believes were the reasons her parents adopted. In this and other ways, these memoirs are cautions against any tendency to idealize adoptive parents. The conditions behind these motivations, class anxiety and depression from sexual shame, contribute to some of the family strain that Harding and Jakiela relate; nevertheless, both memoirists attach to their parents enough to have significant happy memories of them. Jakiela believes she had a "good mother," and Harding that he received "good care," phrases that are repeated. Extrinsic motivation may ultimately not preclude "good enough" parenting. It does not guarantee it. But maybe intrinsic motivation does not guarantee it either, especially in the case of transracial adoption.

3

Constructing Racial Identity

Seeking Ancestry, Exploring Relationships

Deann Borshay Liem, Jane Jeong Trenka, Katy Robinson,
Mei-Ling Hopgood, Nicole Chung, Catherine McKinley, Jaiya John,
Avery Klein-Cloud, Jackie Kay, Rebecca Carroll, Jenny Heijun Wills,
Susan Devan Harness

M ost transracial adoptees' memoirs reveal a huge gap in their adoptive parents' preparation, with sad consequences. Many of them were adopted at a time when belief in the "blank slate" not only emphasized the importance of nurture over genetics but also ignored the fact that these children would experience confusion, at best, because of the ambiguity of their relation to their parents' white privilege.[1] Even the most progressive parents they describe do not expect how much their children would have to struggle with racism, a lack in their education that some adoptive parent memoirists also note with regret. As Kim Park Nelson has shown, the sadness in many transracial adoptee memoirs is a great contrast to the "dominant representation of transracial adoption as an overwhelmingly positive experience marked by familial fulfillment, generosity, and unconditional, colorblind love."[2] Most transracial adoptee memoirists from childhood on experience institutional and personal biases that their parents at worst share and often cannot talk about. Still, they do not ultimately portray themselves as victims. Like those of most same-race adoptees, these memoirs show persistent and largely successful efforts to find birthparents and explore what kind of relationships they can build, while dealing with the further complications of navigating an in-between position and defining their racial identity and their communities.

This chapter will discuss five memoirs written by and one film with script cowritten by adoptees with complete or partly African descent, four memoirs written by and one film directed by adoptees of Asian descent (four Korean and one Chinese), and one memoir by an adoptee who identifies as American Indian and transracial. A brief historical overview and a summary of each precede discussions of commonalities and divergences among them. As Marina Fedosik writes, "transracial adoptees cannot be understood as a homogen[e]ous group any more than transracial adoption can be understood as an unequivocally beneficial or tragic experience."[3]

Early Histories and Summaries

Transracial adoption of Asian children, earlier championed by Pearl Buck, began on a large scale with the Korean War.[4] Some soldiers adopted children as mascots; others left behind children conceived by Korean mothers, who then had to deal with a repressive society without a social safety net. Harry and Bertha Holt founded the extremely influential and long-lived Holt Adoption Agency, originally just for Korean children, in 1955.[5] The Holts' only requirement for prospective adoptive parents was an acceptable response to a form letter asking them to "state in your own words what your faith is and what Jesus Christ means to you personally" (quoted in J. R. Kim 157). They were so adamant about their religious requirement that social welfare agencies complained that they were disregarding home study assessments and endangering the welfare of the children. Soojin Chung details cases where their proxy adoption process led to the abuse and even the death of some children (77–80). But the agency survives.

Many of the couples who adopted from Korea did so because of the influence of their church, seeing adoption as a way to convert the innocent children of the heathen. This converged with the 1950s emphasis on domesticity after the disruption of the war—returning soldiers and their wives wanted to have children—as well as with the American melting pot ideology of the time: Korean children might be educated to fit in as Americans.[6] These practices had their costs. The costs were first publicly revealed to an American audience in a collection of poems, *Seeds from a Silent Tree*, in 1997.[7] Other Korean adoptee writers and filmmakers began exploring their experience around that time. A watershed was the First International Gathering of the First Generation of Korean Adoptees in Washington DC in 1999.[8] Such collective organization was unique among transnational adoptees, and Korean adoptees were leaders in "shifting the discourse toward a more culturally inclusive paradigm in all forms of transnational adoption after this important turning point," as Kristi Brian writes.[9] Previously, only a few parents who adopted transracially and/or transnationally (we will read about some of them in this chapter) made efforts to educate their children about the culture of their birthparents. Few social workers or adoption agencies told them they should. (Still, as early as the 1970s, parents could buy an Asian-looking doll for their child.) But since the late 1990s, memoirs and other cultural creations from transracial adoptees, especially those from Korea, presented experiences of deracination and identity confusion so devastating that, as Heather Jacobson writes, "Contemporary adoption practices, policy, and international adoption discourse now emphasize the importance of culture keeping" and now often "adoption social workers promote cultural engagement among their clients who are adopting interracially or internationally."[10]

Deann Borshay Liem's *First Person Plural* helped make the situation of Korean adoptees widely visible to others; it appeared on National Public Television in 2000, in the series *The Independent Eye*.[11] Borshay Liem's family home movies shows many scenes of what looked like happiness for little Deann, but at the same time reveals how much she tried to look white, like her sister, and shows her family's obliviousness to her experience when they couldn't repeat her Korean name and didn't care that the orphanage had erased her original identity in switching her with the child they had been writing.

The cost of others' failure to acknowledge her history emerges most clearly when the film shows Deann, in college, having disturbing dreams of her earlier life in Korea. These dreams send her on a quest to find out as much as she can about her past. Through Korean television, which has regular shows that bring separated relatives together, she eventually locates her birth family, meets them, and brings her adoptive parents with her when she visits them again.[12]

Since *First Person Plural*, many transnational adoptees from Asia have written memoirs about their experiences. Korean adoptees, the first large group, made up the first large portion of these memoirs. The best known of these is Jane Jeong Trenka's memoir *The Language of Blood* (2003), now as close to canonical as any memoir of a transnational adoptee.[13] In *The Language of Blood*, we see the full-scale consequence of Holt's attitude toward adoption, made more toxic than in *First Person Plural* partly by Trenka's parents' rigidity.

The Language of Blood tells how Jeong Kong-Ah is flown to the United States from Korea when about six months old and, along with her sister, is adopted by a German American couple, becoming Jane Marie Brauer. Raised in a small town in Minnesota, she has little contact with any other Asian Americans except her sister, also a Korean adoptee but more a rival than a support. Both girls feel "haunted by the birth child who was never conceived, this pink-skinned boy who had pretty blue eyes like his mother and a funny smile like his father . . . and by the ghosts of our own dead twins" with their original Korean names (27).[14] While she is in high school, her birthmother starts writing to her. Her college life involves more contact with Asian Americans, but she doesn't feel she belongs with them. Worse, she has to deal with a determined, violent, and racist stalker. Upon college graduation, she visits

Korea and gets to know her birth family. She returns several times, bringing her sister and, after her birthmother dies, her husband. Her adoptive parents' continuing rejection of her Korean family devastates her as they refuse even to attend the American memorial service that she arranges for her birthmother.

Katy Robinson's *A Single Square Picture* (2002) focuses on Robinson's return to Korea to meet her birthfather and try to locate her birthmother. She recalls her disorientation at her adoption into a white American family at the age of seven after leaving her mother and grandmother, and her subsequent family life with a loving mother (who eventually visits her during her year in Korea), a difficult and eventually alienated father, three older brothers increasingly in trouble with the law, and complex relationships with Korea and her Korean relatives. From the fact that the photograph of the title reveals lies told by the orphanage to the question of whether her Korean mother is dead or living in America, the memoir shows the difficulty of finding the truth, especially in dealing with international adoption.

Mei-Ling Hopgood's *Lucky Girl* (2009) recounts Hopgood's growing up and her developing relationship, beginning in her twenties, with the Taiwanese couple who gave her up for adoption and their many, mostly adult, children. She also portrays her loving white American parents, her trip with them to visit Korea with her two Korean brothers, and their trip with her to meet her Taiwanese family.

Nicole Chung's *All You Can Ever Know* (2018) narrates the results of her domestic adoption after being relinquished by Korean immigrants. Early in her life, her birthmother asked for information about her, and her white parents refused to give it. As an adult, married and working for an adoption organization, she seeks and finds nonidentifying information. After she gets pregnant, a searcher helps her connect with her birthparents and the sisters she did not know she had. The sisters, whose point of view some of the chapters tell, have been told she was dead. Cindy, her full sister, was frequently beaten by her mother. That abuse turns out to be the most likely reason her father decided that she, the next child, should be raised in another family. Her birthmother phones her and apologizes for giving her away, saying her husband was responsible. They talk, and although Chung says she does not blame her, she feels she cannot give her peace. Her birthfather writes, telling the adoption story differently. Having already begun to form a close relationship with Cindy, she believes him, and eventually they meet, together with Cindy and her husband and Chung's own husband and daughter. She discovers and feels a strong affinity with his scholarly and literary achievements. The memoir gives vivid pictures of the impact on her of having her own child, and then of the interest in identity and Korea that her daughter Abby also develops.

Jenny Heijun Wills, in *Older Sister. Not Necessarily Related* (2019), devotes most of her narrative to relationships with her birth family after her reconnection—her birthparents get together again, break off communications with her, then reconnect, she is very close to a younger sister, who moves away, she writes many sections as addressed to an older sister to whom she cannot speak in person. The relationship of a younger sister to an older, called *unni*, is an important theme throughout the book. This focus on complicated postreunion relations with many people in a birth family is virtually unprecedented in a memoir by a Korean adoptee. However, she also writes about her earlier life and introduces her memoir with a preface (with no page numbers) declaring, "These stories are not all mine" and presenting herself as channeling the fantasies of an adoptee community that has "only echoes of memories and alibis."[15]

Trenka, Robinson, and Hopgood were adopted from Asia in the early 1970s and grew up in the American Midwest and, in Robinson's case, West (Utah); Chung was born in 1981 in Seattle and grew up in an all-white community in Oregon, and Wills was born in Korea in the 1990s and grew up in an all-white community in Canada. All recount many experiences of racism and sexism. (Wills's sound similar to what the others experienced in the United States.) Borshay Liem was adopted by a family in California in the 1960s. Racism is suggested by her film's voice-over, in which she recalls her own desire to have blond hair and blue eyes like her sister and her family seems heedless of her distress.

Like the memoirs discussed in the previous chapter, all six works show that meeting and communicating with one's birth family can involve many difficulties. But their tone varies. Trenka's and Wills's read as critiques of transracial adoption and Hopgood's as ultimately a celebration of the impact it had on her own life, while Robinson, Chung, and Borshay Liem generalize less. In their presentation of their early life and upbringing, Trenka and Wills on one hand and Hopgood on the other recall, in some ways, opposite experiences, with the rest of the memoirists somewhere between them.

For a long time, transracial adoption of African Americans was rare, whether because of state laws, expected bias, or the belief in formal matching as psychologists gained more influence in adoption.[16] African American children, unless they were part Korean or Vietnamese, did not receive sympathy as war orphans or potential Christian converts.[17] Helen and Frank Doss, whose "one-family UN" of twelve children was made famous by Helen Doss's 1954 memoir *The Family Nobody Wanted*, met too much opposition to adopt even a partly African American child.[18] In the 1960s, however, the emphasis on integration in movements from civil rights to communism encouraged some white parents, such as Jackie Kay's in the UK and Jaiya John's, Catherine McKinley's, and Douglas Bates's in the United States (Bates's memoir will be discussed in the next chapter) to adopt across racial lines. A few months after the assassination of Martin Luther King Jr., whom they admired, John's future adoptive parents were asked if they would accept a Black child and they said yes.[19] Though rare in 1968, transracial adoption became frequent enough by 1972 that that the National Association of Black Social Workers issued a statement strongly opposing it. In making their argument at that time, the social workers did not cite any transracially adopted memoirist who had written about their problems. There were hardly any transracial African American adoptees old enough to publish a memoir.[20]

As with Korean adoptees, before there were memoirs by adoptees of African descent raised in white families, there were fragments of memoirs written as poems. Jackie Kay's memoir-like poetry gained a wide audience, spreading from the UK to the United States, for her representation of the voices of an adoptee who is partly African and her two mothers. Her sequence *The Adoption Papers* was first published in parts beginning in 1986 and was published as a whole, with some other poems, in a book by the same title in 1991.[21]

More U.S. transracial adoptee memoirists would follow. Catherine McKinley's *Book of Sarahs* (2002) discusses growing up adopted by white parents in a white New England town with an adopted white brother. She searches for her birthmother, who she learns is white and Jewish, and her birthfather, who is African American. She develops a relationship with her birthmother, Estie, but is troubled to discover that she seems sometimes to confuse McKinley with another daughter who was also given up for adoption. McKinley's birthfather talks to her on the phone occasionally from Las Vegas, and she eventually visits him. She enjoys a better relationship with her new siblings.

Jaiya John's *Black Baby White Hands* (2002) narrates, from a male point of view, growing up as a Black child and teenager in an all-white environment; John has three white siblings born to the family and a Black brother who was also adopted—in fact, as his parents' main attempt to deal with John's race. John's birthmother finds him when he is in his twenties and later his birthfather contacts him. They are admirable people, with values like his, but contact with them does not solve how he can be a Black son to his adoptive parents, and he feels inner turmoil. However, he works through the turmoil, and ends the book by bringing parts of both white and Black families together for a celebration of his daughter's naming.[22]

The script of the film *Off and Running* (2009) was cowritten by African American adoptee Avery Klein-Cloud and director Nicole Opper. It presents a period in which Avery, a very dark-skinned young athlete raised as Jewish by a lesbian couple, writes to and loses contact with her birthmother, moves from a Jewish grade school to a Black high school, experiences the departure of her older brother (a biracial adoptee) for college, gives up the discipline and training that has won her many awards for track, moves out of her home, gets pregnant, has an abortion, and finally gets counseling sensitive to her needs as a transracial adoptee and returns home for the fall holidays.

Jackie Kay's prose memoir *Red Dust Road* (2010) begins with the Scottish Nigerian Kay in Nigeria for her first meeting with her fundamentalist Christian birthfather, who spends most of it praying for her. *Red Dust Road* intercalates moments in her search for and relationship with her birthparents and other relatives with memories of her childhood, key moments in her life, and early and recent scenes with her beloved white adoptive parents, who, ahead of their time in some ways, always try to give her positive feelings about her African ancestry.

Rebecca Carroll's *Surviving the White Gaze: A Memoir* (2021) describes racial isolation in New England similar to McKinley's, but unlike McKinley she meets her white birthmother when she is eleven—she gives the pseudonym Tess to Jan Waldron, whose version of their relationship, *Giving Away Simone*, is discussed in the first chapter of this book. The memoir shows Carroll's identity development, professional attempts, and search for love and friendship often frustrated by racism. Much of the book is a counternarrative to *Giving Away Simone*, describing the highs and the more frequent painful conflicts, often race-related, of her relationship with Tess. As Waldron analyzes it, her daughter is sensitive to rejection because of having been given up for adoption,[23] but Carroll describes being further hurt by Tess's racist comments. The reconciliation with which the earlier book ends does not last. When she eventually meets her Black birthfather, she is surprised to find that he seems "gentle" and says he wanted to raise her, but she soon feels he is too mentally ill for the relationship to continue.[24] At the end, she is a successful author married to a white man who "understands that black history [his academic field] is American history, and that there are a million different black stories and histories that have never been told by design" (309).

As far back as the early nineteenth century, when President Andrew Jackson adopted a boy named Lyncoya, orphaned because of Jackson's attacks on his parents' community, a few Native American children have been adopted by white people, but their numbers increased significantly in 1958 with the start of the Indian Adoption Project under the auspices of the Bureau of Indian Affairs and the Child Welfare League of America.[25] As we have seen in discussing the history of adoption from Korea, when the war was over, people wanted to start families, and they believed in the melting pot and therefore in assimilation by children of different backgrounds. "There were about twice as many would-be white adoptive parents as there were white adoptable children," writes Laura Briggs.[26] Since 1953, state child welfare systems had some jurisdiction over Native children. Although according to scholars such as Briggs, who cites many Supreme Court decisions, adoptions of Native children should be considered as adoptions from tribal nations rather than from racially different families (59–63), the visual difference of Native children makes their situation more like that of transracial adoptees than like same-race adoptees. Many such adult adoptees identify as transracial. Many are more likely to call themselves Indian than Native, so I use both terms.

Susan Devan Harness, born in 1959, refers to "transracial adoption" in her book's subtitle. She was taken from her Native birthmother and apparently missing white father and adopted by white parents in 1961. More than any other memoir I have read, her book *Bitterroot: A Salish Memoir of Transracial Adoption* (2018) conveys the toll of experiencing prejudice from both the community where she was raised and the community from which she was adopted. Her alcoholic adoptive father calls Indians drunks and frequently insults, slaps, and at least once sexually abuses her. As an adult, she meets her birthmother and many other family members and visits places where they lived, but relationships with them are difficult—a few say she was lucky to leave—and though she learns and tells the reader much about American Indian history, she never feels a sense of belonging on a reservation. However, she constructs another kind of community by interviewing and surveying other American Indian transracial adoptees. She structures the memoir largely through conversations in which she finds out more about members of her birth family and visits the places where they lived, and meetings with each of her adoptive parents and her birthmother close to the time of their deaths.

Talking about Race and Adoption—Denial or Openness?

Parents' denial of race and their difficulty in talking about adoption, reflecting inadequate preparation, is dominant in most of these memoirists' recollections of childhood, with the Hopgoods and the Kays being the chief exceptions. Trenka's parents, most obviously, make many of the mistakes that Cheri Register points out in her book *Beyond Good Intentions: A Mother Reflects on Raising Internationally Adopted Children.* This is not surprising since Trenka was one of the Korean adoptees whom Register consulted in writing the book. "Wiping Away Our Children's Past," "Holding the Lid on Sorrow and Anger," "Believing Race Doesn't Matter," "Raising Our Children in Isolation," "Believing Adoption Saves Souls"—these are all titles of chapters in *Beyond Good Intentions* and habits of the Brauer family in a place Trenka calls Harlow, Minnesota.[27] (The name refers to Harry Harlow, a psychologist whose most famous experiment involved separating monkeys from their mothers shortly after birth and noting their response to wire and cloth substitutes.)[28] Robinson's parents raised her in white Salt Lake City, and she feels that "there was nothing said or done to make me feel proud of being Korean (at least nothing that worked)."[29] Chung's experience was similar in that regard. Wills remembers, when at six she was having cosmetic surgery on an ear, being given a doll about which her parents had said, "It looks like you." It had black hair but "a hard white face and blue, never-blinking eyes" (134).

Hopgood's parents, however, avoided most of these mistakes and are not easily associated with the pitfalls discussed in any of Register's other chapters. This is in spite of the fact that she was adopted in 1974, before there were many transnational adoptees writing about what they needed in their childhood. Their most obvious contrast with the Brauers is in their willingness to acknowledge that their daughter is adopted and has Asian ancestry. The Hopgoods call Mei-Ling their "beautiful adopted baby" (69), adopt two sons from Korea, eat Asian food, hang Asian art on their walls, and have Asian babysitters.[30] While fiction of the 1990s and after often mocks such practices as Orientalist, Hopgood is describing life from the 1970s and '80s, before they were common. Even at the time, she appreciated having an Asian Raggedy Ann doll as well as a Black one, though she and her brothers "just wanted to be seen as American" (77).[31]

The Robinsons want Katy to assimilate to the white culture of Salt Lake City (78), but they take her to an annual Asian festival until she refuses to go (84) and let her write to her Korean mother and grandmother (though the agency returns the letters). Chung's parents eventually, belatedly, get her an Asian doll. The Brauers, by contrast, never say what Trenka calls the a-word (adoption) or the K-word (Korea) (35).

Harness's parents also don't want to talk about adoption, and her father is biased against Natives, though she eventually discovers he has many books about them—his relation to American Indian culture is "love-hate" (174). When she asks him, "What happened to my real parents?" when she was six, like many adoptees she was told, "They died in a car accident" and then, probably more angrily than many adoptees, "We are your real parents" (6). When she asks again at sixteen, he adds, "Drunk driving," and when she wants to know about any other relatives form that family, he mentions an uncle: "He was a drunk, a no-good bum. . . . He and his family would leech off of you for as long as you'd let them" (8). So much for pride in her ancestry. Her mother, when asked, would say, "You don't need to hear about the bad things that happen to people" (11).

Catherine McKinley does not get a total brush-off from her mother when she asks, at eleven, as they are taking a break on a climb up a hill in Scotland, her parents' ancestral land: "Mummy, why did you adopt me?"[32] "Why didn't I get adopted by an African—an Afro-American—family?" But after saying, "We'd waited a long time. . . . There were very few healthy white infants available to couples who wanted to adopt . . . and how could we have refused you?" her mother rushes up the trail: "Come on, let's not waste time." How ironic that their ancestry is worth a transatlantic trip but hers does not seem worth more than a few sentences. Asking about adoption often seems the way to end a conversation with parents.

More devastatingly even than McKinley, Trenka presents a moment when she asks about her history as the moment of transition from believing in her adoptive mother's love to doubting it and her own goodness as well. Having shown her birthmother's photograph and her Korean clothes to her kindergarten class, sitting on her mother's lap in a rocker, she asks, "Why did she give us away?" Her mother stops rocking, stands up, leaves the room, and as far as Jane remembers, the house. She concludes, "I must be rotten . . . I could also be returned to the store . . . I must be very, very good so my mommy will keep me" (22–23). As Wills writes, this anecdote stands out, partly because at this point "the narrator takes on a five-year-old's perspective," and it shows the continuing importance of the "initial rupture."[33] Jane's parents never mention adoption or Korea after this day. They have no understanding of how to give Jane and her sister support against the various kinds of racism they experience. Furthermore, Jane's American family frequently talk about physical similarities in the biologically connected family and she feels left out.

A more open adoptive mother appears in *Red Dust Road*. At the age of seven, Jackie finds out that she is adopted. Watching a cowboy-and-Indian movie with her mother and brother, she thinks, "the Indians are the same colour as me and my mum is not the same colour as me." She asks, "Mummy why aren't you the same colour as me?" "My mum says, Because you are adopted. I say, what does adopted mean. . . . My mum says, It means I'm not really your mummy. . . . I am crying for real now because I love my mum so much and I want her to be my real mummy and I am worried . . . that she is going to disappear or dissolve."[34] Kay's poem "The Telling Part" (ll. 56–57) from her earlier book *The Adoption Papers* gives a dream image for what she feared at this point: "Mammy's skin is toffee stuck to the floor/ And all her bones are scattered like toys."[35] The memoir, however, recounts how her mother sees her pain, weeps in sympathy, says, "Your real dad came from Nigeria in Africa and your mummy came from the Highlands. . . . But your dad and I love you more than all the tea in China, more than all the waves in the ocean and will love you till all the seas run dry. . . . Everyone needs cuddles, so they do. Come here and let your mummy give you a big cuddle" (Kay, *Red Dust Road* 13). In the UK in the 1960s her mother would never think of saying "birthmother" or "first mother"—terms then not yet widely used even in the United States—but she knows how to deal with mistakes and a hurt child. Jackie knows that she is loved.

Later on, her mother not only talks about adoption but encourages fantasies about origins. "Maybe your father was an African chief. . . . Maybe you are an African princess" (41). She tells Jackie that he studied agriculture. These stories and others bind mother and daughter together in their fascination with the other parents. As John McLeod says, this gives Jackie "an opportunity to play with a range of fanciful and possible pasts."[36]

Mrs. Kay, like Mrs. Hickman in the previous chapter, identifies with the other mother: "Not for a single second was my mum thinking that there might be another mother somewhere who never bothered to think about me on my birthday" (45). She is so generous that she even provides a sympathetic perspective on the birthfather's departure: "Although your father loved your mother he would have had to abandon her, while she was pregnant, imagine, Jackie, and return to Nigeria to this woman he wasn't in love with like he was in love with your mother" (42). Later Kay's own attitude about her birthparents is still affected by her mother's approach. She writes, "All anyone adopted really needs is a good imagination: more than genes or blood, it offers the possibility of redemption. . . . All you really need is to think you came from somebody good" (149, 150). Her white birthmother has been cautious about meeting her, and her birthfather refuses to continue their relationship if he can't convert her to his form of Christianity; however, she can still think of them both as good because both, one as a scholar of medicinal trees and the other as a nurse, have spent much of their lives helping people and "have something tremendously kind about them" (150).

Carroll's book, by contrast, stresses failure to help her develop her identity from both her adoptive parents and her birthmother, in different ways. Her parents have no interest in any part of Black culture. While she is in high school, Rebecca asks her father if he ever had any black friends, and he answers that they "preferred to keep to themselves" (Carroll, *Surviving* 141). When she suggests "that might be about self-preservation in a predominantly white environment," he says, "I never really thought about it" (142). In her early teens, she must discover by herself that moisturizing lotion helps her scaly skin (15). Her hair is always a problem. Tess finds her a Black beautician when she is twelve (91), but that is not enough.

It does not contribute to her development of a Black identity when Tess's answer to Rebecca's first question about her birthfather is "basically, he was a dog . . . a jive-ass black man who could bullshit like nobody's business" (65). She talks about race but more stereotypically than helpfully. Just a few years later, she advises Rebecca to choose her "devirginizer" by race because "Black men are the best lovers. . . . They have more rhythm" (102) and suggests a visiting friend in his thirties, present during this conversation, to the four-teen-year-old.

While the Carrolls hardly ever talk about race, Tess, who lives in a more integrated world and often uses Black dialect, criticizes Rebecca when she calls Tess "girl" with a Black intonation (128). When Rebecca, as a student at overwhelmingly white University of New Hampshire, gives a talk on her experience "trying to navigate . . . blackness" (160), Tess says, "It felt to me like you were playing at being black . . . I've been around far more black people than you have." And a dozen years later, when Rebecca is working at Harvard's Department of Afro-American Studies and publishing a book of interviews with Black women writers, Tess tells her, "You came out of my body and I am white, so there's no way that you're gonna just go around calling yourself black" (276). Carroll identifies Tess's viewpoint as part of the white gaze that makes her life difficult.

Racial Isolation

For all the awareness that the Hopgoods have, they bring up their children, as do the Brauers and the Robinsons, in a location where Asian faces occur, if at all, only in special places like Korean school (which the boys hate except for Tae Kwon Do), and Chinese school (which Mei-Ling refuses to attend). The children want to be American, and Asian American is not enough. And it never occurs to the Hopgoods that they can have contact with Mei-Ling's original family during her years of growing up—they could have, because of the connection with Maureen, but no one thinks about the possibility. They are ahead of their time to some extent but not in every way. Hopgood writes, "I never felt separation pains that I can recall . . . the fact that I was not my parents' biological child was never an issue" (*Lucky Girl* 69) but what the ellipsis in the previous quotation replaces is "I felt racially isolated at times," and elsewhere she writes, "I didn't discuss those feelings with my brothers or my parents until years later" (80). Hopgood's memoir doesn't put a lot of emphasis on her insecurities, and so it is easy to neglect them and to notice more her stress on the limitations on women and girls in her family of origin, and the warping of boys and men by their privileges. But her insecurities are a persistent part of her young life.

The lesbian couple depicted in the documentary film *Off and Running* have been far more in denial about their daughter's race than have the Hopgoods. Avery has two transracially adopted brothers (an older one partly African American, a younger one Korean). At the beginning of the film, as she writes a letter to her birthmother, she appears to be flourishing, and emphasizes that she is happy in her family and loves her brothers. But later, in a voice-over, she says, because she went to Jewish schools, "For years I felt so out of place among Black people."[37] Moving to an all-Black high school, she says, "I am very new to Black culture and I don't fully understand it." As the film continues, the birthmother writes a few times but stops, her older brother leaves for college, and her sense of alienation from her mothers increases—"I don't feel that they understand anything about who I am."

In other memoirs, parents make some attempt to acknowledge their child's race, but it is not enough. McKinley's mother tries—she connects Catherine with a Black church where she is accepted and makes friends, but, she writes, "my weekend life as part of John Wesley remained almost completely separate from my life at home and at school" (McKinley, *Book of Sarahs* 51). She complains that her parents want Black culture to be her thing, not theirs, and says that her mother's letters stay on the surface, "never risking any deep admissions" (33). At six, Rebecca Carroll sees a Black woman in real life for the first time, her ballet teacher, and when her mother says, "Isn't it nice that Mrs. Rowland is black?" she wonders, "Had I even heard Mom use the word black to refer to a person before?. . . . Would I go live with Mrs. Rowland now?" (34). She writes, "I still felt other. . . . In my world my blackness made me feel special and treasured, but it didn't seem that was the case for Mrs. Rowland" (35). Mrs. Rowland does not enter into their conversation again. Nor apparently does race, except years later when she asks her father if he ever had Black friends.

All these adoptees experience racism from outside the family. Hopgood writes, "My parents tried to counter any racism. They did their best to explain ignorance and hate, dismissing the offenders as idiots" (78). They were living in a suburb of Detroit at a time when Asians were blamed for the decline of the auto industry, but she says she never felt her physical safety was at risk, though she remembers hostility from kids and from drunks driving by. However, in spite of all her love for her parents, she still feels uncomfortable and isolated as an Asian, for a long time unable to discuss her feelings with her family.

From the very beginning, when she is still Kyong-Ah and being assaulted by her birthfather because of his suspicion of her paternity, the writer we know as Trenka is more of a target than any of the other memoirists. She gives an especially vivid account of suffering as part of a visibly transracial family in public. She includes a play representing a family outing in which white diners in a restaurant first shout questions such as "*Do they speak Chinese*?" then proceed to "I don't want my kids to play with those girls. Go back to where you came from" while their parents stay obliviously glued to their menus (*Language of Blood* 31). Clearly her parents themselves have a significant degree of racism. When she has an Asian boyfriend in high school, even her father mocks his face and his name. She never dates an Asian again.

Trenka endures many metaphorical assaults. But worst is the threat of literal assault from a psychopathic stalker while she is in college. Because of this threat, he has "experienced the fear that my mother had given me away to escape" (69). As Homans has observed, she shows that the effects of "misogynist violence . . . cross national borders" (*Imprint* 167–68). Her parents try to protect her and share her disgust with some observers' gossipy unhelpful interest; the stalker goes to jail for years, but post-traumatic stress disorder remains, and she is occasionally accosted by presumably less violent men who want to pay her to fulfill their fantasies about Asian women. Wills has similar problems with sexism; it is not just a matter of one stalker but fetishistic interest by grown men from the time that she entered middle school (*Older Sister* 144), as well as observers assuming her Canadian father has a fetishistic rather than familial relationship with her (147). This contributes to her sense of confusion and isolation: "There was no one to explain how grown men would look at me" (144).

Chung gets nosy questions about adoption, envies her parents' nonchalance, and works out a simple happy-ending story to tell questioners. This doesn't help her morale. Chung, in Oregon, and Robinson, in Utah, are the only Asians in her respective Catholic grade schools, and both face hostility from their schoolmates. More than the other Asian American adoptee memoirists, they recall hearing racial slurs frequently from their early school years. Chung is more graphic. She recalls that when she was in second or third grade, a neighbor boy from her school taunted, "You're so ugly, your own parents didn't even want you," screwing up his face into a squint, saying, "Me Chinee, me can't see!" (*All You Can Ever Know* 14). She tells her parents about the adoption angle but not the racial one, and they tell her that she should ignore it. In middle school, the leader of a group of white girls asks, "Do you have a sideways vagina? My brother told me Asian girls have those" (18). The attacks come somewhat less often when she moves to another school in seventh grade. She never discusses this taunting or other examples of bigotry with her parents.

All adoptees with Asian ancestry write about discomfort with their appearance in their childhood and youth. Borshay Liem recalls her impossible desire to look like her sister, displaying her white dolls and Westernized pictures of herself as a teenager. She has surgery to have her ears made closer to her head, and when she sees the results, she cries because she still does not look like her family and friends. Robinson writes that she wished she could look like her mother, felt she was ugly, wanted to have surgery to reduce her nose size. Chung was called ugly by schoolmates, wanted blond hair instead of dark and twisted what she had enough to create a bald spot, suggesting to her parents that she needed a therapist. Wills writes to her older sister, "Can you imagine, *unni*, never having seen Korean people when you were young? I think that's why I hated myself at different points in my childhood" (128). No matter how understanding her parents are about finding Asian food, art, babysitters, and even brothers for their daughter, Hopgood is uncomfortable with looking different and doesn't want to make friends with other Asian Americans, from the fifth grade on to her sophomore year in college, when she seeks out her first Asian American friend.

And of course African American or biracial adoptees have to deal with racism. Kay gets physically attacked by racist schoolboys when she is six, and called names many times after, repeatedly defended by her parents. One of McKinley's neighbors won't let her children play softball if she is on the team, so the game is canceled. She feels people are watching her with suspicion in their virtually all-white Vermont town, thinking she is "the welfare kid, my father's little whore, my mother's sign of having been with Black men" (19). Carroll remembers her fifth grade teacher saying, "You're very pretty . . . for a black girl. . . . They're usually very ugly" (53). As a child she is molested by a family friend and in high school by white boys in her class—while other white boys say their parents have forbidden them to go on a date with her or to a small evening pool party where she is present. Later on, if she develops a relationship with a white man, usually he tells her she talks about race too much.

Jaiya John's experience as a child is an even clearer illustration of the problems a transracial adoptee can have. His parents, the Potters, are the first white people in New Mexico to adopt a Black child. They are unaided by any support groups or follow-up education (*Black Baby* 42). They start with good intentions. In her best effort to support his ethnic identity, his mother sings him Negro spirituals and plantation songs (32). The Potters later adopt a second Black child so John will feel less alone (34).

But the overwhelming whiteness of their environment overshadows the companionship between brothers. Los Alamos has Hispanic and Pueblo presence, but "no appreciable Black community existed within 100 miles" (49). By the age of five, when John looked at his classmates in preschool and, he writes, "recognized that my hair was shorter and more tightly curled than that of most other people and that my nose was broader. . . . I was self-conscious of my race to the point of withdrawing" (36). He also feels left out because of the whiteness of the television shows the family watches and the stories his parents read to him—"I didn't find my reflection anywhere I looked" (38–39)—not to mention the hostile comments that he hears from children and adults outside his family. He is constantly wondering what he should do to fit in and how much of himself will be lost. Once, when John is in high school, his parents invite over two visiting Black female college students, but the result, perhaps predictable, is an uncomfortable silence (130). His parents make little attempt to compensate for their adopted sons' difference by making "African American considerations . . . an inherent strand in our family life" (130) with regard to either friends or cultural activities. He says that most of his relatives showed him "the shaded love of people who spent their lives distant from people who looked like me," as he learned to discern the difference between "embrace" and "ambivalence, tolerance, and disdain" (78).

In this all-white community, his hair is one of the most obvious signs of his difference. It causes him "excruciating" physical pain from his mother and the local barbers (none experienced with such hair within a two hours' drive), as well as shame in public (100–101). For a while he uses its ability to hold objects such as pencils and coins to make his (white) peers laugh. He gets approval that way, with other kinds of humor, with frequent smiling, and a generally nonthreatening persona in spite of his feelings of discomfort and anger. As a result he becomes so popular that his white sister, born into the family, feels rejected. Ironically, he hardly notices, let alone enjoys, his popularity (115). He feels even more like an outsider because his parents frequently remark on physical similarities between their three biological children and the rest of the family (127). When he tries to discuss with his parents his feeling that people are staring at him, again his parents miss the opportunity to discuss race. His father frequently says, "People stare at me all the time because of my beard" (170).

Like Trenka, John includes anecdotes that dramatize his pain from racial isolation and the reaction of observers to his family. Sometimes the issue is the failure of observers to see that he belongs to his family. He describes how he would "go into a store with a sibling or parent, and the employee would come up and ask the other family member first if they needed any help. Then the employee would turn to me and ask, 'And can I help you with anything?'" (129).[38]

John desperately looks for sources of racial pride in popular culture: John Henry of the folk song, the Black Panther of the comic book, even hip characters on sitcoms, much to the dismay of his mother. But the figure that he now sees as standing in for his unknown biological father is Muhammad Ali, and his most memorable identification with Ali is listening to the 1978 championship fight along with his father in the mountains on a ham radio. His memory of this is a rare and veiled version of what Kay experienced in sharing her mother's fantasies about the missing parents.

John writes that his growing up was a time of "three constant tensions: (1) fitting in with my White world, (2) needing to feel a part of my adoptive family, and, (3) needing to feel good about my Blackness" (192). One of the few times when these tensions seem resolved is when his piano lessons led him to playing Scott Joplin's ragtime. Another is when "Mom expressed an enjoyment for Nat King Cole, Diana Ross, or some other Black vocalist" (208). But his parents had no understanding of the racism he had to deal with, and he does not recall that they ever discussed Black political leaders.

Growing up with an openly anti-Indian father, Harness also experiences prejudice from fellow students and teachers. She feels her skin marks her to too many people as "stupid or lazy" and maybe dangerous.[39] She is in the ninth grade when she first meets another young person who identifies as Indian. Repeatedly, she is asked to explain the background of her name; no one else is. Anti-Indian jokes are frequent. In college, one teacher tries to send her to a vocational school without looking at her file (104), and an anthropology professor who researches Indians doesn't want her in the class (105). And then, to make matters worse, she finds prejudice against her in Native college students. They call her an apple—"red on the outside, white on the inside" (107), blaming her for ignorance of the traditions that she was never taught. Later, after she has found similar prejudice on the reservation she visits, when a psychologist who is happy about being one-thirty-second Cherokee tells her to be proud, she says, "I'm too Indian to be white and too white to be Indian" (188).

Child-Parent Relations and Physical Difference

The sense of physical difference from their parents strikes these adoptees at different times—and their emotional relations can mitigate it or heighten it. Hopgood's feeling of racial isolation does not seem to have affected her relationship with her parents. She writes of her father, "I was just like him, strong-willed, independent, and passionate" (7). She knows that her father loves "teaching, his students, the union movement, baseball" (45). She has fond childhood memories of dancing with him at the dances he chaperoned at his high school and, though she felt less similar to her mother, going to mother-daughter banquets and being treated with respect as if she were an adult.

The Hopgoods welcome their daughter when she is about two; Robinson, by contrast, met her American parents at seven and described them this way in a letter to her Korean grandmother (one of many sent back rather than forwarded by the orphanage, on the grounds that her address was unknown): "My American mother has orange hair and green eyes like a monster. My American father has no hair on his head" (71). Her relationship with her father would always be difficult, but she soon feels close to her mother, with vivid memories of her "head resting on her cushioned chest, breathing in the tingly scent of Mentholatum on her thin lips" (33). After she leaves her husband, the two women—Robinson now in college—develop a kind of partnership. But she still writes to her mother, in a long-delayed attempt at open discussion, "I do not resemble anyone in our family" (36).

Nicole Chung recounts a conversation with her mother about adoption from when she was about four, in which race is never mentioned (was this so early she hadn't developed the concept?). Sure of her mother's love, she accepts the answer that "your birth parents were very sad they couldn't keep you, but they thought adoption was the best thing for you" (4) and offers this story whenever people ask questions. It helps her believe, as her parents want, that her "birth family had loved me from the start; that my parents, in turn, were meant to adopt me" (5), and it becomes the foundation of her identity. Epitomizing the apparent contradiction, she writes, "I had always felt like the much-adored but still obvious alien in the family" (12). As a college student she formulated her sense of differences beyond difference of appearance: "they were always telling me I worked too much, thought too much, *cared* too much. *We weren't really prepared to have a kid like you,* my mother had said once" (12). Many of the adoptive parents in these memoirs may have felt the same.

Carroll remembers her color difference from her parents as important from early on, though she felt they treasured her because of it. She does not write about finding similarities of any kind with them. Toward the end of the book, her father compares her conflict with the administration at her high school to his similar struggle, but she feels he misses the contrast—"I was fighting not just the academic system but a white supremacist system as well" (286). Similarly, when she meets Tess, she "searched hard for flickers of our resemblance, but found nothing" (63). Tess introduces her into a larger world, and they have some fun times together, bonding especially over popular culture; however, their relationship is repeatedly marred by hurt feelings. In spite of their racial difference, Carroll feels that her adoptive mother has given her unconditional love, while Tess's love is only conditional (153).

Many of the adoptees recall early comfortable times with a parent—John includes a memory of "intimate solitude" (38) as his mother rocks him with a lullaby. Even Trenka imagines that scene in which her mother leaves her in the rocking chair as beginning with her thought "My mommy loves me a lot" (22). And just before she asks the question that her mother doesn't want to follow up with much discussion, McKinley is enjoying looking at the scenery through binoculars with her mother—"together with my mother like this . . . I could chart a world of pleasure and have her all to myself" (8). Ironically, these times of closeness allow Trenka and McKinley to feel the possibility of having the discussion—and then their questions break the closeness.

Harness remembers that once when she was six, she saw her "brown arm . . . against her [mother's] porcelain one," and said, "You have such pretty skin. I wish I had your skin," and her mother responded, "What I would give to have your beautiful, young brown skin." (46). Her father, however, has an opposite attitude to her mother's. When she is a few years older, her father buys and paints a statue of a little girl for the front yard of their house, and says, "I've always wanted a little blond-haired, blue-eyed girl. They're the cutest damned things, and now I have one" (17). Feeling embarrassed about her own appearance, she hates him. "What's worse, I realize I am beginning to hate myself."

Still, her feelings about her adoptive parents improve later in the book. When she visits her father as he is dying, a grief she never expected emerges. Better memories of childhood return—swimming together with him for two hours on Fridays for six weeks, helping him feed trumpeter swans (177).

Her portrayal of her mother also changes. Early in the memoir, remembering her senior year in high school, Harness describes her just-divorced and previously reliable adoptive mother having fantasies of people talking to her through the stereo speaker. She disappears, is found walking barefoot in the snow, and takes planes without telling her teenage daughter. But later, when her mother is close to death with dementia-related memory loss, Harness remembers a page of details of what Mom, the name used throughout the book, did for her and taught her (287–88).

Double/Multiple Identities

The racial isolation of transracial adoptees often produces a sense of being torn between two identities.[40] While same-race adoptees Hipchen and Saffian think occasionally about the people they would have been as Mary Beth Delaney and Susan Morgan, these other identities have less presence in their memoirs since racial difference is not involved. For African American adoptees, double identity can be especially vivid. Sometimes it is dramatized by a change in the child's name. In John's early months in an African American foster family, for example, he was named Scott. Four years after he moved to a white family who adopted him, his name was officially changed to John Scott Potter. Eventually (close to the end of the memoir) he renames himself, making John his last name and adding the first name Jaiya, which comes to him as if from the universe (306).

His sense of internal division begins early in his life. When he does have a "Black sighting" he feels both "excitement, like when you're in a place where no one speaks your language, and finally one person appears who can understand you. And shame, because seeing another Black person reminded me of that same Blackness in me that I was at odds with" (49). Another kind of identity split occurs when he becomes old enough (at ten!) for white people to see him as a threatening African American male: "the teddy bear had become a grizzly bear" (217).[41] Later he feels that when with white people he has "done the mental and emotional two-step. One step toward my true personality under the cover of my private inner world. One step back toward the image I knew others had of me as a Black person" (301).

However, by the time of writing this memoir, John identifies so much with Black culture that he envisions another kind of doubling—dream-like conversations with a figure called Storyteller who comes right out of Black tradition. She gives him messages about spirit, truth, and naming, can turn him into any shape and give him visions, tells a fable about Moses and his Egyptian brother Ramses, changes shape herself, and at one point (304) resembles him. This folkloric figure enables John to double himself creatively and include conversations with himself in his memoir.

Struggle with identity disconnection and multiplicity, eventually resolved, also appears in Catherine McKinley's memoir, *The Book of Sarahs*, beginning with that crucial visit to Scotland at eleven. She sees a group of African visitors in a pub, is attracted to their brightly colored clothes, and has a flashback to an uncomfortable moment in a shop earlier that day when she was asked, "Are you Scottish?" (5) as she, visibly of African American descent, was looking for the McKinley tartan. McKinley's dual identities include those framed by racial-national definitions: the assumption is that no Black person can be "Scottish," and yet McKinley claims her family's Scottish tartan as also hers. Of course it is, given that the McKinleys are in all ways except the biological her family.

She has already, like John, found additional complications at ten, when beginning puberty. For years her mother has washed, dressed, combed and braided her nappy hair every two weeks. She would feel that her mother was "the orchestrator, taking me through a tour of emotions that I could not otherwise express . . . helping me find a grip somehow" and at the end, "she would hold me in her arms with a love that made the whole affair worthwhile" (146). But as her body starts to change, she starts to be embarrassed at the difference of "the purple brownness of [her] nipples" (147), starts to feel hatred of her mother's different skin and smell, humiliation from the difficulties of her hair care, and also further embarrassment about the pleasure in this ritual she has felt earlier.

As Marina Fedosik emphasizes, early in her high school years "the complexity and vulnerability of [McKinley's] racial identification is exposed at a service in the black church she has just started attending" (222), when a Black child visibly rejects her greeting as that of a "white lady" (63). To counteract this alienation, she finds a Black girlfriend whose "attitude and phrases . . . sound and posture" (66) she can copy. "This narrative moment exposes the role of culture as a racializing tool," Fedosik observes (232). McKinley continually seeks Black women she can identify with, if only in fantasy. Away from home in prep school, she even displays a photograph of an African immigrant cloth vendor she has seen once and tells her friends that this woman is her mother (29–30). In her twenties, when she meets or hears of Black people she likes and thinks look similar to her, she imagines they might be her birthparents (36).

But there are further complications when she discovers her birthmother is not Black but Jewish. She writes, "I often think about how I would have *been* Jewish, except that I am Jewish. Or how I would have been Black and Jewish, except that I am. . . . And how would I have also lived in the third world that is mine, the world of the WASPy, agnostic McKinleys?" (51). When she works in New York for a summer and goes to an exhibit at the Jewish Museum comparing Black and Jewish social histories, she feels "no matter how difficult it might have been to walk between these two worlds, it would have been easier than the confusion and denial of growing up adopted and part of neither community" (94).[42]

Now knowing that her father is Black, she discovers women writers from other countries searching for a Black father and imagines herself as part of an international community of "the children of African American men's segregation-era sexual crossing of racial lines" (60–61). She develops relationships with two other adopted biracial women and jokingly calls their community "Friends of the Mulatta Nation" (69).

But her relationship with her birthmother, already vexed, is further troubled, along with her sense of her identity, after she discovers her original name was Sarah Khan. She remembers using the name Sarita and then is startled and angry to discover that her mother had given away another Sarah Khan before she was born and gave the name also to a third Sarah, whom she is raising. She wonders how many of the details her mother has told her of her early life belonged to the other Sarah. And the complexity of her selfhood strikes her again when she travels to Ghana and finds herself considered "a rich, white woman" (286).

As her title, *Surviving the White Gaze*, suggests, Carroll does not present herself as dealing with double identity but rather as learning how to be Black. One of her boyfriends has a sister who is also a transracial adoptee, with whom she sometimes discusses being biracial, but otherwise, she seldom uses that term. She occasionally analyzes herself as depending on white approval, and the blond, rich white boys she likes in high school stay in her life a long time; however, Blackness is clearly her goal. She never discusses the literature of transracial adoptees such as Kay or McKinley. This contrast with McKinley might be related to the greater salience of Blackness in U.S. culture as Carroll writes almost twenty years later, the presence of Scottish and Jewish culture in McKinley's families rather than the generic whiteness of Tess and the Carrolls, or the racism Carroll experiences from white people in both of her families. After she meets Claudia, a Black woman married to a white man and the mother of a college friend and lover who identifies as Black, she thinks she's found "the black mother [she'd] never had, literary-minded, stately, and fearless" (231) and writes in her journal, "Although I am half white and was raised in a culturally white environment, I am choosing blackness, because there is more dignity in that" (232). Soon after this she decides to meet her birthfather.

The issue of double identity is particularly fraught for most transnational adoptees because of the geographic and linguistic differences they deal with. Writing especially of Korean adoptees, Kimberly McKee says that their adoption in the United States is like "re/birth" (*Disrupting* 84) in a painful way as they are "confounded with a new name, language, culture, and family" (85). Their earlier memories are supposed to be supplanted and their life is supposed to begin on the day of their arrival to the West, though some will keep those memories or find they return.

The Language of Blood dramatizes its author's multiple identities from the beginning through a narrative of name change. Very early in the memoir, Trenka begins a paragraph, "My name is Jeong Kyong-Ah," recites the names of her ancestors and her citizenship in Korea, and continues, "Halfway around the world, I am someone else. I am Jane Marie Brauer, created September 26, 1972, when I was carried off an airplane onto American soil" (14). The conflict between these identities is even harder for her because her parents' difficulty in dealing with her preadoption past is so extreme. She has internalized this conflict as well; she wonders, "What does it feel like to pass a mirror and *not be surprised*?" (35). In other words, part of her expects that her face will be white, like most of the other faces around her. Chung mentions occasionally feeling this surprise as well and feeling, when she was younger, "more like a white girl than an Asian one" (16).[43]

Deann Borshay Liem's film *First Person Plural* places multiplicity front and center in its title. Like *The Language of Blood*, the film emphasizes the different names she was called before and after her adoption. But she had a third name (the one she received first) before the adoption agency gave her the name of the girl her future parents had been writing to, whose father had taken her home. As Kim Park Nelson writes, "The inability of Borshay's adoptive family to detect the switching of the child they adopted from Cha Jung Hee to Kang Ok Jin, despite a two-and-a-half year correspondence that included letters and pictures, underlines the white stereotype that all Asians look alike."[44] Her parents resist seeing this switch as a problem when she discovers it later. As discussed before, her wish to change her Korean appearance while in high school also shows her discomfort with her multiple identities; this was still the time of the "melting pot" and assimilation ideals.

Memoirists have varying ways of dealing with the issue of plural identity. Wills has a clear sense of which identity is real. She writes in the second paragraph of her book that she answers to her non-Korean name only out of custom, "not because it suits me" and associates it with being "scrubbed until my skin turned pink . . . programmed to speak English, then French" (3). In a reversal of the image of adoption as rebirth, she writes, "around 2009 I came back to life . . . when my Korean father called me by name, when my Korean mother called me daughter" (4).

As a teenager, Harness made poetry and jewelry about "being Indian and living white" (280). Her possession of two names is relevant to external events more often than that of any other adoptee discussed in this chapter. The Bureau of Indian Affairs oversees a bank account of money for her because she is a tribal member. When she turns eighteen, she has a choice: "keep the account in my birth name and continue to allow social services to administer the account, which meant I needed to request money in writing; or change my name legally to my adopted name and have direct access to the monies themselves" (121). She chooses the first, identifying her birth name as Vicki Charmain Rowan, and after some correspondence, the social service administrator circumvents the law and allows her to learn some of her history and the names of her primary relatives. Her birthmother is still alive, and she tries contact, with no answer. A few years later, though, when she writes a letter to the tribal paper about the prejudice she faces from people on both sides of her identity, she signs her name "Susan Devan Harness (Vicki Charmain Rowan)" and hears from her two birth sisters; she meets them and many other family members, last her birthmother, at a Fourth of July family get-together. She narrates many later meetings with this family. To them she is Vicki. But when she speaks to the Salish tribal council on the Flathead reservation asking for a cultural event to welcome back people separated from the tribe by adoption or long-term foster care, she uses both names.

Mei-Ling Hopgood never mentions a sense of double identity, and her contrast with other memoirists in this way and others suggests how important it may have been that her parents kept the first name Mei-Ling, given her by her early caretakers. Jackie Kay's *Red Dust Road*, like John's *Black Boy White Hands*, narrates a progress in resolving identity issues. Early on, she writes that "being black in a white country makes you a stranger to yourself" (38). She remembers learning racist stereotypes about Africa in school and struggling to remove internalized racism. Reading Fanon, however, she feels "electrified; reading changed the mirror that I held up to myself" (40). She still suggests doubleness when she writes, "the story of your own adoption seems like the story of some stranger" (134), but she also is strongly affected by advice from the African American poet Audre Lorde, in 1984, "that I could be proudly African *and* Scottish and that I should embrace both" (201). Near the end of the memoir, after meeting her brother, she says, "You can't have two lives, you can only have one" (276).[45]

Repression versus Support

In a previous section, I noted that Mei-Ling Hopgood emphasizes her feelings of similarity to her adoptive father and her happy times and sense of respect from her adoptive mother. This is unusual in memoirs by transracial adoptees. Cheri Register, considering Trenka's account of her relationship with her parents, speculates that difficulties inevitably arise when "thousands of Korean children, by heritage seething cauldrons of Han, profound and prideful anger at a history of occupation and oppression, have been or are being raised by placid Scandinavian Americans and tight-lipped German Americans, who struggle to keep the lid down and not get scalded" (55). One may wonder about attributing an inherited temperament to a child only a few months old when adopted, as Jane was, but her memoir clearly shows her adoptive parents as stoic, especially her mother, who tells her father not to cry at his own mother's funeral, and her Korean parents as more emotional (53).

Parents who deny the importance of race and adoption are also likely to deny the importance of feelings of sadness or anger related to race or adoption. This is probably part of why Jane's mother does not answer her question about why her birthmother gave her away. When in the film *Off and Running*, Avery is upset because, during her adjustment to an all-Black school, a brother to whom she was very close goes away to college and her birthmother stops writing back to her, one of her mothers says, showing a similar difficulty to that of Jane's mother in dealing with a child's painful feelings, "It's like something really traumatic happened to her but I don't think anything did." Wills's American mother remembers her as a happy child, but says that one time she "only stopped sobbing when I was slapped across the face. . . . *We didn't know how to stop you; We didn't know what was wrong*" (129).

John's mother also deals with his feelings of sadness harshly; she snaps, "Quit hanging your lip!" This leads him to an even greater sense of rejection (64). At nine, he becomes totally absorbed with the televised series *Roots*, identifying with the characters too much to hide his emotions. His parents miss this opportunity for a discussion leading to more understanding: rather, his mother says, "You've been acting weird. I'm not gonna let you watch that show anymore if you don't straighten up" (158). McKinley also recounts the *Roots* series as a crucial divide: she watches, "powerfully in love with the images on the screen, feeling my sense of isolation and my longing for Black company begin to grow and overwhelm me," while her parents and her brother build a kayak in the basement. To her this dramatizes their "indifference toward people (ultimately me) they were supposed to care about" (13).[46]

McKinley's parents do care about her, but they do not understand the difficulties she faces. They participate in civil rights activism, but she believes that they never had a sustained relationship with anyone Black. They don't see a problem with a photograph of her grandmother as a teenager in blackface. While packing for a family move, she comes across a photo of her cousin Jimmy, also a transracial adoptee, who was "sent back." She explodes at her mother, who walks away, saying, "I'm tired of all this race business" (85). These memoirs provide many examples of lost opportunities for understanding transracial adoptee sadness, fear, and anger.

However, the memoirs also provide examples of more supportive family. John's father and his grandfather on his father's side contrast markedly with his mother and her family. He remembers sitting on his grandfather Potter's lap at the age of seven, reading aloud a story he wrote in school, and hearing his grandfather tell his father, "This boy's going to be a writer!" (81). The grandfather, a year later, writes him a Christmas card note: "I know someday you will be a very important man and will do a lot of good for everybody" (80). These moments of praise help his self-image even if they do not contribute to specifically racial pride.

Kay narrates occasions throughout her life when her parents do promote her racial pride. They give her a poster of Angela Davis for her wall, and in their circle Davis is called a "political heroine" (36). The Kays' neighborhood in Scotland is not racially integrated, but because they are active members of the Communist Party, they meet and host many visitors from Africa: Kay remembers the "dark life lines" on the hands of one who visited when she was four (50). When Jackie meets racism at school, she tells her parents; they complain to the teacher and try to comfort their daughter (*Red Dust Road* 184–85; see also 187, about the time when as a teenager she is insulted by an adult racist; and her poem in *Adoption Papers* titled "Black Bottom"). She remains close to them, and in *Red Dust Road* this closeness is intensified as she describes to them her strange reunion with her Nigerian birth father.

Red Dust Road, which narrates Kay's meetings with her birthparents, her childhood, the broken leg that began her interest in writing, and her decision to have a child with a male friend, is most unlike other adoption search memoirs (apart from those of Jakiela and Harding, where the portrayal of the parents is less celebratory) in that it spends at least a third of its length showing her adoptive parents in relationship to her and to each other. This memoir can, even more than *Lucky Girl*, be described as a tribute to the writer's adoptive parents. Although Kay knows that being grateful is too often imposed on adoptees, in the second-to-last chapter, as she is speaking to them about her second trip to Nigeria, she writes of feeling gratitude, "flooded with love for them . . . like the light across the land" (286), because her adoptive parents are such extraordinary people.

Community, Search, and Reunion

In some ways, the processes of exploring identity and searching for birth family, meeting, aftermath, and resolution present many similar issues for transracial and same-race adoptees, but as with same-race adoptees, experiences vary. Is meeting other adoptees helpful? For Harness, it is crucial that for her MA she interview other American Indians "transracially adopted by white families" (223). She learns, among many other things, that seven out of the twenty-five she interviewed experienced sexual abuse (234), eleven had heard Indians described as "dirty," and only four had heard them described as "intelligent" (233). Sharing the stories of "shame, of heartbreak, of pragmatism, of survival, and of" feels like "a beautiful and valued gift" (228). She turns them into a book that holds "both Native and white societies accountable for imposing identities on us that made us unable to fit into either group.... We were coming into our own and people were going to have to listen to us" (235). This is the way that Harness finds a community. Chung calls an adoption organization for information, gets a job there and meets other adoptees. Robinson, Wills, Carroll, and McKinley benefit from contact with others who are Korean, Black, or biracial, but the adoptee support group McKinley tries is not only all-white but also too fixed on extreme expression of emotions for her (54). A sense of the collectivity of Korean adoptees is important for Wills, but she describes the guesthouse for Korean adoptees where she stayed as not only a place for connections but "also a place of palpable confusion and rage and grief" (21).[47] One of the other Korean adoptees staying there rapes her—she believes that he took her in anger as a substitute for the Korean mother who abandoned him (58).

Is reading helpful? All the memoirists of African descent mention the importance of Black writers—Kay feels that reading Franz Fanon, Audre Lorde, Alice Walker, Toni Morrison, and Ralph Ellison changes her life (40–41). Reading Morrison and Hurston is a revelation to Carroll, and her first book is a collection of interviews with Black women writers. McKinley writes to authors who are racially mixed, including Kay, and Isha-McKenzie-Mavinga and Thelma Perkins, two Black British sisters who wrote a book about their separate searches for their elusive father (58–59). John writes, "Malcolm X, Alex Haley, and Martin Luther King embraced me in kinship from the other side of the Great River as I read about their lives" (261). Analogous literary connections would have been harder to find for the Asian American adoptees, who don't mention any. Chung remembers finding only one children's book with characters who look like her, *Farewell to Manzanar*, a memoir of a Japanese American internment camp (36), but after she sees Asians in Seattle, at ten, she starts writing her own stories about such characters.

McKinley goes through a search process similar to that in most of the memoirs of same-race adoption. She deals with sealed records, hires a searcher, gets, slowly, some help from the adoption agency. When she and her (white, Jewish) birthmother meet in an airport terminal, they immediately start "comparing eyes and teeth, fingers, taking off our boots and stockings to show each other our feet, rolling up our pants to compare our legs.... I had her exact hips and feet" (151–52). But this similarity is not enough to maintain their relationship, for reasons already discussed.

For many transracial adoptees who first meet someone in their own family who is not white, the Africanness, Koreanness, or whatever, or the emotional fact of reunion and their compatibility or lack of it, may be more important than details of likeness. Hopgood does not mention noticing physical likenesses on her first meeting with her birthparents—that stage comes later when she is with her sisters. Robinson looks for resemblance to herself when she first meets her birthfather, and sees none, though she does feel a bond (45). When Kay meets hers, his prolonged prayer for her conversion disorients her so much that it hardly matters that, on his bare feet, she can "recognize my own toes" (5). At her first meeting with her birthmother, she "can't see anything of my face in hers" (63). Early in the book, looking back on her relationships with them, she writes "I have my father's forehead and jaw. I have my mother's hair. . . . What does it matter?" (48).

With Trenka, it takes more than a week, photographs, and the encouragement of her sister Eun-Mi for her to notice "hands that are the same, as well as similar hair color, ears, noses and lips" (112). But then she goes into a "routine of exaggerated mock crying and laughing" (112) to show that both she and her birthmother and one sister are emotional.

Two extremely close experiences of physical resemblance are recounted in these memoirs, with opposite feelings. Near the middle of her memoir, Wills describes how much she hates the similarities to her father's features and expressions she sees in her mirror (111). By contrast, when John sees his birthmother's face for the first time in a photograph she sends months after her initial letter, he writes "I saw . . . myself . . . the spirit beneath her skin and bones was my own" (270–71, first ellipsis his). For him, this parallels how close their values are, how compatible.

Relationships and Identity after Reunion

For these adoptees, as for those in the previous chapter, meeting birthparents is not the end of the story. Kay writes in *Red Dust Road*, "No matter whether the experience is positive or negative—it churns you up. It turns your life upside down" (48). All the memoirists recount discovering details about the story of how and why they were given for adoption, but there are many contrasts in what and whom they find and the sort of relationship possible.

When Harness is thirty-eight, she meets her birthmother, Vic, who has been drinking all that day—she thinks it is because of fear of their meeting. They sit together sharing their pain. A year later, at another family gathering, they try more conversations and eventually bond a little over liking Steinbeck and other authors. Ten years later, they have another strained meeting. Her sister Ronni recalls their mother's cruelty. Later, when Vic is close to death, neither can say anything (303). From her brother Vern, she learns more about their birthparents' alcoholism—while in grade school, he sometimes had to drive them home from a bar—and frequent disappearances. Vern jokes that he might "write a book about [what] it was like *not* to be adopted" (261), but he doesn't convince her that she was better off. When she goes to the reservation to write, she sadly observes some of the same destructive patterns in her extended birth family she has seen or heard about (260). But she is cheered by the companionship of Vern and Uncle Albert and the beauty of the mountain lands with their flowers (317). And she keeps on trying to get possession of the file about her removal and adoption.

The three adoptees with Asian ancestry who were adopted internationally all find birthfathers who are not simply patriarchal but also tyrannical. Homans writes of several Korean adoptee memoirists, including Trenka, Robinson, and Liem, that they find "traditional gender norms and hierarchies . . . far more openly enforced than in the United States" (*Imprint* 167) and Hopgood finds the same conditions. But Hopgood's birthfather, who brings his girlfriend's children into the house though he has given two of his wife's and his daughters away, goes beyond traditional gender norms especially in the way he literally idolizes his first boy-child by blood.

Robinson's father may be less violent and eccentric, but failed to care for children from two different women and is described by his son as a playboy and an egotist (219) and by his ex-wife as "Number One Bad Person in all of Korea" (256). He wants a relationship with Robinson now but strictly on his own patriarchal terms, and she cannot trust him to tell her the truth about whether her mother is alive and if so where she is. In all cases of overseas Asian birthparents language difficulties are further complications.

Wills's relationship with her birthfather is constantly shadowed by what she sees as his mistreatment of her birthmother, to whom she is much more attached. He was married to another woman when she was born, but somehow her search has occasioned a reunion between her birthparents: her mother has forgiven him, but Wills herself constantly observes his failings. After her wedding in Montreal, he is suspicious of any compliment paid to her mother. Wills is enraged at him and he at her. Both parents return to Korea. At the end of a later chapter, as she visits him in Korea knowing he has not long to live, she writes, after he has said something she couldn't understand, "We stood like that for a while, forgiving each other" (200). But later after that, she resents in him "the selfishness I'd tried to ignore because of the cancer" (222). After his death, she imagines asking her sister, born to the wife he left for her mother, "Did you forgive him as he was dying, *unni*? Should I forgive him as well?" (232).

The one Korean father who lives in the United States is very different. Chung's father is the parent she respects more, because her sister has told her about beatings by her mother. She is surprised and happy to discover that he is "a published author, a lover of language and a scholar of Korean literature and linguistics" since these achievements give a family background to her own already "lifelong obsession with writing" (189). She can even see that, contrary to Korean tradition, during their meeting he defers to her and her sisters, and answers their questions, "sharing what he remembered even when it was painful" (193).

Relationships with sisters (five for Hopgood, two for Trenka, two for Chung, two for Wills, of which one is shadowed by their having different mothers), in which communication is usually easier, are unexpected joys for most of the adoptees with Asian ancestry, especially Hopgood. Wills writes that her younger sister, Bora, who was raised in Korea with the same mother but a different father and who later moved to Canada, is "the most important person in all of this" (15). To Bora, she is the *unni*, older sister, but to her own unnamed older sister, most clearly evoked by the book title *Older Sister. Not Necessarily Related*, she can speak only by italicized passages within it, because of their conflicting loyalties to badly behaving parents. Robinson meets a half brother who believes in the importance of the blood they share (253) and, more briefly, a half sister as well as a friendlier aunt her own age who she imagines as living the life she would have if not adopted (242)—but her feelings for her siblings are more distanced. The sister mostly avoids her, and the brother may be lying about her mother (who is not his). After Robinson has to have eye surgery, he won't tell their father the truth about her condition. Chung also thinks of her sister's life as what she herself would have lived, and the violence and instability her sister experienced contribute to her feeling that placing her with her adoptive family was the best solution for her. The sisters develop a close relationship.

It is, however, the mothers whom these Asian adoptees are chiefly seeking, with a range of results. When they meet, Trenka's *Umma* keeps apologizing to her for giving her away, in long Korean speeches that the translator sums up quickly. Umma bathes her in what seems a ritual of purification as well as reenacting the baby baths that were not given, and Trenka finds bliss in sleeping with Umma and her sister on the floor of the Korean apartment, hands held tightly (126).[48] She returns to Korea when she hears that Umma is dying and shares the care with her Korean sisters as much as she can. Hopgood, on the other hand, is struck by a feeling that she will never truly be able to know her "Ma" (212). While Trenka admires Umma for leaving her husband, Hopgood wonders why Ma stays with hers. Trenka appreciates her Umma partly for contrast to her cold American mother; Hopgood finds her Taiwanese mother distant by contrast to her more understanding American one. However, she is glad for the moments when she notices similarities—for example, mosquitoes often bite them both, they both make up little songs.

Wills becomes closer to her Korean mother as the end of her memoir approaches. As she wishes for a child, she thinks it is "so I might be my mother's child again" (184), especially since Canadian immigration policy would then make contact with her mother much easier. Regrets are still there: her mother apologizes for not showing her how to be a good mother. But she ends her book not just with a love letter to her baby daughter but also with imagined questions about whether she is treating her daughter as her mother treated her in the earliest months, and with a Korean proverb, "the daughter follows the path of her mother" (244).

Robinson did not come to the United States until she was seven; she has memories of her Korean mother that recur at various points in the memoir, and even an old picture of her from just before the adoption. She is left with two conflicting stories—that her mother died in an automobile accident and that she moved to the United States and is living in Chicago—and she has seen so much dishonesty in her relatives that she is not sure which to believe. She ends the book by imagining a meeting with her mother, whom she can now imagine as twenty years older than in the photograph, in which she expresses forgiveness and gratitude.

Chung is also left with uncertainty, since her original mother and father separately tell different stories about her placement for adoption. She recounts only two telephone conversations with her apologetic mother and in the first one denies blaming her. She learns that her mother's own father was violent and abusive as well. But she believes that whether she forgives her mother is irrelevant because it was her sister who suffered.

Most of these adoptees would like to bring their adoptive and birthparents together, or at least help their adoptive parents to be understanding.[49] These memoirs show varying degrees of success with this project. The Hopgoods are enthusiastic about their daughter's visit to her birth family and eventually accompany her on another visit. Robinson, by contrast, long feels that her mother never understood her needs as an adoptee—she never responded to her letter trying to discuss this. She feels "unease" (259) about their relationship as her mother comes to visit during her year in Seoul. But when they have dinner with her brother, all goes well, and she finds them both "more endearing than ever before" (267). On another evening, her mother and her half-brother's mother connect not only over their affection for her but also over shared experiences as single mothers.

When Kay returns from meeting her new half brother and tells her parents about him, she says that he's going to visit. Her mother likes thinking that he can call her his "Scottish mum" and says, "Isn't it amazing how rich life is, how our family's expanding" (282), though her father "looks a little uncomfortable." She narrates this in a scene that includes response from the brother she was brought up with, anticipation of her son's return from Guadalajara, and memories of his childhood, dramatizing the expanding net of kinship. Chung's parents do not meet any of her birth family during the time narrated in the memoir, but discussion about the reunion has, she writes "forced my adoptive parents to think about my birth parents not as poor, pitiable immigrants or people who might steal me away, but real people with their own feelings, fears, and failings" (212). Also, they now have more understanding of her own feelings of loss about her first family and knowledge of their roots. Thus the reunion has improved their relationship, and she emphasizes, "No matter what, no matter our differences, they will always be my parents, the ones who wanted me when no one else did" (213).

The Brauers never give Trenka that feeling of being wanted. They never come to respect her birthmother. Rather, they feel threatened by their daughter's relationship with her and even, after the birthmother's vividly and painfully narrated fatal cancer, refuse to come to the memorial service that Trenka holds in Harlow. This refusal leads to a long time of alienation. Trenka tries to get beyond her bad relationship with her parents by asking Lutheran Social Services what sort of education they were given about adopting. The lack of information they provide dramatizes the closed nature of this social service bureaucracy and convince her that her parents were given no kind of preparation for the realities of transracial adoption. The problems she had in her childhood were not necessarily because her parents were exceptionally close-minded (though it seems they were); they were as much because the agency did not officially take the complexities of transracial and transnational adoption into account in their procedures. Dr. Spock would at least have told them that adoption should not be the unmentionable A-word, though he would not say anything about transracial adoption in the edition available at that time.[50] She approaches "something like forgiveness" (202) as she asks, "What were my parents to know of the inescapable voice of generational memory, of racial memory, of landscape—if they had never been separated from their own people?" (208).

Trenka was born as Jeong Kyong-Ah in 1972 and adopted later that year. In 1972, agencies were not educating adoptive parents that they needed to raise their children with a knowledge of Korean culture or develop a sense of pride in a Korean identity to combat the hostility that they might face. In the 1990s, around the time Trenka decided to reach out to Lutheran Social Services, many adoption agencies and social workers were telling parents that there should be some regard "to the child's ethnic, religious, cultural, and linguistic background."[51] When she called LSS, however, they wouldn't let her see her file and didn't have any information about how her parents were prepared to adopt (except that they were invited to a Korean meal) or about a support group for adult adoptees from Korea.

Wills, by contrast to Trenka, devotes very little of her memoir to discussing her current relationship with her adoptive parents. As she is reconciling again with the Korean ones, she summarizes that while she had broken up with her Canadian family, "the cracks exposed the places where repair could be made, and we found each other again and tried to move forward" (173).

That becomes a kind of model for the other reconnection, which is the major concern of the rest of the book.

The memoirs of Asian adoptees deal more with issues of national identity than do those for whom the issue is Blackness. In one of the many letters included in her memoir, Robinson, a few years before her trip to Korea, writes her mother, "I am not one of you. I am not a Connole. I am not Irish. I am Korean and I want to find out what that means" (*Square Picture* 36). But when she arrives in Korea, she realizes that her identity is more complicated, she is an outsider, an "overseas Korean," and the relevant contrast to Korean is not Irish but American (7). She enjoys her birthfather's affection but is uneasy to feel "independence and American identity" (119) dissolve when with him. Meeting her brother and sister, she writes, "I did not see a resemblance or sense a connection with my new siblings" (123). Later, though she now sees a resemblance with her brother, she still feels like an outsider in spite of his emphasis on their "same blood" (136) and continues, "Nor were my physical characteristics alone enough to make me a Korean."

Robinson sometimes connects national identity with personal relationships: after she discovers that her father has concealed his second marriage from her, she writes, "I despised my father and loved him with equal strength, as I did Korea itself, for the strong hold it had on me, while at the same time rejecting me as one of its own" (153).[52] Later, thinking of the shame her Korean mother experienced as a single mother and her grandmother's hopes for her, she is glad for her "infinite freedom to shape the course of my life in ways unavailable to her or my mother" (241–42). Still, during the dinner with her mother and her brother, as she observes one displaying American "individuality" and the other Korean "self-restraint" (267), she thinks that she might have "become more Korean during the past year. One culture was not necessarily better than the other, and for the first time I could see that I contained qualities of both" (267). Somewhat similarly, Chung concurs when her sister says that everything about her "screams American" (221), but she wants to "regain at least some part of my heritage, my cultural birthright, and pass on that knowledge and sense of belonging to my daughters" (217). She cannot recover everything, but, she writes, "My identity as an adoptee is complicated, fluid, but then so is everyone else's" (221).

For Wills, raised in Canada, the situation is somewhat different; Canadian identity, at least as presented here, does not have the strong ideological content associated with identity as a U.S. citizen. She does remember a bizarre encounter with Canadian multiculturalism as a child, which might have happened in the United States also: her town had a large German Canadian community, she ate schnitzel with her uncle Hans, and her mother suggested she audition to be Miss Octoberfest (148). At her college in Toronto, she found multiculturalism extending beyond Europe and began to learn to be a woman of color (152), but she still felt alone. And indeed, much later in the book, after the death of her Korean father, recalling a question about a future burial place from her Canadian mother, she writes, "my body doesn't belong to any place. And it doesn't belong *in* any place" (233).

Like Robinson and Chung, Hopgood emphasizes the elements of choice and freedom that they and many others see as American values: "I didn't automatically feel a strong connection with my birth parents . . . I did feel a special bond with my sisters that was growing stronger, but I was not some passive player. I *wanted* to love them—and I wanted them to love me" (152). . . . "You can't change your past, but you can choose where to go with what you are given" (189).[53] Ma's repeated insistence, about many events in her life, "I didn't have a choice" (231) emphasizes the national difference.

How much Hopgood feels Taiwanese is a complicated question. On her first visit to Taiwan, rather than expanding in ecstasy at meeting her parents and sisters, she writes, "I have always loved—obsessed over—food. . . . In Taiwan I fit right in" (96). For a short time she feels they have a perfect reunion. She discovers sisterly reflections of her big breasts, of her crooked little toe. But soon she feels exhausted and frustrated, ready to leave (109). She finds her other sister who was sent to Switzerland, comes back again to solve more mysteries, and develops a more Asian style of dressing with more security about looking Asian. But the way she writes about living in Argentina is different—"I'd fallen in love with Buenos Aires. . . . The warm culture fit with my personality" (191–92). Her daughter is learning more Spanish than Mandarin. However, Hopgood did not stay in Argentina. After she finished this book, she got a job teaching journalism at Northwestern and wrote a book about child-rearing around the world.

Hopgood is emphatically positive about the greater freedom she has as an American, along with her complex identity. When she thinks of her daughter's inheritance, only a bit of it comes from China, fitting with her own acknowledged food obsession: "I hope she will get my dad's compassion, my mom's athleticism, and my husband's good humor. I already sense that she has inherited my Chinese family's love for eating" (244). Hopgood may well be the kind of person Trenka denies being in *Fugitive Visions*, her following book: "a global citizen, a true cosmopolitan, a person who has accumulated the riches of culture and experience, marketable job skills."[54] When Trenka writes of national identity, she does not convey a sense of freedom. Near the end of *Language of Blood*, she identifies herself as an exile (199) but in *Fugitive Visions*, she writes, with an identification of parent and country comparable to Robinson's, "I sometimes hate this country as much as I sometimes hate my own mothers, whom I also love intensely, and deeply" (188), following this a little later, however, with almost two pages of what she loves about Korea, which conclude "I love Korea because I am Korean" (190).

It is striking to look at Hopgood's memoir together with Trenka's, Robinson's, Chung's, and Wills's and Borshay Liem's film to see experiences that all have in common in spite of their different families and approaches and to see ways they are on a spectrum. The situation represented in *First Person Plural*, like that in Robinson's and Chung's memoirs, might be described once again as between that of Trenka and Wills and that of Hopgood. Borshay Liem, like Trenka, Chung, and Robinson, emphasizes her sense of multiple identity, as the title *First Person Plural* itself suggests. On the other hand, the Borshays become much more understanding than the Brauers, and the film places the sequence showing three names and birthdates for the same woman as something that Deann is showing them. Like the Hopgoods and Mrs. Robinson, they travel to meet the birth family, but like the Brauers, though not as often, they sometimes miss the significance of Deann's experiences, still getting her Korean name wrong and minimizing the importance of the orphanage's switch of her identity with that of the child they had been fostering from a distance. Unlike the three other families, Borshay Liem's and Robinson's parents have raised children who were theirs by birth; as adults Borshay Liem's siblings seem obtuse about her feelings, generally minimizing the importance of her adoption, and Robinson's brothers as adults never enter the story. Borshay Liem's relation with her parents, like Wills's, Robinson's, and Chung's, has been neither as close as Hopgood's nor as antagonistic as Trenka's.

Late in the film, Borshay Liem discusses the difficulty she had accepting her parents after she became an adult, moved away from home, and had dreams that returned repressed memories of her life before the age of nine, when she was adopted. But the film emphasizes that her parents, like Chung's, are willing to learn, and willing to listen when she talks about the unacknowledged losses related to her adoption that she has felt. She feels acknowledging the losses will help in many ways: she can develop a better relationship with her Korean mother when she acknowledges that "for 30 years she was not my mother."

In spite of the difficulties they have experienced, these memoirists conclude with a sense of agency and hope. Margaret Homans observes that Hopgood, Trenka, Robinson, and Borshay Liem all end by emphasizing their authority as artists (writers and filmmaker) and their role in family continuation on their own terms (177). Chung too writes of finding the courage to "seek and discover and tell another kind of story" than what she had been told (222). All these women conclude by evoking their children, mainly daughters, real or imagined, in a parallel to the emphasis on created families found in many same-race adoptee memoirs previously discussed.[55] We've seen this in Wills. Trenka imagines herself flying along with her Umma (mother), her fantasy daughter, and butterflies, which she has earlier invoked as symbolic both of Asian women and of metamorphosis and migration. Hopgood looks at her actual daughter, seven months and three weeks old, as she herself was when she left Taiwan, and contrasts her happiness at her daughter's birth with how her birthmother felt about hers. Robinson also invokes a continuing, if ambivalent and partly fantasy, family as she imagines her Korean mother: She is "kind and patient" but "her children will doubt her, just as she doubted her own mother and my child will someday doubt me. There is a comfort in the cycle that will connect generations of women, Korean and American" (297). Chung's daughter, at five, is old enough to ask, "Mama, am I a real Korean?" (214), to wonder why she doesn't know the language, and to want to learn it. This insistence motivates Chung to investigate schools and tutors. The memoir concludes with them writing the Korean alphabet together.

Though there are similarities, the contrasts among the five Asian memoirs and the further story told in the film are reminders of the many possibilities of variation in adoption experience. How a child is cared for before adoption; at what age and how many times they are moved; how empathetic, prepared, and open about adoption parents are; how much children feel temperamentally matched in the adoptive family; how much parents and neighbors emphasize ethnicity and family physical resemblance; whether there are resources available that help a child develop interests and skills; and many other variables, including what characteristics the child has inherited and what the mother's physical and mental conditions were during her pregnancy are all factors that determine what the impact of specific adoption circumstances will be. And there are as many variables in determining what the impact of meeting birth relatives again will be. Adoptee anthropologist Elise Prebin concludes from her own experience of meeting her Korean relatives, "blood alone does not create a relationship. It involve[s] time and effort" (181). Chung writes that after spending three informative days with her birthfather, her half brother, and his wife, "I did not feel like a reclaimed daughter" (198).

The aftermath of meeting is also complicated for adoptee memoirists with all or partly African ancestry, but they too, like the adoptees with Asian ancestry, can by the end of their memoir develop an image, fantasy, or ritual to define their identity and sense of family. McKinley finds that neither of her birthparents can provide her much of a relationship. As we have seen, she finds an extremely unreliable mother. Her African American father, who lives across the continent, is a charmer but also a mobster and liar and seems to have difficulties dealing with her being a lesbian. Sometimes she loves seeing parts of herself that look like Estie and Sarah, and sometimes they trouble her; then she feels in some way being adopted was easier for her because "it must be torture to grow up never feeling free of other people's legacy—however proud or horrifying" (199). A resolution in which she will construct her own legacy comes later.

In the middle section of her memoir, Kay is similarly skeptical about the results of her search. "You cannot find yourself in two strangers who happen to share your genes . . . you are made up from a mixture of myth and gene. . . . Finding a strange, nervous, Mormon mother and finding a crazed, ranting, Born-Again father does not explain me" (47). She can enumerate similarities, both physical and temperamental—for example, "I have my mother's hair. I have my father's sense of humour, gift of the gab" (48)—but still asks "What does it matter?" Whether it will actually tell her something more about herself or not, she has enough curiosity that she chooses to continue to search.

Though her meetings with both of her parents are uncomfortable even with her birthfather's rejection, she does not give up. While she has seen physical similarity to herself in her birthparents, the feeling of recognition missing in the earlier meetings finally comes to her when she sees the "red-dust road" (213) of the Nigerian home village of her father, and in a further "almost ecstatic" way when she meets her brother. She feels "ambushed" (272), because this feeling is such a surprise. McLeod sees it as part of the "perpetual surprise of the transcultural adoptee's ongoing journey . . . not amplified as the teleological goal of tracing heredity nor deleted as having no significance at all" (*Life Lines* 222). Yet the end of the memoir, as we will see in a few pages, suggests a kind of resolution.

Of all the adoptee memoirists discussed here, Jaiya John meets the birthparents who are the most compatible to him and admirable according to his values. His birthmother, Mary, writes him, and after graduating from college, he visits her. She cooks him a feast, and he learns about her Blackfoot and Cherokee ancestry and her studies at a seminary and also sees her "passion about racial justice and spiritual dignity" (279), with which he strongly identifies. He feels that as he learns more about her he is "becoming familiar with myself" (280). When he meets his birthfather, Whitfield Jenkins, whom she had also written, he learns about his grandfather and the American Indians in this part of his ancestry and meets his extended family. He enjoys seeing their proud acceptance of their dark skin (darker than his) and their big feet and Whitfield's distinctive way of getting into a car (like his), and finds another model for his own commitment in his father's work on the Florida Human Relations Commission and NAACP.

Still the aftermath fits Kay's prediction about upheaval. After John meets and gets to know Mary and Whitfield, and becomes part of a Black family, and a Black community mostly elsewhere, he feels some turmoil about his relation to his adoptive parents. They are unfamiliar with Black people and attached to their white cultural heritage, and they can see when he returns to visit that he is even talking differently. Finally he has to have the difficult conversations—he gets them to talk about their attitudes toward race in relation to adopting him.

John's father recalls that when he was long ago asked by an African American man about how he would prepare his son for a racist society, he had acknowledged his ignorance and limited perspective, saying, "All I can do is try to teach him what my father taught me, and hopefully that will provide him the tools and the strength of character to figure out the rest on his own" (287). His mother remembers that when growing up, she was taught that "Black people were dirty and unclean" (286), but later she says, "I tried to treat all you kids the same" (296). In other words, John writes, she had tried to deny "the facts of our adoption and race." As they said when he asked why they adopted him, they "wanted to give a child a better life" (292), but with the limitations of their experience, his parents had no idea what they were getting into. Although they showed their belief in racial equality when they agreed to adopt him, his mother's behavior, especially, exemplifies the deep-seated nature of implicit bias, which research shows can go against one's conscious beliefs.[56] Neither of his parents understood their own privilege as white people, a lens of analysis that was not yet widely known, but which clarifies the difficulties of adoptees in this and most of the other memoirs discussed here.[57]

John's reunions and subsequent relationships with his birthparents are among the most satisfying for a searcher in these memoirs. His final identity includes being a full participant in several Black communities, not an ongoing sense of hybridity or a self-image as a traveler like that we will see at the end of Hopgood's and Kay's memoirs. His concluding situation is so different from his early life that Fedosik sees the memoir as structured like a conversion narrative, or a narrative of escaping from slavery.[58]

But John's conclusion is not just a critique of his adoptive parents. Like virtually all these memoirists, he has gained more empathy for them. He has also come to appreciate their "steady support" in spite of their lack of understanding and concludes, "Mom and Dad gave all their children a precious and rare gift: the permission to be ourselves" (302). He sees that he has learned valuable things from them. "I was Dad's son, with his same irreverence for conformity. . . . I was Mom's child, with her willingness to sacrifice comfort in order to nurture and protect what she believed in" (332). In what he calls an "Afterthought," he writes of a phone conversation with his mother, recalling her early singing and massaging of him as a young child, which gave him the "energy of encouragement" (349) to complete the book telling his story. Close to the end of the book proper, he describes the celebration of his renaming himself Jaiya John and naming his new daughter, during which his adoptive parents "Mom" and "Dad" and his birthfather, Whitfield, and his wife, called Mother Loretta, bond with each other as well. He is the only adoptee with African ancestry whose adoptive parents meet one of his birthparents. Since his daughter's mother is not mentioned and John works closely with social service agencies committed to the Black community, it seems likely that he has adopted this child.

At the end of her book, after a childhood and young adulthood filled with anger, McKinley has a calmer evaluation of her adoptive parents, which resembles much of John's summation, though her parents had more sense of her needs. She writes: "I can see that I had a childhood unnecessarily complicated by my parents' choices and circumscriptions. . . . [They] valued independence and integrity . . . their emotional steadiness . . . was a bedrock as I wavered and grieved. My parents gave me the tools to go forth and figure out an American Black woman's life. My bond with them is as simple and as automatic as love; as vexing and as intractable as our distances" (289).

McLeod writes that McKinley learns how to "fashion singular plural being from the intercalated traces of biogenetic and adoptive heredities" (178). She cherishes the color and fabric indigo, which links her to her biological, adoptive, and fantasy families as well as a beloved Nigerian teacher. She summarizes, "WASP and Jew and Choctaw and Africa mark me with ferocity" (288) and lines up photographs of all her families, but it is the one of her adoptive family, including her brother's Filipina wife and daughters, about which she says, "I like the picture. I like the people in it" (288).

McKinley brings the parts of her identity together in her fascination with indigo and in her private ritual of lining up photographs. The Asian adoptee memoirists we have considered, as we have seen, end their memoirs with what might be considered private or fantasy rituals involving their children, real or imagined. Although Avery is only a coscriptwriter for *Off and Running* rather than a director, and her plot is shorter than those in the memoirs and *First Person Plural*, this film also suggests the importance of ritual in ending with her return to her parents' home for the Jewish fall holidays. John, uniquely among these memoirists, is able to have a successful large celebration involving many people (the previous chapter notes Hickman's descriptions of family celebrations of various kinds near the end of his memoir, but his tone is more ambivalent). In the next chapter, about adoptive parents' memoirs, we will see another public celebration, a transracial adoptee's wedding, mixing Black and white families. Memoirist Douglas Bates hopes that this is a foreshadowing of better race relations in the whole country.

Other adoptees place different rituals near the end of their memoirs. Two Asian adoptee memoirists want to affirm their complex identities and the bonds between their families with a religious ritual. Chung, who remembers feeling a sense of connectedness and comfort in Catholic faith and rituals in her childhood, concludes her first visit from her sister and her husband with candle-lighting and prayers at a Marian chapel in the National Sanctuary to Our Sorrowful Mother (196). By contrast, Trenka would like to have a ritual attended by her adoptive parents, whether her wedding or later a memorial for her birthmother, but they refuse to participate.

When her memoir is about to be published, Harness finally gets her tribal welcome ritual from the Salish Kootenai people, with a dance, shawl, and an honor song. Kay's parents are not religious but brought her up with a commitment to social justice, and it is in keeping with that that, close to the end after she tells her parents about her brother, she dances with them to "If I Had a Hammer," which she learned in the socialist Sunday school choir (285). And she also has a private ritual—she walks by herself in a forest she loves, puts a gold coin in a "perfect hollow" (288), in an oak tree, and imagines growing an African moringa tree transplanted to her house in Manchester. Earlier she wrote that being adopted never ends, but in imagining the transplanted tree flourishing for years, she creates another celebratory version of herself—what McLeod calls "adoptive being" (224). She thinks of herself as a traveler like the tree, and links her own traveling to that of all of her parents, as when she picked a name meaning "good journey" from the Igbo names her father offers her (Kay 107; McLeod 219). Although she never directly calls herself lucky, she uses that word for the sound of the trees under her feet in that walk, and in planning to transplant the moringa she says, "I will chance my luck" (Kay 289).

Close to Kay's inclusiveness is the passage near the end of *Lucky Girl* when Hopgood connects her plane rides with "all the trips that my family, in all of its many forms, has made then and now, crossing land, sea, and the globe, searching for a different life, a new perspective, peace of mind, a place to call home" (238), feeling part of "a collective tapestry so intricate that one string cannot be untangled from the other." Still, another sign that transracial adoption really does make a difference is that none of these adoptees expresses, even momentarily, the feeling of being related to everyone that strikes Homes, Strauss, and Harding as they pore over public records. Transracial adoptees may need to look in a different set of records, especially if they are also transnational. However, somewhat as Homes writes, "The quest to answer the question Who am I? is not unique to the adoptee" (152), Chung writes, "My identity as an adoptee is complicated, fluid, but then so is everyone else's" (221).

A folkloric fantasy about meeting birthparents is that it will lead adoptees to a permanent return to their homeland, rejecting adoptive parents. This seldom happens in adoptees' memoirs—even in memoirs by transracial adoptees, where one might expect it more often because race is such a salient category in American life. These memoirs, like those in the previous chapter, show how much more there is to identity than genetics. Considering shorter essays as well as memoirists Robinson and Trenka, McKee shows that "for many adoptees, return to Korea evokes feelings of cultural inauthenticity. . . . Adoptees remain cultural outsiders" (91). Dorothy Roberts reminds us of the complex interactions in which environment determines which genes are activated and writes, with regard to African Americans in particular, "defining identity in genetic terms creates a biological essentialism that is antithetical to the shared political values that should form the basis for unity . . . we have considerable freedom to decide how much importance to give our genetics, family history, and social relationships."[59] Thinking of the desire that African Americans might have to use genetic tests to find and connect with their relatives, either African or white, Alondra Nelson writes, "DNA can offer an avenue toward reconciliation, but cannot stand in for reconciliation: voice, acknowledgment, mourning, forgiveness, and healing"[60] (164). This qualification is also relevant to adoptees, who may seek reconciliation with both (or all three) of their families.

Like the memoirs of same-race adoptees Homes, Strauss, Saffian, and the separated twins, almost all these memoirs end with some kind of synthesis, including recognition of what the adoptees have gained from their adoptive parents. Even Trenka thinks of how unprepared her adoptive parents were and writes that she offers them "something like forgiveness" (202). She remembers that her mother got "only crumbs" from her parents and wanted to give her "the whole pie." And she does recognize that from adoption she has gained "the freedom that America has to offer, the opportunity to have the same rights as a man" (200).

But the syntheses that most of the memoirists recount with fewer reservations have not been easily achieved and might not have been possible at an earlier stage of their lives. Barbara Yngvesson, after interviewing a number of transnational and transracial adoptees and observing her own son in his late teens, writes of their return to their birth country as occasioning moments of "a space of nonidentity and the double vision it produces[, which] can be excruciating, sometimes unbearable" (176).

And Carroll, who has cut off contact with her birthmother, ends without a gesture of synthesis. Rather than paying tribute to values that her parents gave her, as do McKinley, John, and Kay, she has described them as losing their focus on their children after Tess arrives and writes that she experienced "acute lack of guidance or structure . . . no grounding in culture or religion or aspiration" (98). In her epilogue, she remembers performing a kind of ritual of *removal* of most of the photographs of her in childhood, except for one which her four-year-old son Kofi thought was a photo of *him*. She recalls his questions on the way back from a later Christmas visit with her parents about why there was "no black art, books, or music" in their house. "Does that hurt your feelings, Mom? . . . Shouldn't they care more because Mom is black?" (314). She agrees that "it wasn't a best case scenario."

Another adoptee memoir also presents a definitive choice of a life connected only to ancestry. In *Looking for Lost Bird: A Jewish Woman Discovers Her Navajo Roots*, adoptee Yvette Melanson moves to a Navajo reservation. However, this is a special case, because she was literally stolen from a Navajo family, her adoptive mother died when she was twelve, and her father remarried, blamed her for her mother's death, and in effect threw her out. Even she has a moment of remembering her dead adoptive mother and forgiving her father in the ritual of acceptance into her Native tribe at the end.

Harness, who also forgives her father, remembers her dead adoptive mother with more warmth and has a ritual of acceptance into her Native tribe but lives in a condo in a white area, writes about the independence of others' views of her that she gained, and a kind of synthesis through "the role social memory plays, by determining what is remembered but, more importantly, what is forgotten. Social memory is what ties all these generations together, allowing them to be regifted from one generation to another" (334). In other words, she remembers some things from each of her families. Writing of her white extended family, she uses a Native word, *Qene*, meaning "grandmother," to describe the importance to her of her role in it.

Wound of Adoption? Wound of Racism? Wound of Early Instability?

Some of the adoptees discussed in the previous chapter, Winterson, Homes, Jakiela, and Hipchen, attribute their feelings of being unwanted, wounded, marked by loss, never fitting in, to being given up for adoption, while Strauss, Saffian, Harding, and Bernstein write that they did not feel that way. In this chapter, the sense of not fitting in is more objectively based because of the memoirists' visual difference and American, Canadian, and British racial bias. Hopgood emphatically distinguishes—she didn't find being adopted in itself a problem, and got along with her parents very well, but she did feel racially different and inferior. Chung similarly felt isolated by her race though she says that as she grew up she felt loved by both her adoptive parents—temperamentally different though they were from her—and her birthparents (4). Harness, John, Carroll, McKinley, Borshay Liem, Robinson, Klein-Cloud, Willis, and Trenka clearly had many difficulties in their childhood that could be attributed directly or indirectly to their parents' lack of understanding of their racial issues.

Kay's parents were not only loving people but also better about introducing her to cultural heroes of her race and speaking up for her against prejudiced behavior. Still, she writes that that being adopted gives her an extra "layer of aloneness" (46)—"no matter how much she loved me, no matter how much my dad loved me, there is still a windy place right at the core of my heart.... I sometimes even forget it" (45–46). Yet something changes. At the end of the book, after having found in her Nigerian brother a compatible relative, she writes, "The empty ghost, the wraithlike figure that has stalked me for years ... disappears" (276). Before her first departure for Nigeria to meet her father, she makes a ritual of placing a coin in the "hollow" of a tree, with twin trunks, but when she returns from Africa the second time and wants to memorialize her meeting with her brother, in a gesture analyzed by John McLeod, she chooses the hollow of a different tree, not one that is a double (288). McLeod (223) relates this gesture to metaphorical filling up of the "windy place" Kay wrote of earlier. She now neither feels stalked by a double nor identifies with a double tree. She had, for whatever reason, the persistence to keep on with the search until she could find one Nigerian family member who would accept her. While she feels gratitude for her particular adoptive parents, unlike Hopgood she has connected her feelings of aloneness not only to race but also to adoption, yet she suggests that they have finally disappeared.

Among these writers, Trenka and Harness feel the worst about adoption as an institution, having experienced its large-scale imposition on Korean and Native children. Chung shares the belief that the Korean adoption system is problematic, though she feels in her own case things turned out for the best.

With regard to the suggestion that being given up for adoption inevitably results in a feeling of loneliness, it is worth considering the instability that many adoptee memoirists discussed in this and the previous chapter experienced early in their lives.[61] The worst experience of preadoptive life is recounted just after the title page to *The Language of Blood*, in a long letter Trenka's mother wrote to resume their relationship after about twenty years. "Your father was saying, 'Who is father!' 'She is not my baby!' . . . Your father tried to suffocate Kyong-Ah as using a comforter" (7). She was temporarily sent to an orphanage, where her mother found her at the brink of death. Her father insisted that she could be taken home only if she and her sister (four years older) were sent to the United States. Soon eight-month-old Kyong-Ah joined the Brauer household and became Jane; her older sister became Carol. There are many reasons why the Brauer household was difficult for the girls, but instability before their adoption could not have helped.

Harness was neglected in her chaotic birth family. Robinson also experienced insecurity, though not intended murder, before her adoption; her father was married to someone else when she was born and never married her mother but left her for a third woman. She had been moved into her aunt's house, then back with her mother and grandmother, and then to an orphanage by the time she was seven, and finally was adopted. Like Trenka and Harness, she long felt uncomfortable in her adoptive home. Jackie Kay was born with damage from a forceps delivery and had to stay in the hospital for five months, with her (adoptive) mother regularly driving the forty miles from Glasgow to Edinburgh to pick her up while wearing a mask to guard against infection. "The doctors were apparently amazed at my recovery" (26). Regardless of whatever problems might result from early separation in itself, about which psychologists disagree, many of these experiences provide material for a lifelong sense of instability and loneliness. Kay focuses on the positive, the persistent loyalty of her mother through this period, but that is her mature reaction, not necessarily what she felt most of the time as an infant.

The Hopgoods located little Mei-Ling because a friend knew an American nun working as a midwife in a Taiwanese hospital. Sister Maureen's loving care for little Mei-Ling, along with that of the other nuns in her community, is one of the many ways in which Hopgood sees she is lucky. (Here we see a very different picture of a Catholic institution than Jakiela and Hipchen present in the previous chapter.) Maureen's attachment shows in her letters about the baby quoted in the book: "She laughs out loud if you tickle her and her body is beautiful, strong and fat. She *loves* to be bathed" (59).

Chung was born ten weeks premature and medically vulnerable. Her birthparents had no insurance and were worried about the cost. But she had one similar trait to Mei-Ling: "she was a favorite of the nurses," and though she weighed less than six pounds, at two and a half months she was already talking a storm when her new parents took her home (25).

The care that little Mei-Ling received from Sister Maureen for almost all the first eight months of her life is arguably one of the reasons why she related so well to her adoptive parents—in addition to their warmth and insight—and why as an adult Hopgood writes that adoption in itself was not a problem for her.[62] Possibly the fact that Chung was "a favorite of the nurses" helped her to believe in her adoptive parents' and even her birthparents' love. Maybe even Hickman, discussed in the preceding chapter, was able to attach to his adoptive parents in spite of his difficulties with them partly because of the happiness he experienced in his foster home.

Transracial Adoptees' Conclusions

Most of these memoirs, like many memoirs, focus finally on the identity that the adoptee author has developed and the way they have come to terms with their past. John, for example, writes, "It was a good life. It was a life embroidered with pain" (348). Kay ends with the image of a healthy Nigerian tree, "magical" and "splendid" in Manchester, a transformation of her sense of doubleness into a proud identity as a traveler (289). But transracial adoptee memoirs in particular illuminate the racial faultlines of our society as well as the failure of many social welfare institutions to acknowledge them and help those caught in them. John is not the only transracial adoptee who feels the need to break silence and discuss racism with his parents. Close to her conclusion, with an attitude like John's, Chung discusses how she now feels that she must talk more openly with her family about racial issues. Beloved relatives speak with casual prejudice, and she feels she can no longer ignore it: "It feels like my duty as my white family's de facto Asian ambassador to remind them that I am *not* white, that we *do* experience this country in different ways because of it, that many people still know oppression far more insidious and harmful than anything I've ever faced" (208).

Transracial adoptee memoirs include some astounding pictures of cruelty, like Trenka's parents' refusal to attend her wedding and her mother's memorial service and Harness's father's abuse, and more astounding pictures of generosity, like Kay's and Hopgood's parents. And even more pictures of parents like the Potters and the Borshays, who just want an ordinary family life and show ordinary parental obliviousness and ordinary parental generosity at the same time, unaware of the suffering they are causing. Those two sets of parents, at least, seem to gain more awareness, unlike the Carrolls.

Two clichés about adoption are that it is a rescue and that adoptees are lucky.[63] After hearing about her Nigerian father's attempt to exorcize her, Kay's parents feel justified in saying, "By God, did we rescue you!" (11). We have seen that Kay invokes the idea of her good luck at the end of her memoir, and she clearly expresses gratitude to her parents though she knows gratitude is too often imposed on adoptees. Hopgood more directly calls attention to the idea of her good luck in her title. She feels lucky most obviously to no longer be in a society in which girls are openly considered second-class, but also not to be a boy in her birth family, either, because of Pa's weird and disabling way of raising his sons, for example still bathing the second at the age of eight. But her luck also appears in the distinctively happy and understanding home into which she was adopted—not the kind of home one would necessarily arrive in as a Taiwanese person in 1974.

Chung, having learned about the violence and instability in her sister's childhood, also counts herself as lucky (153). She now believes "Being adopted probably saved my life" (210). Theoretically, she could have been raised by her father along with her sister, but she thinks that would have been difficult too: "I don't know if I ever would have measured up to his standards" (211). However, the stock phrase that being adopted gave her "a better life" (211) eventually seems too simple to her. There are so many uncertainties, so many possibilities. Though she knows now more than her parents earlier thought she could (as the title suggests), some things she will never know. But her empathy and acceptance are striking when she says of her father, "He had—like my adoptive parents—done the best he could" (211).

Harness feels not lucky but cheated (212). She writes, "I don't know why I was taken from a chaotic family filled with alcoholism and dismembered relationships and placed with a family filled with alcoholism and dismembered relationships" (211). Trenka refuses calling herself the "lucky adoptee" that she claims to have once thought she was (199). She asks, "How can I weigh the loss of my language and culture against the freedom that America has to offer? . . . How many educational opportunities must I mark on my tally sheet before I can say it was worth losing my mother?" (200–201). She has had a terrible loss and cannot weigh it against the "burden of gratitude she feels for her adoptive country and parents." Gratitude itself is a burden rather than a good thing.

The issue of gratitude as an expectation for adoptees looms large in McKee's book about Korean adoption, as she analyzes the effects of the popular idealization of transnational adoption as rescue. McKee writes that "to assume that adoptees should automatically be grateful results in their oppression" (94) and observes that this assumption ignores or would silence their honesty about experiencing racism. Chung comes places near the beginning of her book a memory of her conflict of feeling when she is questioned by a couple wanting to adopt. She remembers as a child twisting her hated hair and being asked a racist question by a fellow schoolgirl but won't speak of those memories: "I still had to think of adoption as an unqualified good . . . because to do otherwise felt like a betrayal of my family and their love for me" (20). Her just mentioned belief that "being adopted probably saved my life" came from discoveries about her specific situation rather than about a large cultural faith in adoption.

Trenka's attitude is thus different from Hopgood's or Chung's, neither one of them part of a great wave of adoptees from Korea or China. Hopgood, especially, was adopted outside the usual system. Her parents were idiosyncratic and unusually insightful; she knew they were on her side and respected her other family. Trenka's parents, on the other hand, were more typical of parents sought by adoption agencies during the great wave of Korean adoption—devout churchgoers who believed they were doing missionary work. Robinson's and Chung's parents were perhaps somewhere in between—adopting through Pearl Buck's Welcome House or a church contact rather than explicitly as missionary work. Trenka is the one memoirist who emphasizes that motherhood was the only career for a woman in the culture of the time and portrays a pastor persuading her parents to adopt internationally as a way to spread Christianity. (*Language* 18, 24).[64] They would have preferred to adopt a white boy domestically, but none was available. This sense of religious duty may be a more common extrinsic motivation for adoption than getting money from a relative or distracting from trauma, seen in the previous chapter; Trenka stresses that it is far from giving a child of a different race a sense of belonging. Other memoirists in this chapter, and most in the previous one, apparently take their parents' desire to adopt as authentic rather than imposed—or else, like Harness, don't mention it.

Thus it makes sense that Trenka's book shows more awareness of widespread problems with transnational adoption, including the lack of adequate preparation for would-be adoptive parents. In addition to narrating many frustrating exchanges with Lutheran Social Services, she frames her return to Korea with quotes from the Child Welfare League and International Social Services. She includes material from Korean history early in the book and, after explaining why she was given away for adoption, writes, "Almost every Korean family has such a story. The characters are always the same: starvation, lost family members, bitter cold, poverty, men unable to support their families, drunkenness, disappointment, despair" (44). Trenka feels a strong identification with the international community of Korean adoptees, and has been very active within it; her book's critique of the system that has caused pain to so many of them is revelatory, and she followed this by helping form a group called Truth and Reconciliation for the Adoption Community of Korea, which brought cases to the Korean Anti-Corruption and Civil Rights Commission, with limited success (*Fugitive* 93).

Robinson also has some criticism of adoption procedures: the single square picture of the book's title is evidence that Welcome House lied to her parents. She "had not been abandoned at birth and left at the doorstops of a Pusan police station with a note . . . had not grown up in an orphanage, as the adoption records indicated" (64–65). By contrast, giving up children to be adopted was not quite as frequent in Taiwan when Hopgood was born as in Korea when Trenka was, and when Hopgood gives a larger context to her parents' story, it is to their history in war-torn Taiwan as well as to cultural devaluation of women. Chung, dealing with American adoption procedures, notes that the lawyer who helped her parents was relatively inexperienced and the social worker had difficulty communicating with the birthparents and no sense that there were any special issues in raising a Korean child.

Some other clichés about adoption often invoked by adoptive parents and remembered, sometimes critically, by adoptee memoirists are that it is like a miracle, it comes from Divine Providence, or, in perhaps more secular language, the matches are "meant to be."[65] Theology is beyond the scope of this book, but some consideration of the role of religion is not. People can use religious faith to go beyond their racial and other boundaries and believe that we are all God's children, and this is one of the reasons that so many orphanages and adoption agencies have religious affiliations. But people can also use religious faith to try to convert other people to be like them, and that is another reason why so many orphanages and adoption agencies have religious affiliations.[66] And people who have either a nominal or militant commitment to their religion can combine it with hatred or at best unconscious prejudice against outsiders. In *The Child Catchers*, Kathryn Joyce shows some such problematic elements in the recent evangelical crusade that claims to follow a biblical command to adopt orphans from all over the world.

Many of these dimensions of religion register in Chung's memoir. She knows her parents believe that she is God's gift to them, and this contributes to her belief in their love. Yet it is in a Catholic grade school that she first meets prejudice, from her schoolmates. She writes, "My family's devout Catholic faith had often functioned as a kind of substitute for the Korean heritage I had lost . . . there was rhythm and ritual in my Catholic upbringing, a sense of purpose and interconnectedness. I had long found comfort in it" (46). But in high school, she asks her father, "Did you ever wonder how I ended up with you and Mom as my parents, and not someone else?" and is dissatisfied with his answer, "God wanted us to have you" (45). She wonders why God didn't care that her birthparents wanted to keep her.

Language about fate or about God's will is often used to justify events by people who have benefited from them, to forestall a clearer study of more immediate causes. As Chung writes, this view makes it "easier to gloss over real loss and inequity, to justify the separation of a parent and a child" (47). And she thinks it also helped her parents to be patient with difficulties in raising her. But from a practical, human point of view, which she takes later in the book, she was given up for adoption partly because her mother couldn't afford therapy and wouldn't have found a doctor who could speak Korean, and "the child welfare system that took charge of my placement overlooked the opportunity to look closer and see children at risk, a family in crisis" (211). And the system also overlooked the opportunity to educate her parents about the needs of children who were visibly Asian and the possibilities of preserving contact with their birth family or at least their birth culture.

How Can Adoption Be Improved?

Near the beginning of this chapter, I noted that some of the memoirs discussed in this chapter have influenced the advice many adoption agencies and social workers now give adoptive parents. Robinson notes a related change: "Adoptive parents increasingly recognize the importance of interweaving their children's birth culture into the fabric of their family's daily lives" (36). But this is not something simply accomplished by buying dolls and food associated with their ancestry. Ideally the family would also have adult friends of that ancestry, something complicated to achieve in our segregated society. There have been attempts: some adoptive families have tried to build bridges with Korean Americans by working with a service organization, Friends of Korea, and a newspaper, *Korean Quarterly*.[67] But this takes effort.

Also challenging is the new kind of adoption Trenka surprisingly imagines at one point, in which the adoptive family regularly talks about the Korean family left behind as part of their extended family, and the American parents travel with them to meet and keep in contact with their Korean family. But we have seen Kay's mother approaching the first step when Jackie was a child, and at the end she speaks of her "forty-five-year-old Nigerian son"

(284) who plans to visit them. In the next chapter we will see a few adoptive parents who take the second step.

One of the main lessons of this chapter is that people who adopt trans-racially need guidance. Chung repeatedly emphasizes this. Telling her parents' story, she writes that in their preadoption interview with a social worker, they asked whether there was anything special they should do for her because she was Korean and were told only, "I'm sure you'll all be fine" (28). She recalls her mother's surprise "the day I came home from school and told her how much I wished I knew other Asians" (119). Even Hopgood, whose parents understand her needs more than many, feels uncomfortable about her Asian appearance until she meets her sisters, and all the other adoptees discussed in this chapter feel unease about their own faces for many years. Adoption agencies should emphasize how difficult it is for children to live in a place where there are no adults who look like them. Linda Seligmann finds that some parents who adopted transracially have begun "not just to move into more integrated neighborhoods or schools but also to make black friends in those neighborhoods and confront racism" (159). More do now than formerly, but not that many parents are willing to move. Transracial adoptees would benefit from knowing other transracial adoptees growing up, but they also need to have adult models who can help them deal with the deep racial bias, including unconscious bias, that many people they meet will have. Adoption agencies need to explain this. Research in recent books by Elizabeth Raleigh and Kristi Brian shows how inadequately adoption providers still deal with racial issues. Raleigh writes that "market concerns lead social workers to downplay the significance of race, often conflating discussions of racial power and privilege with more palatable discussions of multiculturalism."[68] We see agencies not doing their job of preparing, supporting, or selecting parents in the memoirs of Trenka, John, McKinley, Robinson, Chung, and Harness and, in the previous chapter, Homes and Winterson. Winterson's social worker saw her prospective parents as "not what you would call modern," but that seems too mild a phrase for their violently punitive behavior.

Robinson's memoir stresses another frequent irresponsible act by an adoption agency, misrepresenting her as an abandoned child. In addition to lying blatantly as here, orphanages and agencies very often do use the term *orphan* with deliberate ambiguity, meaning that living parents are too poor or ill to raise the child, knowing that potential parents will probably think that the parents have died.[69] As Deann Borshay Liem's documentary *In the Matter of Cha Jung Hee* shows, they also sometimes lie about the identity of a child—if a couple has been supporting a child who has been adopted, that child's name may be given to another child who is still available. They may misrepresent to birthparents the meaning of adoption to Americans, allowing them to assume that their children are going away to be educated and as adults will return to support them.[70] And as Trenka and Harness narrate, they frequently refuse to give adult adoptees their records. Many countries have found so much corruption by adoption agencies that they have denied them permission to place their children. More regulation is necessary. And so is a challenge to the idealization of adoption, which McKee identifies as reinforcing the transnational adoption industrial complex that requires adoptees to appear happy and grateful at all times (77).[71] Challenging the accompanying mythology of adoption as rebirth, research shows that in most cases adopted children benefit significantly from having continuing relationships with one or more birthparents from an early age (Grotevant et al. 79–101).[72]

This is particularly difficult to accomplish with children adopted transnationally, and in fact, as memoirs of adoptive parents show, some choose transnational adoption specifically to avoid contact with a birthmother whom they imagine will want to take her child back.[73] But in domestic transracial adoption, it is possible, if challenging. Some writers believe that for domestic cases, at least, often better than adoption that cuts contact with birthparents would be a model in which parent and child are adopted together into a new family (Grand 144–47). Harness would support adoption that keeps the child in the extended family, agreeing with Judge William Thorne, who she quotes as saying, "If a child needs new parents, we can replace their parents, but that doesn't mean we have to replace aunts and uncles, cousins, or their siblings" (332). Her memoir shows good reason for ICWA's preference for this kind of adoption or, at least, adoption within the tribe. Would any adoptive parent memoirists support these models? Many are dissatisfied with current practices and feel that they could have used better preparation.

As I was finishing this book, I read Angela Tucker's "You Should Be Grateful": Stories of Race, Identity, and Transracial Adoption.[74] This is not a memoir, but it includes many stories from Tucker's life illuminating issues in transracial adoption, along with discussion of those issues and stories of other adoptees. Tucker's adoptive parents are more like the Kays and the Hopgoods than any other parents of transracial adoptees we have read about. She writes, "I always knew I belonged in my adoptive family, and I've always longed for a genetic sense of belonging" (79). An expert in paradox and both/and, she opens her book with an adoptee manifesto. The first two items are

1. We can love more than one set of parents.
2. Relationships with our birth parents, foster parents, and our adoptive parents are not mutually exclusive. (xi)

In the next chapter, we will find a few adoptive parents who would accept this.

4

Many Ways to Be an Adoptive Parent

Theresa Reid, Ralph Savarese, J. Douglas Bates, Sharon Rush,
Jana Wolff, Kay Trimberger, Michael Dorris, Ann Kimble Loux,
Jesse Green, David Marin, Melissa Fay Greene, Claude Knobler,
Emily Prager, Jeanne Marie Laskas, Jeff Gammage

M any adoptee memoirists, we have seen, write that their parents were
not sufficiently prepared. Most adoptive parents writing since the late
1980s agree and would like to have had more information about their
child's previous history and the challenges they would face as parents. This
emphasis contrasts strongly with the stress on their own competence and
the ordinariness of adoption that Rachel Raines Winslow finds in memoirs
adoptive parents, including some who adopted transracially or internationally, wrote in the 1950s and 1960s.[1]

However, there is considerable variety in the plots and emphases of memoirs by adoptive parents now. Many of them convey the message "Raising an
adopted child is harder than I expected—still, it is worthwhile," but the kinds
of difficulties vary enormously; a few seem quite defeated by the undertaking,
and others apparently find it all enjoyable. Like most memoirists discussed in
previous chapters, more adoptive parent memoirists now consider an adoptee as having two sets of parents, even if they can't meet the birthparents—
but several would emphatically deny that this is true. Most agree with adoptee
memoirists that it is important for adoptees to learn about their heredity or
at least their ancestral culture. However, some do not. Reading many adoptee memoirs may lead to a prediction that these adoptive parents may be in
for conflict about such denials as their children grow up.

In the 2002 book, *Adoption in America*, in her chapter "Adoption Stories,"
Barbara Melosh observes that of the many perspectives in adoption (adop-

tee, birthparent, adoptive parent, and so on) adoptive parents have written the most memoirs.[2] More than twenty years later, with many adoptees having found communities and voices, this may no longer be true, but adoptive parents continue to write. Their more recently written memoirs place comparatively less emphasis on the search for a child through infertility treatments and adoption agency tests than those Melosh discusses. More now go beyond the "ending of family formation" and, like a few she discusses, "deal with parenting of children in nonmatching families" (224) or children with disabilities.

In recent years some adoptees have argued that to write a memoir about adopting and raising a child is to take away the agency of the adoptee, who alone owns the story, especially if the story goes past childhood. This is an understandable reaction to the historically more prominent public voices of adoptive parents, many adult adoptees' lack of legal access to the records of their birth and adoption, and their continued labeling as "adopted children." However, for prospective or new adoptive parents or for those interested in improving the lives of adoptive families, some memoirs by adoptive parents are helpful because they reveal the efforts required to meet some children's needs, and others are helpful as cautionary because they show adoptive parents continuing with practices like those that adult adoptees protest, in memoirs and otherwise.

Since Melosh wrote, there have been many more memoirs by parents who adopted internationally or from American foster care as well as by single and gay and lesbian people, whose relation to fertility is obviously different. This increase in adoption across national borders and from foster care is partly for demographic reasons: there are now fewer healthy white babies available for adoption. And the domestic adoption of a healthy white baby by a married white mother is ordinary enough in itself (even if it involves a difficult journey with rejections and failures on the way) that publishers are unlikely to think of it as an interesting story, though a gay man's domestic adoption narrative has an audience. I did not find a memoir by a straight adoptive parent whose relationship with a child, same-race, same-country, nontraumatized, is as simple as the relationship that Strauss's and Saffian's parents seem to have had with their daughters, who have the happiest memories among same-race adoptees before, in each case, one of their parents died. Transracial and transnational adoption, special needs adoption, and open adoption add complexity.[3] While transnational adoption is becoming less frequent, other kinds are becoming more so.[4]

I make no claim to discuss a statistically representative sample of adoption memoirs in this chapter, but I portray a diversity of situations, occasionally showing similarity across categories, sometimes showing how adoptive parents in somewhat similar situations write differently. Most of them tell stories that contrast with those Melosh identifies as the dominant pattern— "ending with family formation."

Privilege versus Social Commitment

Let's begin with a brief contrast to hint at the range of attitudes in these memoirs. The memoirist closest to the "ending of family formation" pattern is Theresa Reid, who finishes her memoir with the picture of her two young daughters happily crawling into bed with her and her husband. But she has, unlike Melosh's examples, adopted internationally, in her case from Russia. Indeed, she chose Russia because she wanted a white child whose birthparents would be far away.[5]

The parent memoir most different from Reid's is Ralph Savarese's *Reasonable People*.[6] Savarese and his wife, Emily, a therapist, chose to be foster parents to a speechless boy Emily was helping who had been removed from his birthmother's custody. After years of trying to help her get her life together, they decide to adopt DJ, knowing his continued difficulties and some of his history of trauma and neglect. They teach him to communicate electronically even if he can't speak, decide to focus on him rather than trying to raise any other children, and help him mature emotionally. After learning to attach to them, he also learns, by the age of twelve, to separate from them enough to develop independence and friendships outside the family.

Reid and Savarese contrast in their attitudes to their economic privilege, contact with birth family, and loss and trauma in adoption. Different as they are, both Reid and Savarese say that other people often consider them saints, and they reject this designation, as would the other memoirists. They do not feel selfless or perfect. Reid writes that having a healthy family is her prime motive in adoption, and so she says no to a hypothetical child with anything on the adoption agency's long list of possible diseases and turns down two children presented to her as possibilities because of her pediatrician's diagnoses of them through photographs; she also specifies Caucasian because she wants adoption to be invisible to others and, she hopes, even to her. Savarese sees adoption as a form of social commitment and has "hopes of reconfiguring family, making it less like the genetic version of a gated community than a shelter of shared intimacy and support, open to the needs of the world outside."[7] Neither of them fall into Larissa MacFarquhar's category of "impossible idealists" who are "drawn to moral goodness for its own sake."[8] Savarese's openness, shown in his attempts to sympathize with DJ's birthparents and keep them in touch, involves a struggle against his understandable repulsion at their irresponsibility.

But both are clearly writing books with messages. Reid says explicitly that she writes partly to "encourage other people to adopt the world's parentless children" (3). Thus her inclusion of all the difficulties she experiences along the way, including her doubts about her ability to love her second child, is directed at telling the reader, in effect, "If you have these problems, you can get through them too, and the end will be worth it." Savarese is interested in broader social change: he supports not only open adoption but also the idea that children diagnosed with autism have much more potential than is often recognized and deserve to have care that will permit them to flourish—and wants this for all children in poverty and children with many other kinds of disabilities.

Other adoptive parent memoirs have different messages, some of them ambivalent. Several memoirs of adoption across the color line show that such adoption is more difficult than the authors expected, mostly because of widespread racism, conscious and unconscious. Meanwhile, other memoirists who have adopted children with disabilities have experienced much less sense of achievement than Savarese shows in his memoir; rather, they have encountered frustration and critique the failure of doctors and adoption agencies to give parents accurate information. Some memoirists emphasize their child's loss and trauma and try to maintain their relationship with birth families and/or birth countries, and others write with a comic tone, stress their own happiness, and/or argue the similarity between adoptive families and biological families.

Domestic Transracial Adoption

Douglas Bates adopted the African American daughters he portrays in *Gift Children* in the 1970s, Kay Trimberger adopted her son in 1981, and Jana Wolff's *Secret Thoughts of an Adoptive Mother* and Sharon Rush's *Loving across the Color Line* focus on the 1990s.[9] Many of the anecdotes in all four portray the authors' lack of preparation for how much racism their children would experience, and they are reminiscent, especially, of the experiences narrated from the adoptee's perspective in *Black Boy White Hands*.

Bates clearly frames his book in the larger context of American race relations—the subtitle is "A Story of Race, Family, and Adoption in a Divided America," and he surveys his early experiences of race before he describes his and his wife's adoption of two Black girls after two white boys have already been born to his family. Rush's framing is similar—the subtitle is "A White Adoptive Mother Learns about Race"—though she is a single parent and a law professor with fewer anecdotes about her preadoption life. Trimberger, also a single parent, writes that "as a white, idealistic supporter of the civil rights movement, I believed that white families who adopted nonwhite children would help integrate society" (7). She finds out that the issues are more complicated, but she ultimately places what she learned about race second to what she learned about behavioral genetics.

Wolff, who is married and had no children before she adopted, explicitly presents her volume as an advice book, with the "hope that by sharing my story, yours will be even better" and no clue in the title or subtitle that hers is a transracial adoption (3). Unlike the other memoirists, she connects (through an agency) with a pregnant woman planning an open adoption. Present at childbirth, she knows that the child would not have traumas or neglect from an orphanage or foster care; on the other hand, she doesn't know what the child will look like; she expects olive skin, like his (as it turns out) mother, as opposed to freely choosing a Black child, and she would have preferred a girl.

Bates, Wolff, Rush, and Trimberger all emphasize that they lacked preparation for the racism they come to deal with.[10] Bates is told by a social worker that "it would be extremely important for us to work hard to help her develop black pride and a black identity, both sorely needed to grapple with society and racism" (*Gift Children* 46). This is more warning than most of the parents discussed in transracial adoptees' memoirs have.[11] But the Bateses have no idea how hard this will be, given that they have "no black acquaintances" (95) in white Eugene, Oregon. The one Black worker among the three hundred employees in Bates's workplace says he also has trouble meeting Black people and quits for a job in Houston soon after they talk. Bates moves his family from white working-class north Eugene to white-collar south Eugene, which he thinks will be less prejudiced, and is disappointed. His daughter Lynn is a senior in high school before she can find someone who can do her hair (as the memoirs by Jaiya John and Catherine McKinley show, this is a big issue for many transracial adoptees). Trimberger, who arranged a private adoption without a social worker, discovers in Berkeley, then 19 percent Black and apparently more progressive, "how hard it was for a teenager to figure out where he fit into the complex race and class relationships of Berkeley and its surroundings" (109). She realizes that even in a mixed-race community it is difficult for him that her family and friends are all white.

These memoirists experience several dimensions of racism in their culture. Sometime it is what Wolff calls "'friendly' racism" (131), like being asked if her son wants to be an NBA player when he grows up, Rush's daughter being drawn as pink by a sidewalk artist, or Bates being told as a compliment that his daughter was "much, much lighter than I expected" (67).[12] Sometimes, as in Trimberger, it is a larger issue—the frequent sight of dead Black men. Her son deals with this in part by a preoccupation with guns. Much later, she discovers that he got his first one in eighth grade.

Sometimes hostile racism is even closer. Bates's uncle, an adoptive father himself, compares Lynn to "polluted, muddy water" (65). Bates's mother-in-law is uncomfortable with Lynn and apparently "heartsick" (84) about their adopting the darker Liska. Even Wolff's nieces and nephews seem curious about the baby as if he were an "exotic animal" (90). All the memoirists have prejudiced neighbors, including children. Both Bates and Rush remember their daughters being accused of theft.

Dealing with institutional issues, Rush has to fight hard to get her daughter accepted into gifted programs, the main jobs for people of color in her school are janitorial, and her daughter knows from experience that "you have to be White" to get the Student of the Week award.[13] Both Rush and Wolff comment on the higher value given to the white Power Ranger in the popular series of action figures. Bates's daughter Lynn, in her early years, feels confused about not looking like her new parents (102) and worse about the mockery and racial isolation she experiences in her school. She wears her hair in an Afro on the first day of third grade, and when students are told to draw one of their peers, everyone draws her unflatteringly; she doesn't try another Afro for years. Wolff ends the details of her narrative before school is important, but both Bates, writing of the 1970s and 1980s, and Rush, writing of the 1990s, comment on how ill-prepared their teachers were and how racially isolated their daughters were. Trimberger, in a better situation in Berkeley in the 1980s, still has problems. She finds a private elementary school with a multicultural curriculum in which five of the twenty students in her son Marco's class are nonwhite, but only one other of these is a biracial boy, and his white mother gives Marco marijuana. While many of the teachers are male, all the full-time teachers are white.

Another kind of institutional racism classified Rush's daughter as "special needs" because she has a white mother and a Black father. Beyond this and the fact that her daughter was in foster care for less than a year before the adoption, Rush knows little more about her daughter's ancestry and history. She comments, "The state allowed us to become a family because we were both 'imperfect' in its eyes" (137)[14] and, though saying very little about the other mother, seems to respect her: "My love is proof positive to a young, adopted child who needs to feel loved by both moms that race had nothing to do with her being placed for adoption" (21). Nevertheless, Rush deals more with race-related issues than specifically adoption-related ones, such as loss of parents: many of the events Rush narrates might have happened if she had had her daughter biologically with a Black partner, and even those adoption-related issues seem to be entangled with those of race, as she writes, "My daughter suffers from the absence of racial connectedness between herself and a Black parent" (138).[15] Rush has an advantage over Bates and Trimberger in that she has Black friends, colleagues (she teaches an African American Studies course), and neighbors, though even she writes, "My White liberal views on race and relations were inadequate to comprehend how profound and pervasive racial inequality is in our society" (5). Her daughter, at five, jumps up and down with happiness when hearing that new neighbors visiting are Black, always asks if Black people will be there when going to an event, and gains confidence when visiting their Black friends.

Wolff builds her son's pride by discussing racist bullying with him and getting him to practice standing tall and saying, "I like how I am. If you don't, scram" (133). Later she writes about moving to a more diverse neighborhood (not so difficult in Hawaii, where she lives) and participating in adoptive family groups. She and her husband go with him to culture camps and heritage festivals.[16] In another article, written when he is seven, she writes, "In looking toward his black friends for clues, he lands on the symbols that they value most, and he makes them his own."[17] A buzz cut on the sides with a Nike swoosh on top makes him walk "as if he had grown a foot taller." Though she wants to expand his horizons, she realizes that stressing non-athletic ideals, for example, won't necessarily give him more self-esteem the way approval by his friends does.

Bates and Trimberger both carry their children's narratives past childhood in their memoirs, and both have many complex issues to deal with. Past neglect and abuse are serious problems for Bates's daughters. He is told that Lynn's mother was white, nineteen, pretty, addicted to heroin, and in jail for its possession—the baby was taken to care three days after birth, with white foster parents. Lynn spent four years in that unloving home, full of conflict and fear and various other foster children, all white in the one available picture (31–32). Bates is surprised to learn that no adult pointed out colors to her, read her a book, taught her how to brush her teeth, or told her about her Blackness (58, 102). Liska's birthmother was white and fourteen; like her birthfather, she was a migrant farmworker. She married another man soon after Liska was born. Liska "suffered daily neglect and physical abuse for the first eighteen months of her life. Scars from those early days are still visible on her body today" (77). The two homes that she lived in for the year and half after that were better, but one was always intended to be temporary and the second one, an attempted adoption, did not work because the close-knit surrounding community was so openly racist. Bates and his wife give both girls lots of love. Liska accepts love easily but Lynn, who does not like to be touched, is wary for a long time. The parents thought she would like having a sister, but instead, she is resentful.

Rush and Bates both try to be positive to their children about their birthparents but have never met them and have little other information. The Bateses tell Lynn as a child "that her mother was a pretty white woman and her father was a handsome man who was part white and part African-American" (103). Only when she is in her twenties do they tell her that her parents were in jail for heroin use. Bates includes, close to the end, words from both

Lynn and Liska, now young women, about their birthparents. Lynn begins "I think about my biological parents all the time" (253), but she is afraid to meet her birthfather, although she knows people from his town who have told her they know who he is and where. Liska says she does not want to find her birthparents. "But they will always be in my heart, because there are always going to be unanswered questions" (254). Near the end of the book, she asks to go to Yakima, her birthplace, and in the Yakima public library, because she was the first baby born there in 1969, they see a picture of her on the microfilm of the January 2nd local newspaper. They visit the hospital, and she is treated like a celebrity. Her birthmother's name, though without a picture, is also included in the article. Bates points out that perhaps they could meet, but Liska replies, "I already have all the parents I need" (257). This, of course, is what he wanted to hear.

In Wolff's memoir, we are in a different world because the adoption is open from the beginning.[18] Although she recalls initially feeling hostile to Martie, the Mexican American intended birthmother, fearing that she would change her mind, Wolff's attitude changes drastically because Martie wants her there for the birth. She feels in awe at this bravery, and empathizes with the loss that she expects Martie to feel—"She was going to go through all of this only to go home empty-handed" (50). The birth seems like a miracle, but the baby is fragile—only a four out of ten on the Apgar test. Although the baby's father is biracial, Wolff is surprised at how dark the baby is and feels fear at the complications of "a baby that not only came out of someone else's body, but out of someone else's culture" (58). Instead of love at first sight, she feels more like "pity at first sight . . . I am feeling like an impostor, like an intruder" (62). But she stays in the hospital while he has tests, holds him as much as possible, endures medical advice that she can still change her mind, worries that Martie will change *her* mind. "She felt awful about leaving the baby I felt awful about taking. The grief of adoption is not lost on the woman who brings the baby home" (78). Wolff's empathy here is striking, a marked contrast to the single-minded joy recalled by many adoptive parents. Her original empathy permitted her to choose an open adoption in which she was present at the birth and then increased in response to that experience.

Once home, she introduces the baby to her extended family, feels like she doesn't know enough about child care, and looks at him and talks to him a lot. By his first birthday, she writes, "my feelings exploded into the fiercest of passions" (98). She thinks surprisingly often about Martie, wondering how she feels and which baby pictures she should send, whether they will hurt or comfort. On every birthday and Mother's Day, they look at his baby book and see a picture of Martie pregnant in front of the hospital. When he is three, she and her husband invite her to meet them while they are staying at a hotel in her city. Martie reads to and plays with Ari, they share small talk and pizza and take photos, and all four "seemed stunned by the relaxation of such an extraordinary relationship" (145). While Wolff sees Martie's flaws—she has trouble keeping a job or a boyfriend—she is glad that her son will be able to see her as a real person and that Martie will "help her answer Ari's questions in the years ahead" (140). Pediatricians now often support open adoption for similar reasons.[19] In her last words before the epilogue, she writes of the resemblances between Ari and Martie: "from time to time, I'll recognize her face in his" (146). While many adoptees and birthparents write about hereditary physical resemblances, this and Trimberger's are the only memoirs by an adoptive parent I have read that mention noticing them.

Trimberger finds a child to adopt through contact with an experienced adoption lawyer, who knows a Louisiana doctor who knows a white seventeen-year-old pregnant by a Creole man of color. With information about the family of the mother (all siblings went to college, one has a PhD) and having herself sent a short bio, she meets the doctor and the five-day-old baby at the airport and takes the baby home. She calls him Marc, but he soon comes to be called Marco, perhaps, though she never says this, because it suggests his dark skin might come from Latino or Italian ancestry, more familiar in California than Creole.[20] When he is twenty-five and at loose ends, she is able, with a finder's help, to contact both of his parents, and he meets them again. Soon after that point, she learns much more about them, and the change in her understanding of her son afterward becomes the main emphasis of her memoir.

Rush and Wolff both end their memoirs while their child is still young. Though they emphasize that they underestimated how much work it would take to combat racism, they mostly describe problems in the external world. Bates and Trimberger, with their longer narrative, acknowledge more of their own mistakes and, indeed, seem to make more from early on.[21] Trimberger's often has a tone of regret that could be compared to that of some birthmother narratives; Bates ends with more affirmation of overall success in spite of difficulties. Bates includes recollections from his daughters and invited them to share memories of each other and their brothers, who respond in turn. Trimberger includes an afterword and a few other comments from her son.

The most notable confession that Bates makes is of his own racism. He assumed that a break-in was by an African American boyfriend and learns that a neighbor saw a white boy do it. Later, he recognizes that he still feels racist suspicion of Black males after both of his daughters have bad experiences—one a violent man and one who, after marriage, subjects her to his parents' repressive religiosity. By the end of the book, however, he is fine with his daughter Lynn's marriage to an African American who, he notes, has survived a background of poverty and a broken family.

Bates acknowledges some of his other mistakes, for example disengaging from his children in favor of his work (240). He is disappointed when none of his children is enthusiastic about college. Showing further middle-class attitudes, he is negative about anyone in his family living on government assistance rather than getting help from him, and at the end, part of his happiness about Lynn's career plans is that, by contrast to an earlier job that meant a lot to her, they don't involve hair.

Early in the book, he looks back on his initial expectations, which include "successful careers for Lynn and Liska, along with happiness and wonderful sons-in-law—probably black, and that was just fine" (10). The memoir shows he was too naive about how indirect the path to these goals would be. Bates may come across as a little too judgmental still, with attitudes complicated by class issues, but the most significant marker that his racial consciousness is dated is the title of his last chapter: "Love Is Colorblind." However, the word *colorblind* is never actually used in the chapter, which describes the festivities at Lynn's wedding. That last chapter and the epilogue move from a recollection of a stranger's query about Rodney King's beating—"Do black people bruise?"—to anxiety about a party in which "most of the white guests had never been around many black people and most of the black guests had never been around many whites" (263), to a celebration in which the tough bride unexpectedly breaks down in tears, to an after-reception dance party with rap, rock, and hip-hop in which everybody dances, even the bride's white step-grandfather with her new Black husband's sister. After earlier tension and awkward remarks, the day ends with a reconciliation between sisters, a proposal to the younger sister, and a family plan to visit Africa. As Bates notes, the wedding and party are examples of integration—but he believes that his family has moved beyond that to "assimilation," a word that he wants to mean Blacks and whites both changing (268), although that is not its usual meaning. In fact, there is a contradiction between his positive words about assimilation and his recounting over and over in the book events in which white people show they do not know how to deal with difference. However, Bates at the conclusion is still concerned about racism in the United States, not looking for a fairy-tale ending. Referring to the party after the wedding, with Black music, he urges that we "remember not to leave the party before the real celebration begins" (270).

Bates probably uses the term *colorblind* in the chapter title as a familiar metaphor rather than literally, since he is very explicit about noting the races of the participants at the wedding. As a nonacademic who has always lived and worked in white settings, he is less familiar with the sort of explanation that Rush makes about why the image of color blindness implies unconscious racism. "Seeing racial differences is inevitable, but if seeing racial difference does not cause one to discriminate against Blacks, then why pretend there are no Blacks in society?" (37). But both of them believe that in their family love has enabled them to transcend racial difference—"transformative love giving me a visceral not just intellectual experience of the harm of racism" (138), says Rush, while Bates says, "In our family, relationships have transcended race" (268).

The last event Trimberger describes in detail in her memoir is also a racially mixed ritual, mostly involving her son's birth relatives, but rather than a wedding, it is a funeral for a half sister who died of a heroin overdose. Trimberger writes positively about working in the kitchen with women in the extended family, but addiction is the shadow that hangs over most of the book. Like Bates, she begins with the assumption that her child would share her middle-class values and attend college. From early on she likes his extroverted personality, in childhood appreciates his abilities in theater, music, and art, all different from hers, and enjoys backpacking and hiking with him. When at eight he asks about Louisiana, where he was born, she introduces him to a friend who tells them both about the Creole culture there that is his birthfather's. Yet although they live in an integrated neighborhood, she has no Black friends she regularly sees. Unlike Bates's daughters, by the time Marco finishes high school he not only resists planning for college but also regularly uses and sells drugs (first sold to him by white boys in a Young Explorers outdoor program). She tries various ways to help him, without success. But when he is twenty-five and she proposes employing a finder to locate his birthparents, he is willing.

His white Cajun birthmother and his Black Creole birthfather, who have not seen each other for a long time and are married to other people, are both open to meeting him, so he goes to Louisiana and is happily introduced to both extended families. His birthmother has a warm personality like his, and his birthfather looks just like him and, like him, is nonviolent and artistic. But, also like him, his father is a crack addict. His birthmother also has addiction in her past. What happens when the three of them meet again? They get high. He has several long visits with each of them, and Trimberger goes with him once and returns by herself later to connect with the extended families.

Clearly his birthparents' warm acceptance is far from healing Marco's addiction. Back in Berkeley, he tries various rehabs and living arrangements, none of which are ever secure; his most regular employment is on marijuana farms. A close friend who has one in his backyard is killed; a sister in his birth family dies from a heroin overdose. His life spirals downward. Trimberger eventually finds a rural inpatient rehab place that fits Marco; he follows time there with time in a sober house, joins AA, gets a job at "an upscale grocery chain," and writes at the end of his thoughtful afterword to the book, "I have a way to go, but I now have positive energy when thinking about my future" (159).

Finding birthparents who resemble and welcome him does not cure Marco, but it motivates Trimberger to research why his similarity to them seems so deep, and what she learns about this is the memoir's main emphasis. Writing against the view that adoption is inherently damaging, she is also writing against the view she had formerly held, that infants are pliable clay and addiction results from parental failure to mold them properly. Thus the book has some elements of a conversion memoir.[22] Trimberger learns the high heritability of vulnerability to addiction, discovers behavioral genetics, which analyzes the way environment can protect against or evoke an inherited trait and often involves the study of adoptees, and considers various ways Marco's childhood experiences she could not control might also have affected him.

For example, her idealism about communal living led her to share a house with friends who were a couple, and after she adopted Marco and they had a child, tensions about child-rearing methods arose and the household broke up, leaving Marco with a sense of instability and loss. Also, though she scrutinized his preschools, considering racial inclusiveness as well as flexible gender norms, and several times transferred him when she found him unhappy or them disorganized or too comfortable with talk about "whipping," psychologists eventually conclude that he was probably sexually abused at one of them.

She finds that childhood experiences of divorce (comparable to the breakup of their communal household) and sexual abuse are among many factors that might activate a hereditary tendency toward substance addiction. She learns, on the one hand, that she was too naive to do more of the monitoring that might have protected him and, on the other hand, that her parenting was sometimes "over-reactive (harsh)" and therefore ineffective (113).[23] She knows she should have sought counseling for herself, but she was in denial. Perhaps counseling would have helped her understand how the stress of being Black in a racist white environment might also have contributed to his addiction.

She hopes that presenting her experience in relation to behavioral genetics will contribute toward helping other adoptive parents and adoptees in the future. The conclusions in his afterword can help validate this. He writes, "Reading research that shows that some things are inherited eases my pain at letting her down. Even though it made me relive the disturbing abuse in my younger years, reading this book led to an uplifting feeling" (158). However, like Liska's words to Bates, his praise might be considered too much under pressure to be reliable.

Trimberger, like many adoptees but few adoptive parents, seeks out and forms relationships with others in her son's birth families besides his birthparents and finds some of those relationships more compatible, though she is reaching across boundaries of class and often of race, and more helpful. She writes, "I wish I'd had this vision of extending family when I adopted. . . . My biological family was his adoptive one; his biological family could have been my adoptive one" (146–47). She recommends that other adoptive parents attempt this, concluding with advocacy for a model in which "adoptees, adoptive parents, and birth parents all have relationships to each other and to relatives beyond the nuclear family" (171). Wolff's memoir shows a little of this, though the families live a plane ride apart.

This generous vision, however, is somewhat clouded by Trimberger's limited awareness of the effects of racism, no matter how much she has learned about it.[24] In her research on behavioral genetics, she admittedly relies on research done on white families who adopt white children. She does not venture into the research suggesting that the stress of racism is transmitted genetically. So she does not consider that his hereditary vulnerability to addiction might have been evoked by the stresses of racism in his environment, and the same might also have been true of his father.

Any one of these memoirs should convince a reader that adopting a Black child is difficult even if you have Black friends. Rush does, and she still finds blatant prejudice in her school, such as seating her daughter, the only Black child in the class, in a place where no one can see her, on the day when parents visit (57).[25] But Rush also writes of experiencing "transformative love" (138) and has raised a daughter with an indomitable spirit, who can write, "I don't care how long it takes, I will stop all racism . . . [if I don't] I would die and my spirit would go into the right person, and if they didn't reach it before they died, then their spirit would go into someone else" (174–75).

The fact that Lynn and Liska still think about their birthmothers, and Trimberger wishes she had contacted her son's earlier, suggests the advantages of Wolff's open adoption with its connection to the real rather than the fantasy person. "I wanted my son to see his birth mother not as a beautiful princess who would let him eat candy all day and then watch ten videos in a row, but as a beautiful person who created a baby she loved but couldn't care for" (140). Being in touch with the birth family, as Wolff and Trimberger are, and as Lynn and Liska sometimes think of being, does, however, have complications in terms of class as well as race. Though Bates and Trimberger write more explicitly of class issues, it is obvious that class as well as race affects Wolff's relationship with Martie, as class will complicate the way other adoptive parents discussed in this chapter feel about birthparents. As Linda Seligmann writes, class differences have a more visible impact when adoptive parents are in touch with birth relatives; Wolff makes great efforts to imaginatively reach across this gap, as we will see Savarese does also.[26]

Domestic Same-Race Adoption, Trauma, and Disability

While Trimberger's son and Bates's daughters experienced early trauma and abuse, and these probably had long-lasting results in their problems as young adults, their problems were much less visible while growing up than those of the children, none of them African American, adopted by Ralph Savarese, Michael Dorris, and Ann Kimble Loux.

The sense of victory Savarese shows in the achievements of his son DJ, discussed at the beginning of this chapter, is in marked contrast to the emphasis in the two others' earlier narratives about neglected and disabled children: Michael Dorris's *The Broken Cord* (1989) and Ann Kimble Loux's *The Limits of Hope* (1997). Dorris, single graduate student soon to be hired as junior faculty at Dartmouth, adopts a three-year-old boy who has been neglected by his heavy-drinking mother and is failing to thrive after two years in hospitals or with guardians. He feels a special bond with this child, whom he calls Adam, because they share Native American ancestry, but eventually that ancestry and the high incidence of excessive drinking in Native communities will provide him a context for the possible role of fetal alcohol syndrome (FAS) in Adam's difficulties. Loux and her husband, junior academics who already have three young children, adopt Dawn, two, and Margey, three, from foster care, where they have been sent because of their alcoholic parents' abuse and neglect. Loux and Dorris stress that the expectations they had for their children were never fulfilled; as adults, Adam, Dawn, and Margey continue to have severely impaired cognitive abilities and cannot learn what seem like simple things from experience.

While Bates and Rush place some blame for difficulties in raising their children on their own naivete about race relations, Loux and Dorris emphasize the lack of information that they received from professionals. Loux writes, "Providing parents with as much information as possible about the child's life prior to the adoption might be the best way to help high-achieving parents develop realistic expectations."[27] Dorris remembers his pediatrician as untroubled by Adam's condition before his first seizure at four. He complains that he did not receive a copy of the report identifying Adam as learning disabled. However, he admits that he "trusted no diagnosis that wasn't encouraging" (76) and blamed Adam's problems with tests on his teachers or racism in test design.[28] Savarese, by contrast, when a graduate student met DJ as one of the children with autism Emily, his wife, helped as a special needs therapist, so he has a better idea of what they are undertaking as they first foster and then adopt him.

The Savareses decide not to have any other children by either birth or adoption because they can see how great DJ's needs are. Loux and her academically ambitious husband have three children already when they adopt children not much younger. The mix does not work well. The adopted children are not interested in the neighborhood games the older ones organize; she eventually learns that the older ones beat up the younger when no adults were around (30, 32). Dorris adopts two other children as a single man and finds them somewhat better learners; he eventually marries another Native American writer, Louise Erdrich; the memoir briefly mentions the birth of two more children to the couple.

Loux, like the other memoirists in this section, vividly recalls difficulties from early in the relationship with her children. Having met Margey and Dawn for trips to the zoo and the beach, Loux and her husband are taken aback when, after they join the family, they can't stop eating. Dawn refuses to leave the table; Margey refuses to stop dumping sand from their sandbox in heaps all over their yard. The Catholic Charities adoption worker dismisses Loux's concern, saying, "You're making such a good home for these girls. God is going to reward you" (11). When a social worker tells them that Dawn was hospitalized for malnutrition at three months, and the two girls had been removed from their original home so often that they had been in foster care at least six months of every year, Loux can see why the children are so disturbed— they had never had consistent love.

But knowing this does not help much when Margey constantly takes others' possessions and Dawn continues to sneak food. Margey does not like to be touched; Dawn touches everyone indiscriminately.[29] The happy life Loux and her husband previously had with their children disappears because Dawn and Margey have too many emotional and cognitive needs stemming from earlier deprivation. Loux later discovers research showing that "a history of rejection and neglect slows down cognitive development" (35); this explains why the girls burned out one toaster after another by buttering the toast first. Also, she feels, "It never seemed that Margey had any real desire to please anyone else" (71).

Loux sends Margey away to board in high school, but she can stay for only a year. Arrested as a runaway at sixteen, she is sent to the city jail and a juvenile detention center. Later she gets some help from The Corners, a mental hospital for adolescents. They too can keep her for only a year, and then she goes to a halfway house. At the end of the memoir, she is supporting herself as a prostitute, and Dawn, who always wanted to be a mother, has an intellectually disabled child who will need her forever.

Dorris and Savarese adopt their sons with no other children at home, so the interaction is simpler. At three Adam speaks only a few words and is not toilet trained, but he seems to Dorris initially to be "pure affection, totally at ease" (12). He happily puts them both to sleep with a story of them and their dog as the Three Bears, and Adam, waking in the fetal position, wants to hear more. But he has cognitive problems; at four, he begins having seizures, and he can't learn pronouns, colors, or numbers. With some good teachers, he learns to read but with little comprehension. His sweet disposition makes it easier to disregard his problems in school, but "in eight years at the

Cornish School he never received so much as a phone call or an invitation from a friend" (120). When he graduates from grade school, he still cannot add or subtract, make change, or name the place where he lives (127).

High school is much more demanding, and after a year, a psychologist says there is nothing she can do to help. After Adam transfers to a vocational high school, the program relieves some of the tension. However, by the time he is twenty-one, when the memoir ends, he has been unable to keep jobs in fast food, outdoor maintenance, or dishwashing for more than a few months. Socially, he seems withdrawn, passive, and sullen, though quite willing to help strangers who ask. The book concludes on Adam's twenty-first birthday after Dorris tries to convince him not to drink though he is of legal age, because of the bad effects alcohol has on him. Dorris silently recalls all the hopes that he has had of the celebrations for each of Adam's milestone birthdays, none of which turned out as he had planned. As Laura Briggs writes, "Dorris never really accepted who Adam was but took refuge in dreams of a boy who might have been."[30]

Savarese is more successful with his son, although DJ is never able to speak, and in their early meetings does not seem to understand spoken language. When Savarese tries to reach him by tickling, DJ's delight in it means that he can learn the sign for "more." Savarese is so preoccupied with DJ, so much enjoys seeing DJ enjoying something, that one of his friends says "You've fallen in love with that boy" (67). When he turns from foster father to adoptive father, one of the first things he buys is a trampoline so they can jump together. Meanwhile, he and his wife are introducing DJ to language through facilitated communication on a computer, a practice in which he is enabled to use a keyboard a helper who may touch his hand or arm or simply keep their own nearby. Savarese frequently refers to research that refutes criticism of this practice.

DJ's emotional and behavior problems are severe. For much of his childhood after the adoption, he frequently hits his parents, his helpers, and other people. Savarese realizes that as DJ learns to understand language, it brings both insight and panic (152). About this time, he hears his parents discussing the book that Savarese is writing about him and then remembers more vividly the loss of his sister, whom his birthfather took when he left the rest of the family. In a complicated development, DJ's "emergence into language" (165) occurs at the same time as he hears frequent discussion of adoption. He tells Savarese that "he sees Rhonda [his birthmother] when he hits" (185), and later he more often has flashbacks to the sexual abuse that he experienced from Kyle, another boy in his foster home. Savarese cites research to support the idea that DJ's autism was originally caused by trauma and maintained by intrusive memories of trauma. While he was already diagnosed with autism at a year and a half, "his life with his mother had been violent and unpredictable" (202). Savarese believes that his apparent withdrawal is really the result of "hypersensitivity to stimuli" (201) and that practice in sensory integration, which he is receiving, is helping him reenter the social sphere.

Of these three memoirists, Dorris makes the least attempt to understand his child's birthmother. The main way in which she enters his thoughts is as the "adversary" (45), dead early from her alcohol addiction, which he believes caused Adam's deficiency.[31] He has abandoned his earlier awareness of the likely role of anti-Native racism and environmental deprivation in her vulnerability, which could also be seen as genetic.

Other memoirists, who also know about damage to their children from their first mothers' behavior, find a little more understanding possible. When the girls are teenagers, Loux writes that she "sympathized with Margery's and Dawn's mother in her struggle to love her children. No doubt she tried hard and felt miserable when she failed" (138). This is what Loux is experiencing herself. Eventually Dawn contacts the social worker involved with her adoption and gets enough information to find her biological mother again. Margey meets her also. Dawn had high hopes, but now, Loux writes, both believe "that they were taken away from their biological mother for some pretty good reasons" (253). Somewhat like Wolff, who does not want her son to see his first mother as a beautiful princess, she says it is "helpful . . . to have the biological parents solidly in the background and not wandering through the attic haunting the inhabitants" (253).

Even more vividly, after he and his wife decide to adopt DJ, Savarese thinks of Rhonda as "an injured party" left behind by their "noble ambulance run" (75). His wish to blame her for damage to DJ is in conflict (as in "an old-fashioned duel") with awareness that she "had been sexually abused as a child and abandoned by her own mother" (75). He imagines Rhonda "calling out for help in every way she knew how, and having no one, absolutely no one, come to her" (87). His attempt to see Rhonda's perspective is comparable to the way that in previous chapters we have seen Trenka and Winterson try to forgive their own mothers (adoptive and original, respectively) because of the hurtful ways they also had been treated while growing up.

Both Savarese and Dorris, like Trimberger, extend the memoir form to include research and policy advocacy relevant to their sons' problems, though Savarese's research is about the successful use of facilitated communication and other help for children with autism and Dorris's is about FAS, its cause in drinking while pregnant, and the prevalence of such drinking especially among Native American women. Dorris commits to this issue when he first travels to a reservation in South Dakota and sees other children with the same facial and bodily characteristics Adam has.

As Tom Couser writes, this similarity leads Dorris to the "conclusion that his adopted son's most significant kinship group is . . . the multiethnic 'family' or 'tribe' of victims of Fetal Alcohol Syndrome."[32] Couser sees this as a classical anagnorisis (recognition, in Greek drama often, as in *Oedipus*, the discovery of unknown relatives). He emphasizes that it is also a diagnosis, after which "Adam tends to become a type and his story a case history" (425–26), and Dorris writes of him in terms that deny him and other similarly disabled people full humanity (433). Instead of focusing on Adam's specificity, he recounts speeches and attendance at conferences on this issue and includes his conversations with experts. FAS includes mental deficiency, growth retardation, and many other side effects, including epilepsy. Dorris presents research unambiguously making maternal alcohol consumption the central problem, though other sources say that FAS symptoms have genetic causes and practices like smoking, drug ingestion, and poor diet, all of which may have cultural, social, and economic roots, may make it worse. He does note that Native American women have in recent years been following the excessive drinking habits of Native American men. Since there are not enough rehabilitation centers to help all the women who need to stop drinking, he makes the drastic recommendation that they be jailed during pregnancy.

Dorris's views are controversial. Savarese's have also been challenged. Some researchers have claimed that facilitated communication is a hoax and the helpers are doing the typing, but Savarese cites much testing that refutes this charge, in addition to his own experience. He also argues against the assumption that people with autism cannot form emotional connection with others or empathize, showing DJ's love for his sister and his feeling for his bereaved aunt and uncle when their baby dies. Advocating for inclusion, he shows that DJ can function well in a regular classroom and can enjoy social life with his classmates, who enjoy him as well.

Loux too has policy and practice suggestions relating to her experience, but they are more various. She writes that parents who plan to adopt a child of more than a year should first work directly with troubled children, tutor children with learning disabilities, become foster parents, and question social workers, adoptive parents, and others who have had experience with traumatized children. "Perhaps many older abused and neglected children should not be 'adopted' but should instead become members of surrogate families in which the knots to the family can be tied more loosely. . . . [They] would be expected to encounter periods where it would be advantageous for everyone to consider a period of separation: summer camps . . . a boarding school perhaps; or a period in a group home or residential treatment center" (261), places that would help the children and provide respite for the parents. A child should not have to sever all ties with previous families in order to be adopted, a recommendation she shares with Trimberger, Wolff, Savarese, Harness, and others quoted in the previous chapter, and children should have choices about where to live at different times.[33] If a child of a year or more has not learned to attach to or trust others, years of effort with professionals will be needed. Adoptive parents should speak out to challenge "the larger society's denial of the difficulties of adoption" (264). Perhaps some children might be "better served in an optimal group home where the standard of comparison was others like themselves" (264) than in a family where there are also children who belong by birth.

Loux has read *The Broken Cord* and finds its discussion of FAS helpful in explaining her daughters' difficulties (239). But when Dawn's child, Billie Ray, is diagnosed with Williams syndrome (having specific physical and some mental deficiencies, overfriendly with adults, impulsive), she thinks that Dawn may have the syndrome also, and this possibility too helps her sympathize with her daughters' first mother. While Dorris notes his own flaws in not admitting problems near the beginning of his memoir, Loux acknowledges her own limitations close to the end: "I am far from being satisfied that I have been able to love the girls enough by *any* standard, certainly not by the measure of how much I love the biological children" (263), because Dawn and Margey have been too damaged to love her. At this moment, she sounds surprisingly like Reid, who also admits that she cannot love without reciprocation. Nevertheless, she bonds with Dawn over helping Billie Ray and her second child, and admires Dawn's somehow acquired ability to get all the help the system affords to parents of children with disabilities.

By the end Loux has also, amazingly, changed her evaluation of Margey: "She has a knack for finding sweet men who are delighted to take care of her—who yearn to rescue her . . . she has lucked upon a match between her talents and tastes and the job requirements. . . . She can't pay bills; she couldn't run a house. But Margey can provide a spectacle" (255, 256). Margey can even write verse about being a prostitute. Though she is in jail at the end of the book, Loux expects her to be out soon. She emphasizes that communication with both her daughters is now much better, though it would never work for them to live with her and her husband. They seem better able to function than Adam. They are less visibly disabled than DJ, but they don't have his sense of mission.

Unlike Adam, DJ comes to have friendly interactions with his classmates and others. Also unlike Adam, he is able to think in conceptual terms about his life, though such progress involves struggles. Savarese writes that DJ has "to separate recovering from trauma from his initial abandonment . . . and his subsequent attempt to grow up, to get distance from us" (346). He needs to learn to communicate with his friends independently and not depend on the help of one of his parents, and it is a struggle for him not to fear the idea of being "on his own." While the last chapter of *The Broken Cord*, written by Adam, is an accumulation of detailed memories of events, without a sense of what is important, the last chapter of *Reasonable People*, written by DJ, has reflections about his own history, ending with "in the future I hope to encourage students who don't speak to free themselves through writing. I also hope to read my speeches outloud. Until I freed myself through writing, people thought I had no mind. Freeing kids who are estimated as retarded is my hope for the future. Years of fresh start have begun!" (442). After the events recounted in Savarese's book, DJ graduated from Oberlin Phi Beta Kappa and collaborated with a filmmaker on a documentary about his life.[34] He is a published poet.

These three memoirs, together with parts of Trimberger's, describe the most difficult experiences of parenthood I have read. Dorris increases his bitterness by the insistent memory of his higher hopes for Adam. (Three years after the book was published, the boy he calls Adam died in a car accident; in 1997, Dorris killed himself, alienated from his two surviving adopted children.) Loux struggles bravely to accept her children's limited versions of success. Savarese shows the advantage of knowing in advance some of the problems your child has. He also shows the advantage of being able to focus the energy and imagination of two parents (plus a team of assistants) on a single child. The Savareses' efforts are heroic, and it is good to see what DJ can accomplish with their help. But the difficulties in these families, as well as in Bates's, whose daughters had also experienced trauma before being adopted, reaffirm the conclusions of Christine Ward Gailey's research that many adoptive parents are in crisis and need help in "developing support networks, finding relief when the tensions were too great, or locating or organizing workshops through state or private agencies."[35]

Single or Gay Men Adopting Latinx Children

Two adoption memoirs by David Marin, who is single and straight, and Jesse Green, who is gay and in the course of the memoir forms a partnership with a gay adoptive father, portray less challenged children than the last three memoirs discussed. They describe problems coming from the external world's prejudices, though also, in Marin's case, the children's previous experiences. Still, Marin in *This Is US: The New All-American Family* (2011) and Green in *The Velveteen Father* (1999) often recall familial bliss.

After an early adulthood of travel, golf, and skydiving, half Puerto Rican but red-haired Marin applies to adopt three Latinx siblings, two, four, and six, from foster care in California. As a single man, he is discouraged from adopting by his boss and fired when he persists. Neglected and abused by their alcoholic and drug-addicted mother, the children were frequently placed back with her. The youngest doesn't speak at two and a half; they all have nightmares, don't want to sleep alone, and expect a beating for potty accidents (78). However, they are not disruptive and enjoy his attention. He faces gender prejudice: he begins the book with a vignette in which strangers in a restaurant have difficulty thinking of his relationship to the children as paternal. They wonder about kidnapping or sex trafficking, concerns heightened by the children's brown skin. But his children, unlike Adam, Margey, or Dawn, recover from the worst of their traumas. Craig, the youngest, catches up with normal development, is exceptionally curious, and at five wants to be an astronaut and adopt five children.

Often Marin feels he doesn't know what he is doing, but he enjoys the children and gets support from his mother and sister, friends, a social worker, and Google, which he consults so often that he nicknames it Brittany (81). His memoir emphasizes the inefficiency, carelessness, and cruelty of the welfare department, especially in giving his children's birthmother too many chances—ten times in ten years someone reported her bad treatment of her children, and ten times either the complaints were ignored, the children were sent to foster care only briefly, or she was just asked to take parenting classes. These children do have the ability to attach to him—perhaps because they received love from their older sisters, who have been adopted by others. Marin calls his daughter Adriana "a child raised by children" (85).

Marin includes statistics about the Adoption Assistance Program that might encourage people to adopt (37). Critical of the operations of the California foster care system, at the time holding ninety-eight thousand children, he notes that vetting people to do foster care takes six to nine months, which seems unnecessarily long. He quotes research showing that of every one thousand people contacting Social Services about adopting, only thirty-six do, most of them, he thinks, put off by bureaucratic policies like mass fingerprinting at the initial orientation meeting (194). However, memoirists have reported that some children are traumatized by their treatment in foster care—perhaps from states that educate or screen foster parents less?

While memoirists such as Loux, Dorris, and Bates emphasize that their adoption was more difficult than they expected, Marin, who says he began knowing nothing about child-rearing, takes problems in stride. As someone whose father died when he was seven, who repressed his grief and frequently got into trouble, he identifies with the children—if one throws rocks in anger, it doesn't seem awful to him.

Marin's memoir ends, like the earlier memoirs in Melosh's summary, soon after the adoption becomes final, but in his case, this is some time after the children have been living with him. Near the official procedure, a member of the birth family turns up and apologizes for not being able to take any of the children, a Spanish-speaking social worker calls the children's foster mother asking to see them, which makes him feel the adoption is threatened, and their birthmother seems likely to make a final appearance but does not. Instead, the children can have a happy reunion with their older sisters (Marin's heroic social worker has told him not to see them while the adoption was still pending). Marin takes all five of them to Disneyland, the same symbol of family happiness that Florence Fisher's newly discovered birthfather chose more than twenty-five years earlier for a celebration trip.

The narrative is dotted with examples of Marin's observing (and trying to refute) prejudice against immigrants and against men raising children alone. The first is an even bigger issue now; however, a suggestion that the second prejudice may have lessened is that Marin wins his lawsuit against the boss who fired him for planning to adopt. Green also deals with suspicion of men as adoptive parents, suspicion more explicit because the author and his partner are gay. And Marin confronts potential prejudice against Latinx ethnicity, an ethnicity he shares in part but not visibly. It is not coincidental that two unmarried male authors would write about adoption of Latinx children. Single, and especially gay, people who want to adopt are often steered toward "hard-to-place," which often ends up meaning Latinx or African American children (as in Rush's case).[36]

Green devotes most of the first quarter of the book to telling his future partner Andy's adoption story. Before they meet, knowing that a single man is not at the top of the list for healthy white babies, Andy goes to an adoption agency in the Southwest that deals primarily with mothers who are Latina or mixed race and is quickly matched with a newborn who is basically healthy but has tremors and brings him to his home in Brooklyn.[37]

Green as a young journalist has the AIDS epidemic as his main subject, so in his work as well as his friendships he is constantly dealing with grief. Taking care of his infant niece is a welcome contrast. He spends more and more time with her and his later-born nephew—and talks about them frequently in their absence. Then he meets Andy and his recently adopted son and falls in love with both.

Green narrates complications in forming their nontraditional family: he has to get past his caution about leading the boy, Erez, to expectations of permanence that might not be met. He keeps his apartment in Manhattan but spends most of his time with Andy and Erez, admiring the way Erez makes Andy fulfilled and happy. He ponders the ambiguity of his relationship to Erez, father-like but not so named, though he is more involved in child care than most of the men in his own father's generation. Ultimately, Andy adopts a second child, and Green moves to Brooklyn near them and begins the procedure for two second-parent adoptions.

From the time that Green describes his first holding Erez, his delight in the child is clear. Green calls him "like all happy babies a faith healer."[38] He loves to watch Erez sleeping, feeds and bathes him gladly, and plays games like chasing him. But he also gives a realistic picture of the midnight wakings, the difficulty in getting Erez to sleep, the projectile vomiting and worse in a new car.

Green is much engaged in a critique of traditional gender roles, in which a man is supposed to supply only money while the woman cares for the children in every other way. At a number of points, the question of whether to adopt a child or not becomes a springboard for discussion of what gives life meaning and what makes a person an adult. Like Marin, Green gives background on the overloaded foster care system, and reading his book, like Marin's, suggests recent social change in some areas. It is a given in 1999 that gay people cannot be legally married in the United States, but since the Supreme Court *Obergefell* decision of 2015, they can. Some of what Green says about the infrequency of seeing gay men with children may also need to be revised, though there are still some agencies that do not work with gay and lesbian people.

Green recounts several times when he is surprised by how friendly people are when they see him, or him and Andy, with Erez. The increasing acceptance of gay parents and families by straight people, at least in New York City, is one of the most emphasized observations in the latter part of the memoir. This is in spite of the fact that early in the book he claims that "it cannot be overstated how ham-handedly American culture pushes parenthood on heterosexuals and how stingily it withholds the idea from gay men, like an unscrupulous mountebank" (33) and comments that the unfounded belief that most gay men are pedophiles causes this prejudice. Apparently the visual evidence of a happy family makes a difference, and "fatherhood trumps gayness" (155), though he sometimes feels this is because "we were no longer gay to straight people" (159); strangers often hypothesize that he and Andy are brothers or divorced pals.

Middle-class Jewish men who can afford to live in New York, Green and Andy are aware of their obvious privilege. Some gay men scorn them because they see adopting children as buying into the heteronormative system, and Andy goes to one party where he feels "we were no longer gay to most gay people either" (159), though on the previous page he describes lesbians there welcoming him and especially Erez. Readers influenced by queer theory might claim that *Velveteen Father* makes too much of a case for gay people becoming like straight people. Arguing that equality of rights should not depend on sameness, they might say that Green and Andy are striving for homonormativity.[39] Others would say that the book is, rather, showing the diversity of what kinds of family, what kinds of life for gay people, are possible. The book shows that having a child often increases one's social acceptability—something also true for straight people—and this may suggest the ethically dubious possibility of seeking a child chiefly for that purpose, treating the child as a commodity.[40] But on the other hand, though he had experienced it before when caring for his niece, Green seems to have found social acceptance as a father a pleasant surprise.

Like the Velveteen Rabbit in the children's book after which his memoir is named, Green feels he has become real not only to the child who loves him but to others as well.[41] If the comparison works, he is the child's possession, and it is the child who has the agency to make him real. The Skin Horse's foreshadowing observation, "Generally, by the time you are real, most of your hair has been loved off, and your eyes drop out and you get loose in the joints and very shabby" (15–16), resonates with Green's emphasis on the importance of scars to identity (when they were children, Andy's face was burnt when his brother sprayed lighter fluid on a barbecue and Green was seriously injured in a soccer game because of a pencil in his pocket) as well as on the messiness of child-rearing. A new car is "christened" (142) by Erez's vomit, and Green's new suit records his holding Erez at a picnic with "little red amoebiform blobs. . . . . One way or another, a child marks you forever" (160).

More problematic than whether Green is trying too hard for acceptance is how Green and Andy relate to other minority groups, birthparents and Latinx.[42] Very early in the book we learn that Andy refers to the birthmother of the unknown child he will adopt as "Concepción," expecting that she will be Latina (understandable because of the agency he chose) and wanting "to define her by her biological role in the endeavor" (5). This is the sort of attitude that, as we have seen, birthmothers who write about their experience with adoption hate, because, like most women, they want to be seen as more than their biological role. And Green calls the birthfather "Don," short for donor (6). Any birthfather who is later interested in meeting or learning about his birth son would hate that as well. Andy twice chooses a closed adoption and unofficially gets some information about the birthparents but does not think about making it possible for Erez and Luke, their second son, to find out anything about them later, though Green expresses ambivalence about the erasure of the birthparents when he sees Luke's birth certificate (216–17).

They have models of different practice: they happily attend the baptism of the child openly adopted by their friend Mercedes, also a birthmother, whose twenty-one-year-old adopted-out son is present as a godfather. Nevertheless, though he writes of Erez "even at birth he had the high almond eyes and light-brown-sugar skin so typical of the Latin American mélange" (5) and Luke has similar coloring, Green feels this ancestry is less obvious than that of his friend Emily's daughter adopted from China, who will always be seen as Chinese. He does concede, "If later they want to learn Spanish, fine; first they will learn a bit of Hebrew" (229).[43] Their situation as Latinos is probably more fraught now than it was when Green wrote his book, because of the heightening of white-supremacist nativism under Trump.[44] Raising his children as if they were white Jews may not be as problematic as the upbringing given to Avery in *Off and Running*, but the comparison is worth making.

Are Green and Andy using their children, born in poverty, as possessions to gain social acceptance? Some might think so, but overall the book gives a convincing sense of their generosity as parents. The problem of seeing a child as a possession is several times discussed: Green writes, "A child is not something of one's own," as he argues against using children for one's political agenda, even if that agenda is the right of same-sex couples to adopt (157). He writes happily of Erez's interest in girls as showing independence in following his own passion and concurs with the legal construction of adoption as attachment rather than ownership (211). Yet with regard to learning about ethnicity and ancestry, Green cannot imagine the future perspectives of his children.[45]

Both memoirists, more than any other discussed so far except Savarese, emphasize the joy they have found in parenthood. Part of its intensity is in its surprise—Marin as a male and Green as a gay male had not expected children would be so important to them. Both had feared to be alone, both find parenthood overcoming past sadness—Green from the death of many friends from AIDS, Marin from the early loss of his father. Marin explicitly recommends adoption to his readers; Green explicitly does not: "Having children guarantees nothing. I don't recommend it except, like art, to those who feel they simply must" (233). But perhaps his recommendation is more subtle, as his jokes are. He feels "there wasn't very much in the world more satisfying than showing a child a good time" (232).

Another kind of surprise is one reason why there is less emphasis on happiness in some other memoirs of domestic adoption. Bates and Loux expected that raising adopted children would be like the child-rearing that they had already done, and it was not. Many of these memoirs are written largely to present the complications of adopting children with racial difference and/or earlier trauma in our society. Certainly Savarese, Wolff, Trimberger, and Bates feel that the joys are worth the efforts, but they don't want readers who contemplate adopting or think about adoption in other people's lives to assume that it is easy.

Adoption from Europe and Africa

Transnational adoptions are different from those discussed so far not only because they cross national boundaries but also because they provide more obstacles to later contact with the birthparents and because they are more expensive. Adopting parents are likely to be moved by the idea of adopting an orphan, without realizing, as noted previously, that that term is often used, especially in transnational adoption, to refer to children with one or perhaps even two very poor living parents. Several memoirs portray international adoptions that are considerably eased not only by the wealth of the adopting family, but also by their access to expert guidance. This is especially true of two recent memoirs whose authors were advised by Jane Aronson, a physician who specializes in the care of orphans worldwide and of internationally adopted children.

While Loux, especially, complains about not getting good advice prior to adopting, Melissa Fay Greene and Claude Knobler benefit from their interactions with Aronson, as well as others, connections enabled in part, it seems, for Greene by being a writer and for Knobler by his wife's work as a fundraiser for adoption-related causes. Partly because of Aronson's guidance, these two memoirs show adoptive parents welcoming meetings with birth family. Their writing has a much more buoyant, often comic, tone, even more than that of the men just discussed.

Greene, who has four children already, loves raising them and has also published several books of nonfiction journalism, pitches a magazine an article about international adoption of postinstitutionalized children and interviews Aronson, who says that there is always a risk involved but emphasizes that for emotional health a child should have had the experience of attachment, of feeling loved, before being adopted.[46] She sees a video of a child who was seventeen months old when he entered the orphanage (and therefore may have had a stable home for most of that time) and now smiles, happily reaches for a stuffed rabbit, sings a song on request, and when given a muffin in reward examines it curiously in every dimension but restrains himself from eating—all good indications of his spirit. He is from Bulgaria and has "the black eyes and dark hair Donny and I had come to expect in our children": in Bulgarian terms this means that he is probably Romani and the target of prejudice, but from Greene's view his coloring will help him fit better into her family.[47]

In spite of these positive signs, he suffers from institutionalization. At four, he is uncertain of his name—he is called Chrissie but thinks his name may be "Tian," and he does not know colors or numbers. He wants to explore everything in their apartment but is afraid of the teddy bear she wants to give him and frequently at night wakes in fear and has to rock himself back to sleep. When at home, he seems like the chaos-creating "magically animated broom in *The Sorcerer's Apprentice*" (63), and he is enraged if she takes a bit of food from his plate for another child. In an airplane, he is uncontrollable. He has rages four or five times a day, and understandably she is depressed and wonders if she loves him. After a short trial she is told that he is clearly not ready for preschool. But he is endearing as well as difficult, for example in his attempts to make up for asking for a bagel that she cuts herself preparing (he gives her a plastic knife). Yes, she does love him.

Jesse, as he is now named (his name was officially "Christian" but this would be too ironic since Greene's is a Jewish family), can play and can pretend to be "Gercules" or Jackie Chan, so he appears happy; however, he does have difficulty reading, and Greene learns about ways to prepare children for literacy—letting them see and hear letters and feel their shape in addition to reading to them. Jesse learns to write his name legibly, even if the *es* are backward. The family seems stable.

Greene would like another child, and she learns about the AIDS orphan crisis in Africa. She and her nine-year-old daughter Lily, who wants a sister, see a picture of five-year-old Ethiopian Helen in a newsletter and then see her in a video, singing and hopping with excitement. Like Jesse, this is a child who has had family love. She has not been at the orphanage long. Raise a Black child? They live in Atlanta. They seek advice about transracial adoption, and Greene's biracial cousin Julian says, "You can definitely raise an African child in Atlanta" (119). Greene pitches a story on AIDS orphans in Ethiopia to the *New York Times Sunday Magazine*, and the pitch is accepted. They adopt Helen, and Lily continues to be close to her.

In Atlanta, there are Ethiopian workers in many stores (198); Greene wants Helen to talk to them in Amharic, but she is shy. However, after Helen, they adopt three other children from Ethiopia, all boys. The first one is Fisseha, a nine-year-old from the same orphanage as Helen, also taken there recently after, it seems, knowing the love of a family. Two more arrive upon the urging of their son Lee, who is doing an internship there. The Ethiopian-born children presumably have less need for others who look like them since they make up such a large part of Greene's family now.

Having learned from Korean adoptees about the need to feel rooted (199), Greene thinks seriously about how her children will form their identities. She discusses how important it is to acknowledge that a child was born to other parents and not to pretend that their life began with adoption and recalls their attempts to get all the ethnicities, from birth and adoption, into any school assignment about a family tree. She writes, "A person's sense of self rises out of a simmering stew of traits, talents, events, sensations, looks, chance, discoveries, books, relationships, beliefs, and memories, from nature and from nurture. A person's racial, ethnic, and/or national identity is one ingredient" (200). Knobler makes a similar comment but often seems to deny the importance of race in a way Greene does not. She looks with her children at pictures of their countries and asks them about their memories. She is glad to know the specific region and/or people that they came from, but she is aware that the children also need to know more about "how twenty-first-century citizens live in that country [and] how they live as immigrants in America" (201). In a sense, she has constructed a little Ethiopian immigrant community in her own home. And in addition, partly because of Greene's research for future writing, the family or part of it several times returns to Ethiopia and can join in celebrations there.

When opportunity arises, she is eager to connect her children with their Ethiopian relatives. While there to get Fisseha from the orphanage, she takes him to see again and introduce her to Tsehai, the woman who acted as his grandmother and brought him there when she could no longer take care of him. They see her again when they return to Ethiopia five years later, and with some anxiety, they meet his mother, who is still alive. (Orphanages and agencies in developing countries frequently represent children with surviving family members, even parents, as orphans.)[48] It turns out that he was given to the orphanage to save him from revenge that another family would have taken for a death at the hands of his relatives. Another family member confesses that they lied about her death to the orphanage, and Greene tells them she understands their difficulties and the orphanage would have accepted him anyway since his Ethiopian family couldn't support him (266–70).

After this, Greene hires a private investigator to find Jesse's birthmother, since he has long been curious about her and he is the only family member who has neither memories nor photos from their original family. They discover that she is happy to be found and looks just like Jesse, and after contact, she sends them many more family pictures. Jesse says to Greene, "I love you both the same" (323). She admits a moment of hurt recollection of how much effort she has put into mothering him, but concludes by finding in his words "the path to wholeness." He is saying, she believes, "I love my life as a child of our family and I love my history and my people and my first family. I love both aspects of myself" (323).

The celebratory and often comic tone of the book is epitomized by the last chapter, "DNA," in which Greene enumerates, for five pages interspersed with photographs, many different characteristics along with which of her children share them, showing that often some bio and some adopted children are similar in some ways. For example: "Allergic to cat: Seth (bio), Lee (bio), Daniel (Ethiopia), Jesse (Bulgaria). Horseback riders: Molly (bio), Daniel (Ethiopia)" (348). The book ends, "By joining this family, through birth or adoption, family life was regained or enlarged, enlivened, and enriched: all of the above" (351).

The family life recounted here, dependent on being able to afford to raise nine children and repeatedly fly to Ethiopia with several of them (sometimes partly supported by the *New York Times*), is out of the reach of most readers. Greene is unique among these memoirists in reporting that she and her husband contribute money to help support members of Fisseha's Ethiopian family. However, since these gifts come after the adoption and were not promised, they need not be considered an example of child-buying but rather contributing to the welfare of relatives to whom they now have family bonds.[49] Margaret Homans strikes a balance in writing that Greene locates "the child in an economic transaction—we could even call it a swaggeringly imperialist one—even as it makes his dual identity as Ethiopian American a more readily lived reality. Sending money home is something any good son and grandson might do."[50]

Claude Knobler's book *More Love (Less Panic)* is literally indebted to Greene partly because Greene's article about Africa's AIDS orphans first gets him and his wife thinking about adopting and, specifically, adopting from Ethiopia, in the first place. *More Love*, like *No Biking*, begins with a story of adopting a child more emotionally healthy than many because he had more time with a loving family than he had in the orphanage. This five-year-old was brought to Knobler's attention because of his connections: "Because she was trying to raise money for adoption-related causes, Mary [Knobler's wife] was in contact with the adoption agency's director. . . . One day the director told Mary that she thought she might know of a little boy we might like."[51] They see him laughing and gesturing in the video, ask their kids what they think, their son asks his friends (saying "He was born on Hallowe'en, isn't that cool?"), and getting everyone's approval, they go ahead (28).

Furthermore, like Greene, Knobler gets some advice from Jane Aronson, "the Orphan Doctor," who tells him that they have to meet the family of the boy they are adopting. He argues with her, but knows she is an expert and is convinced; when he does meet Nati's mother, his perspective shifts drastically (49). He feels that she is the "bravest woman [he] will ever meet" (54), which resembles Wolff's impression of her son's birthmother, but unlike Wolff, he probably will not see her again.

In his new home in the United States, Nati's good spirits continue. He has the "confidence of a four-star army general and the charisma of a young Elvis" (97). Nothing is what Knobler expected—he realizes that he needs to change his attitude toward parenting, giving up his expectations of control and his worry that children's behaviors that don't match his preferences will lead to disaster in their future lives. Indeed, Knobler frames his memoir as a book of parenting advice, applicable to dealing with all children, not just adoptees. He believes that his job as Nati's father is "to help him be the best possible version of who he already is" (138), and this approach will help others approach parenting with the attitude of his title: "More love, less panic." This is an admirable emphasis, but what if it is not so clear who the child already is, what the child needs? Knobler insists that the important influence is "nature, not nurture" (136), but his view is not always quite so simple, because he believes that his older children benefited from living with Nati's different temperament (94). Still, this effect is not something he foresaw or a kind of nurture that anyone intended.

Before writing his book, Knobler spent "twelve years writing and performing comedy acts for radio stations" (137), and like Greene, he fills his book with many funny family anecdotes, about his children by birth as well as by adoption. But for him all problems are solved if a parent just gives up on the idea of controlling children. This is too simple. Greene is not a control freak, and she describes her depression when her first adopted son has rages four or five times a day as well as her desperation years later when the three oldest children are away at college and she asks a neighbor to intervene in the angry conflicts that have emerged among those remaining (281–86).

Knobler is also less thoughtful than Greene about complexities of identity. He does say, "That Nati is a young black man being raised by white parents is important and significant and something he will always carry as part of who he is, for better and for worse" (84–85). But he moves from this to the topic of how geography (they live in Los Angeles) and family size and parents' occupation affects adopted children also. He is happy to recount how the children in Nati's kindergarten class chant his name with enthusiasm, but he doesn't mention the racial composition of the class. He tells us that when he turns down a request from now adolescent Nati, the response will be something like "Really? Is it because I'm black?" (83), and he treats this as an ongoing joke. He tells us about people staring at his family and relatives showing they mentally locate Nati in the NBA or *Shaft* (82–83), the sort of behavior Wolff and Rush complain about, and in effect says, "Lighten up." I wonder how Nati would tell this story. *Black Baby White Hands* discusses gaining popularity by being a clown and may provide some insight into Nati's jokes.

In *Two Little Girls*, a contrast to the two memoirs just discussed in many ways, avoiding birthparents is an important rationale for international adoption. Reid believed that if birthparents and children found each other, "We doting adoptive parents would be out in the cold, childless again" (17). She says she changed her mind about this later, but as she introduces a discussion of how she talks with her daughter about her birthmother, she says, still ambivalent, "I love her for her incomparably precious gift; and I would like to meet her—as long as there is an ocean between us" (54). However, like Knobler and many adoptive parents, she emphasizes the idea that her daughter was given up out of love so she could have a better life.[52]

Knobler does not call attention to his financial situation, and Greene to some extent underplays hers by crediting advances for her writing for some of her trips to Bulgaria and Ethiopia. Reid, however, stresses to the readers and also to orphanage personnel her money as well as her expertise.[53] Her husband is "an endowed professor of pediatrics at an excellent medical school," and she has "run a national organization for professionals in the field of child maltreatment"; they "make a good living, live in a lovely home" (3). When the Ukrainian orphanage is being difficult because a Ukrainian couple wants the girl they are looking at, she asks the orphanage staffer who is driving her around, "Have you told her that we're doctors, that we have plenty of money, that we have a house full of toys?" (155), and her husband makes a similar argument for their claims a few days later. Worst of all, when her first daughter, from Russia, resents the attention given to her second daughter, she says "We have given you the greatest gift we can ever give you by bringing Lana home. We have given you a sister, and it cost a fortune, and even though it might not seem so right now, she will be your best friend for your whole life" (253).

Reid writes that she hopes to show the reader "that even if you are filled with doubt and confusion, even if towering obstacles—from inside and out—block your path, you can bring one of your dearest dreams to life by adopting a child" (3). Part of her strategy of encouraging the reader is to be open about all the struggles and discomforts and anger she experiences, hoping the reader will see that "your own doubt and hesitation and confusion and selfish consideration and anger are not evidence that you should not adopt. They are a normal part of the process—at least for those of us who yet have a very long path to sainthood" (5).

Reid, who worked in nonprofits helping maltreated children for years before she adopted, writes frankly about her strict limits on the kind of child she could raise and openly acknowledges that her attitude toward children is narcissistic (she claims that all parents are). However, she reveals more narcissism than any of the other adoptive parent memoirists.[54] Greene is upset when her child has rages several times a day; Reid feels grief merely because she cannot "claim authorship" of her child (53). That child, her first daughter, Natalie, was described to her as "princess of the orphanage," chosen especially for her (23). When she goes back to adopt a second, she says to Lynn, the director for international programs at their agency, "We're not getting any story with Vera, you see? It's just, 'Here's a child, she's kind of cute.' Do you understand? We're just. . . . It just doesn't feel very special" (82).

Various international concerns, including the aftermath of September 11, 2001, intervene, and they don't take Vera. Instead they go to Ukraine and are referred to the girl she will call Lana, whose weight is well below average, though her head is big enough to indicate normal brain growth. Sometimes she sees Lana as having an "amazing spirit" (179); at other times, she worries "she does not make us feel proud—of her or of ourselves. . . . Natalie's glory reflected well on us. Lana, in contrast, puny and sickly as she apparently is, fails to elicit the pride that could jump-start the bonding process" (221). After getting custody, in their apartment in Ukraine, she looks at Lana sleeping and worries again about feeling less for Lana than for her sister: "When will I find this body adorable?" (234).

Reid's bad mood is more understandable when Lana is out of control on the plane trip home and when their home is full of screams from both of their daughters. The problem is heightened because they are trying to keep their house in shape for buyers so they can leave the city she loves for a job her husband wants, and because he avoids the domestic conflict, spending the day at work. "Surely I should be able to manage better" (52). No explicit critique of expected gender arrangements here!

But things calm down, and then she complains because Lana goes to strangers indiscriminately. This is something child psychologists sometimes diagnose as showing a lack of attachment, often the consequence of conditions in an orphanage, but against the background of Reid's other complaints, it is reminiscent of Browning's ominously controlling speaker in "My Last Duchess": "She had a heart—how shall I say—too soon made glad."[55] Reid realizes her own limits: she is "not interested in bestowing love without reciprocation. I want something back for so much of me and I want a lot back—I want the same amount back. You should get what you pay for" (263). This nakedly transactional attitude does not bode well for the future. What finally convinces her that Lana loves her? "Lana walks away, and Lia comes over and takes Lana's place between my knees. . . . In a flash, Lana is back. 'No,' she says to Lia putting both hands on Lia's upper arm and moving her away from me, 'This *my* mommy'" (266). Finally Reid sees in Lana her own possessive form of love. She observes it in Natalie as well: "I feel that I need to show affection to Lana freely, but I feel guilty every time I love her up in front of Natalie. This seems like wanton emotional torture of my beloved first child" (253). She frames her relationship with her two children as like an adult love triangle, but it also recalls the self-consciousness birthmothers Dusky and Seek describe about how affectionate they can be to their birthchildren in front of adoptive parents, in an open adoption or one that has been opened after long being closed.

In describing these dynamics, Reid contrasts markedly with most of the memoirists discussed previously, such as Marin, who unself-consciously sees himself as giving love to which his children are responding. Interestingly, Wolff, another woman, also remembers doubts about whether she loves a child enough, but they are not motivated by the child's disturbing behavior—she was expecting an olive-skinned girl and was given a dark-skinned boy. Still, are women more likely to have doubts about their love of their children because passionate mother love is more a cultural ideal than passionate father love? Or is there something unusually demonstrative about Reid's version of love, which might provoke more jealousy? Lots of adoptive parents describe their affection, but more dramatically Reid and her husband "steal into [Lana's] room now in the middle of the night and kiss her all over her sweet face" (268). The impulse must be awfully strong to win out against the rational desire to let a child sleeping in the middle of the night sleep on. And she apparently wakes up: "In the morning, she makes a joke of wiping off all our kisses." Is this—like Nati's perhaps ambiguous joke, "Is it because I'm black?"—dealing with something the child finds problematic?

While Greene, for her first adoption, seeks a child with dark hair and eyes like those already in her family, she does not try for similarity of appearance in any of the others, nor does Knobler in his. Reid, by contrast, writes that having a child who looks like her is very important. This is partly for privacy, so everyone won't know her child is adopted, a common reason for parents to choose Russia, but she admits that it is also out of denial.[56] They hoped that "if we were not reminded, every time we looked at her, that she did not come out of us, then we could just quietly elude all those 'adoption issues' that dozens of experts say are unavoidable" (14).[57] She does have a further connection with Russia, "the country of origin of Marc's family . . . the country whose history and culture we knew and loved well—well enough to teach a child" (18).[58] However, the memoir does not show her attempting such education. And similarity of appearance seems to end up meaning white skin.[59]

Greene cites the testimony of South Korean adoptees on the importance of celebrating adoptees' birth cultures and other issues (199–200). Reid, by contrast, says nothing about the writings of adult transnational adoptees. She refers with some respect to "the terrible pain of adoptees who were not told about their adoptions until—if at all—they were adults; whose adoptions were shrouded in secrecy and shame" (57). But she writes in the same paragraph, "I want to believe that this pain is not endemic to adoption but to a type of adoption practice that, thanks to adult adoptees' protests, has changed forever." While telling children about their adoption when they are young is important, this increased openness does not deal with every problem, as many adoptees' memoirs show, and Reid ignores this in her distrust of "the adoption 'search' literature" and "the single-factor explanation" (57, 58).

I include Reid's memoir largely as a cautionary example of unwise adoption practice, though when she ends it, no problems have appeared. But the image of the couple and their two children in bed at the conclusion epitomizes her desire to escape from the complexity of the outside world and the children's ancestry and past. Knobler may be minimizing problems by making jokes and, having apparently escaped the difficulties described by Rush, Bates, and Trimberger (partly because of Aronson's guidance) is giving advice that might not be so helpful to others, but he is willing to undertake an adoption impossible to hide as well as to recognize the bravery of his son's other mother. Greene's "little Ethiopia" may be on balance a good use of her financial privilege, and her acknowledgment of her occasional desperate need for help with her children's conflicts is bracingly honest.

Adoption from China

For years, after the initial prevalence of Korean adoption, the largest number of American transnational adoptions were from China. More than in adoptions from most other countries, these children have overwhelmingly been female, because of the combination of traditional male dominance and the government's one-child population control policy. (Since July 1, 2021, China has allowed married couples to have up to three children.) Three recent memoirs of Chinese adoption—Emily Prager's *Wuhu Diary* (2001), Jeanne Marie Laskas's *Growing Girls* (2006), and Jeff Gammage's *China Ghosts* (2007), are set at different stages of family development. Prager's diary is structured around a trip taken when her daughter was six, back to the town where she had lived before being adopted; Laskas describes returning to adopt a second Chinese daughter, and Gammage begins with the first trip to China to adopt. I will begin by contrasting the two female-authored memoirs since the issue of motherhood is so salient for both, and then discuss Gammage's, which is more like Prager's in attitude though different in scope.

Both adoptive mothers locate themselves in relation to the (never seen) birthmother and (more visible) Chinese culture, an emphasis that we have seen before mostly in Greene, among international adoptive parents. The memoirs of Prager and Laskas make a sharp contrast with regard to their initial attitudes toward their daughters' birthmothers, and this contrast continues. A page into the text of *Wuhu Diary*, Prager, the only single parent among these three, includes the short note left by LuLu's birthmother and speaks of "the people who created her" in entirely positive terms: "they were musical. They were expansive. They had great, strong voices, lovely long legs, and remarkable hands. They were eternally cheerful, smart, and good-looking. They had wills of iron and were awfully good-hearted."[60] She imagines the birthmother suffering at leaving LuLu, and considers reasons such as being unwed, poverty, and China's one-child policy.

On the other hand, almost as close to her book's beginning, Laskas tells us that "I stopped thinking about her [older daughter's] birth-mother the same day they drove us by the spot on the street . . . where Anna was found when she was just a few days old. I just couldn't bear to think about that ghost-woman anymore. What good would it do to keep worrying about her and hating her for what she did?"[61] In her previous memoir, *The Exact Same Moon*, Laskas doesn't mention feelings about Anna's birthmother and does tell us something about the background information she received explaining Chinese women's difficulties with the one-child policy. She even says of those who leave their children somewhere they will be found, "mothers in China are making the most difficult choice imaginable."[62] But in *Growing Girls*, we learn more of her anger and her denials. With her second daughter, Laskas says, "I was already used to blocking out the ghost-women of China, so I put Sasha's birth-mother in that convenient vacuum" (4–5).

Of course, if you write that you are putting someone in a convenient vacuum, you are being self-critical. Laskas admits her denials and, unlike Reid, sometimes tries to get beyond them. She includes in her chapter "Meeting the Ghost-Mother" a newspaper article by the journalist Xinran in which a Chinese woman who has given up her baby girl says, "You don't know how hard life is for a girl in the countryside as the first child of a poor family. . . . My love will live in her blood and my voice in her heart" (*Growing* 45–46). After quoting this she writes, "I can't hold on to the fact that my daughters were once cradled by the women who gave them their biology" (47). And yet she goes on to imagine solidarity with the birthmother: "We want to meet one day, as old women, alone in a coffee shop. We want to embrace and fall into sobs. We want to verify in each other the fulfillment of every mother's pledge: we did the best with what we had" (47).

This is a brief moment in Laskas's book. Prager, by contrast, puts a similar fantasy at the very end of hers, and it expresses the attitude that she maintains almost exclusively. It is found in a letter that she wrote to the birthmother, at her adoption agency's request, seven months before she saw LuLu's photo. She admits that she doesn't know what to say "to a woman whose greatest tragedy is my good fortune" (237). She promises that their shared daughter will be loved, educated, and prepared for adulthood and that "she will know of your courage and love in leaving her alive so that I might raise her," pledges to teach her to love China and identify with its people, and asks forgiveness "for my part in ripping off the Women of China and in particularly, of course, you." She too imagines a meeting, embracing "as one family," but in the afterlife (238).

The difference between these two memoirists results in part from the fact that Prager lived in Taiwan as a child and has always been interested in Chinese culture. No other internationally adopting memoirist I discuss has extensive previous experience so close to the country where her child was born. Laskas has a shorter and more ambivalent history with China.[63] In *The Exact Same Moon*, describing her visit to get Anna, she was pleased to find it "more colorful than [she] had imagined" (263) and to hear the orphanage director speak of joining in a "net of love" (272).[64] She feels that she has "this privilege and this challenge of raising a girl . . . with respect for a heritage that, at best, I can know only as an onlooker" (268). In *Growing Girls*, she writes, "we speak of China as a shared family heritage" (117).

But when she and her husband go with the girls to Chinese classes, the parents don't do well, the girls are disorderly, and they give it up after a month.[65] For her girls, she says, China is "a homeland that was not, in the end, a home" (121). She's not one to dress her daughters in Chinese silks, and has to control a rage about her daughters' abandonment that sometimes makes her want to scream, in a way that seems directed at the whole country, "What is the matter with you people?" (121).

Prager has a more sophisticated sense of the difference between people and their governments. She is not uncritical of Chinese culture: in her first published book, *A Visit from the Footbinder*, the title story is an exploration of a certain kind of internalized oppression: what it is like to be a little girl who looks forward to footbinding as a sign of her growing up. In her letter to the birthmother in *Wuhu Diary*, she writes, "That you should have your daughter forced from your arms by a government who I then must pay to envelop her in mine is the stuff . . . which I have fought against my entire career" (237). But she knows and loves the long history of China and feels a closeness with the Chinese people because of the kindness and hospitality they gave her when, as a lonely child in late 1950s Taiwan, she saw how hardworking and poor her neighbors were. Laskas can sound like this for a moment but quickly becomes self-conscious about the terms in which she imagines her daughter's inheritance: "a ruggedness earned in my imagination by ancestors toiling in rice paddies, wearing hats made of bamboo and shaped like lampshades—a cliché" (147).

Much of the contrast between their attitudes probably results from the contrast in their daughter's conditions when adopted. LuLu seems to have been perfectly healthy when Prager first met her, "with black, sparkling, mischievous eyes," immediately displaying "the most adorable, grand smile of hello" (5). Laskas's first adopted Chinese daughter was also cheerful and lively from very early on. However, at their first meeting, the second, Sasha, has pleading eyes, seems profoundly malnourished, won't touch toys, won't eat, and howls if left alone even for a moment (*Growing*, 49–51). At three she still has trouble speaking. "Some people would say brain damage and some would say the orphanage did it. Or the ghost-mother who left her on the steps of that pharmacy" (114). The cause is never to be known, and Laskas says, "At times I feel an anger toward the orphanage workers, toward all the ghosts, that turns into brittle, hot rage." But "there's no one there to fight," and she doesn't want to turn her child into a victim. Sasha turns out to have great social skills in spite of her speech problems. She's "a popular kid with a ready laugh and two best friends and a sister and a gonkey" [her pronunciation of donkey] (115).

Sasha has a gonkey/donkey because Laskas and her family live on a farm, and much of the book is about caring for animals. Her girls, Laskas says, have seen that "all babies come out of women's bellies [this includes female animals] and some go on to be raised by other moms, goats and sister ducks and dogs" (*Growing* 249). So, she thinks, their own adoption, their coming out of other mother's bellies, doesn't seem remarkable to them. But when she hears a lamb and its dying mother calling to each other, she hears "Anna and Sasha and the ghost-mothers of China, the loss, the loss, the loss" (*Growing* 191). And she feels powerless.

Prager sees responses to loss in her daughter from close to the beginning and finds ways to talk about them. LuLu, apparently unlike Laskas's daughters, occasionally comments on how different she and her mother look. When

LuLu falls in love with Miss Ling, her teacher at an all-Chinese preschool, Prager guesses that LuLu felt in Miss Ling some of the Chinese mother she had lost—an impression heightened by LuLu's devastation, at three, when Miss Ling announces that she is going to get married and move to another state. At a Thanksgiving dinner at the school where everyone else is Chinese, LuLu runs aimlessly about the room and refuses to sit at the table with her classmates. After they leave, Prager asks, "Are you embarrassed because I am not Chinese?" and LuLu says, "Yes" (22–23). It's time to have more of a talk than just saying "You're adopted, too" when an adopted child appears on *Barney* (23).

She tells LuLu for the first time her adoption story—the choice by the adoption ministry, the phone call asking, "Would you like to meet your baby?" and how LuLu had bowed and smiled when they met. LuLu asks to hear the story every night over and over for the next few weeks, and Prager tells it. And here we see again that she is not totally unlike Laskas, who thinks of her daughters as "girls with a history that really only begins with me" (*Growing* 147): at first Prager cannot bring herself to mention the birthparents. However, while LuLu is still three, she starts with the "nice Chinese couple" she calls LuLu's "first parents. . . . They wanted to keep you. But they couldn't, so—" (25). She suggests explanations such as poverty or the government and, instead of the reality that LuLu was found near a police station, invents the fiction that "they took you to the Wuhu Children's Institute and told them to find the best mother for you . . . I am so happy to be your mother."[66] She has to explain that she is crying because she is happy.

Prager adds the Chinese parents to the story she tells every night and, amazingly, writes that after this conversation LuLu became noticeably calmer. From this point on, LuLu initiates a series of games to reenact birth and adoption, asking her mother first to pretend that she is getting her new adopted baby, then to "pretend I'm in your tummy" (27), and then to pretend to have her baby. Soon LuLu wants to pretend she is giving birth, and they do, and Prager buys "her a baby doll so she could have a new adopted baby of her own" (28). LuLu reenacts scenes of loss, has nightmares, and expresses sadness that she will never see her Chinese parents. Then Prager develops a game involving three stuffed pandas, representing the baby and the two mothers. LuLu takes every role. But mostly she is the baby, and the game provides Prager the opportunity to explain more about poverty, China's lack of land for food, and the government's one-child policy, hoping to lay the groundwork so that someday LuLu would understand. After months of this game, LuLu announces, "Okay, I'm going to call you Mama instead of Emily" (29).

Throughout the book Prager is ready to see the losses LuLu has experienced that she can't do much to mitigate, even though she can provide love, care, and education. She can give LuLu no specific knowledge of her parents or other relatives, and on the trip, Prager comes to see living away from China as itself a loss for her daughter. When LuLu spends time with other people in China, Prager thinks of it as filling up the places of experiences "stolen from her memory bank as an infant" (120). By the time they return from China, LuLu's occasional frantic behavior and anxiety have vanished.

People who deal with adoption professionally and personally disagree among themselves about how important it is for children to think about their birthparents and get in touch with their birth culture, though the sense that it matters is increasing. Prager clearly finds these issues more important than does Laskas, though they are also responding to the different temperaments of their children. It may well be that Laskas's two Chinese daughters, having each other as well as the ongoing image of substitute animal parenting she discusses, don't have the psychological needs that LuLu does as an only child in New York.

But the persona that Laskas presents in this book will have to grow somewhat if they ever have such needs. Reading an essay by an angry Korean adoptee critical of transracial adoption, she tries to imagine what it would be like for her if her daughters grew up to say such things, how difficult it would be to cheer them on for being independent thinkers. She lists people who might have something to say about her and her daughters and concludes, suggesting once more that she knows she is in denial: "Listen, girls, for now, at least, it's just us" (159).

Laskas's memoirs are full of apparent inconsistencies, which can make them seem honest and complex. She writes about her loneliness and declares, "Feeling like a bad mother is the only way to be a mother" (11).[67] But she ends *Growing Girls* saying, "Motherhood was my rescue" (272), telling the story of a nursing dog who saved an abandoned human baby in Kenya after most of her puppies had died. The dog, like her, was rescuing but also—more temporarily—given what she needed in someone to care for. In *The Exact Same Moon*, holding Anna for the first time, she says, "She's so calm she's calming me down" (257).

Gammage does not have the history with China that Prager does; like Laskas, he decides against domestic adoption partly because he thinks it involves competing for birthmothers and chooses China because its adoption process seems simpler.[68] He thoroughly researches China and gives a lot of geographical and historical background. He also discovers that the Chinese adoption system requires dealing with a lot of uncertainty, children described as orphans generally have living parents, and seeing their poverty in the orphanage has a long-lived emotional impact. He acknowledges learning from the anthropologist Kay Johnson about, for example, the impact of economic insecurity on Chinese families.[69]

Like Prager, Gammage is basically sympathetic to his daughter's birth-mother: he invents several detailed fantasies about her and expects to wonder about her the rest of his life. While he originally feared any contact with her birth family, he says "I came back certain that my child and her birthparents should meet. Soon. Or that at the least they should be in touch" (238).[70] He admits that he sometimes gets angry at them, but mostly, overwhelmingly, he is grateful because "they gave life to Jin Yu, the person who has come to define my existence, and they suffered for it" (239). But when Jin Yu, around six, asks about her birthmother, "Why didn't she keep me?" (221), he doesn't say that or make up a fantasy or a guess like "They couldn't take care of you and wanted you to have a better life," but goes for truth: "I don't know" (221).

Unlike Laskas in *Growing Girls*, he is, overall, grateful to China, though angry at their inadequate "social welfare" system. Usually a nonreligious person, he takes her to Buddhist temples in China and then Chinatown for blessings. His wish to maintain the Chinese connection works. Jin Yu is grateful to the nannies who took care of her there, and they keep in touch. She takes a course in Chinese lion dancing, likes to watch *Mulan*, wants another trip to China.

While Sasha has serious developmental delays, the bad effects of Jin Yu's early experience are more ambiguous. Behind her ear, she has a mysterious scar, which receives various diagnoses; the most convincing one is that it is an infected insect bite (71). Gammage, somewhat like Laskas, is inclined to blame the orphanage for poor medical care, but his wife discovers IV scars on Jin Yu, and someone else may have seen her with a bandage on her head, so perhaps her injuries did get serious attention. A doctor's words, "Whatever it was, it's healed" (126), may apply both to the mysterious scar and to other scars she has from loss and neglect. Jin Yu may not have had much practice walking in the orphanage, may not have seen a doll there, but she enjoys both walking and dolls now and is curious and obviously intelligent. Suggesting loss issues like LuLu's, Gammage remembers frequent disconsolate night wakings, and special anxiety about a story in which Curious George loses his bunny, but he also remembers her struggling to get through the noise of a thunderstorm by herself, in spite of her fears (183). And once when he hears her talking in bed at 1:30 A.M. and goes in to check on her, her response is "Daddy funny" (166). When she is six, "Jin Yu is the girl with whom all the other kids want to play" (219).

And yet she occasionally says to her mother, "I wish I had white skin" or "I wish I had a pointy nose like you" (221). We have heard this before in the previous chapter, most notably in Mei-Ling Hopgood's memoir, where her loving parents' ahead-of-their-time interest in Asian culture cannot keep Mei-Ling from feeling uncomfortable about looking Asian. Gammage writes that he and his wife feel that taking her to the Chinese lion dancing class is important because it helps them know what it feels like to be in the minority, as she usually is. Will she, like Hopgood, later find more of an Asian community and even Asian relatives who reconcile her to her appearance? Will she also have to be in her twenties before that happens?

Like many memoirists, he briefly deals with the critique of international adoption: he agrees that "Jin Yu deserves to grow up in the nation of her birth. She deserves to be raised among fellow Chinese, in the home of the two people who created her" (96). On the other hand, he says, "If she were to stay in China, she would spend her childhood as a ward of the state, scratching out an existence in a leaky, rundown orphanage" (97). Domestic adoption of girls does happen in China, but it did not happen to Jin Yu in her time there (Johnson, *China's Hidden Children*). Like several internationally adopting parents, he calls his adoption "selfish" (96), though elsewhere he, like Knobler, describes it as done at his wife's urging.

Gammage, somewhat like Laskas, articulates apparently opposite feelings related to adoption at length. Both say it has brought them happiness. He writes at length of his love and admiration for his daughter. But both authors are aware of the suffering of separated mothers and children in China. As Laskas remembers the ghost mothers, Gammage says to himself that every year on your daughter's birthday "you'll think of a nameless woman across the ocean, and know that, for her, this is a day of grief" (107). He writes that the brochures of adoption agencies "don't tell you that the children of the orphanage are all coming home with you. That these kids with their wan smiles and growling stomachs are going to follow you across the ocean, move into your house, inhabit your dreams" (106).

On the other hand, he writes, "Jin Yu makes me comfortable in my soul" (179). He writes at length of his love and admiration for her. There is never any doubt such as Reid expresses about whether he loves her enough. He does occasionally worry about such things as whether he will discipline her too strictly or not strictly enough. But he does not have the fear of being a bad father, as Laskas fears being a bad mother. Like other adoptive father memoirists, he finds the all-embracing love that he experiences for Jin Yu is something he never expected. As Laskas frequently discusses her relationship with her mother, he meditates on his relationship to his father and how different his involvement in child-rearing is than was his father's.

Gammage has one surprising likeness to Reid: he is happy to think that Jin Yu looks like him and has a similarly stubborn personality, and therefore that "the people at the CCAA [China Center of Adoption Affairs] are really good at their jobs" (115–16). (There is a similar remark about parent-child match with regard to Laskas's first child in *The Exact Same Moon*.) He feels she has been chosen specifically for him, as Reid feels about Natalie. But his continuing interest in the children, and the parents, left behind puts him in a much larger world than Reid's, even if it is a more troubled one. It is a telling contrast also that he likes to observe Jin Yu being generous. He and his wife are fine with the fact that the first time Jin Yu says she loves someone it is not one of them but a girl from her orphanage.

None of the memoirs of Chinese adoption has a single message, as some of the others may; these present a complicated picture. Perhaps there seems more unresolved in Prager and Gammage than in the memoirs of Greene and Knobler because the Chinese birth families seem irretrievable while the picture of China itself is so vivid—or perhaps it is because the children adopted from China are younger when the memoir ends than are Greene's and Knobler's children.[71] But while Laskas uses the image of the ghost-mother only with sadness to represent her children's lost birthmother, Gammage feels connection more than loss when confronted with a ghost image: he imagines that an old woman who unexpectedly appears in a family photo from China is actually Jin Yu's long dead ancestor checking on her well-being. He concludes his book by imagining that Chinese adoptees, when they grow old enough, will band together and insist that China change its practices. This is reminiscent of Savarese's support for DJ's activism and Rush's pride in her daughter's hope to end racism. And we can remember, with hope, that China no longer punishes parents for having more than one child.

Gender and Adoptive Parents

Barbara Melosh writes, "Motherhood still figures more prominently in women's social and cultural identities than fatherhood does in men's, perhaps explaining the overrepresentation of female authors in adopters' accounts."[72] The balance may have changed slightly: Gammage, Marin, Knobler, and Savarese all published their memoirs more recently than her 2002 book. She discusses Bates and Dorris, but she does not mention Green, whose book appeared in 1999.

But there are still signs in these memoirs of gender difference in the positions of adoptive mothers and adoptive fathers. Four memoirs have particularly memorable descriptions of parents feeling overwhelmed: those by Dorris, Reid, Loux, and Greene. Dorris is a single parent to a child with severe disabilities and therefore particularly vulnerable. Reid, Loux, and Greene have husbands whose role in child-rearing is hardly ever mentioned—Greene's meltdown when most of her eight teenage children, half biological and half adopted, are in conflict is solved with help from a female friend. Laskas describes feeling like a bad mother—no male memoirist describes feeling like a bad father. Rather, they think about how much more involved they are than their own fathers were. Marin and Knobler, especially, enjoy their children while brushing away many possible anxieties. Reid and Wolff at times worry, for different reasons, if they love their children enough; no man does. Gammage especially is surprised by how much love he feels.

Several articles in the collection *Adoption and Mothering* emphasize the potentially adversarial relation between adoptive mothers and birthmothers, but most adoptive mother memoirists avoid this.[73] Prager, Wolff, Trimberger, Greene, and at times even Loux—and also Knobler—express strong empathy with their child's birthmother; Green, by contrast, joins his partner in calling her Concepción, to reduce her to a purely biological role. Dorris focuses on his son's birthmother's excessive drinking, in spite of her youth and oppressed condition. In addition to Dorris, Savarese and Marin, who have also adopted from foster care, express the most criticism of their children's birthmother's behavior, which merits it, but Savarese tempers his criticism with awareness that she was abused by her own mother. On the other hand, Laskas and Reid, two who seldom mention their husband's help and who feel especially guilty about not being good enough mothers or not loving their child enough—and thus it seems are most strongly bound to the Good Mother ideal—both write about wanting to keep the birthmother at a distance, as their choice to adopt transnationally virtually ensures.

Adoptive Difference and Racial Difference

In all the memoirs except those by Loux, Dorris, and perhaps Trimberger, adoption is presented as bringing more happiness than unhappiness to the memoirist, though for a while it is a close call for Bates. For Gammage, however, happiness is complicated to some extent by sadness about those left behind, including birth families, and such thoughts also occur in Savarese, Greene, Knobler, and Prager. Wolff, Bates, Rush, Greene, and to some extent Trimberger see the well-being of their children complicated by racism and want to help others similarly adopting to be better prepared. Prager and Laskas never mention anti-Asian racism; it enters Gammage's narrative only in the internalized form of Jin Yu's own discomfort with her appearance.

Racial difference and adoptive difference are elided with each other and then denied by a few of the memoirists. Laskas remembers being told "that being adopted outside of your native culture means forever holding the contradiction of belonging and not belonging, of feeling at home and wondering where home is" and thinks, "Perhaps that is the contradiction of being human" (*Exact-Same Moon* 269). Adoptee Nicole Chung, we saw in a previous chapter, makes a similar generalization: "My identity as an adoptee is complicated, fluid, but then so is everyone else's" (221). From Chung this seems modest, but from Laskas it comes off as oversimplified, though she does say "perhaps." Knobler insists the most explicitly that raising an adopted child is like raising any other child. His emphasis on helping children to be the best version of themselves is a good ideal, but stopping there seems like the denial that his career as a comedian would have encouraged, though he does write about the difficulty of learning to respect each child's individuality (56–57). Most of the other memoirs show that parents don't automatically know what this means for their child. A white parent who adopts an African American child will probably have some issues such as those discussed by Bates, Rush, Trimberger, and Wolff. Greene thinks about the proximity of same-race adults before she adopts from Ethiopia, but among the adoptive parents of children from China, Prager takes this concern most seriously—her experience suggests that the lion-dancing class may not be enough for Jin Yu, though having a sister may help.

Adoptive parents often don't initially know much of their child's previous history and the needs that result from it, and this is an issue especially for Savarese (though he knows more than most when he adopts), Dorris, Loux, Bates, Marin, Laskas, Gammage, and Trimberger, who wishes she had known more about Marco's family history. Reid also has a sense that raising an adopted child is different, though she is not sure whether this is due to probiological bias. Arguably her self-questioning about whether she loves Lana enough, and her insistence that her older daughter should love Lana partly because she "cost a fortune," would not occur if her children were not adopted (though she might possibly refer to the money she spent on fertility treatments or surrogacy).

Many memoirs by adoptive parents end when their children are quite young. In our selection, this is true of Gammage, Laskas, Prager, Green, Marin, Wolff, Knobler, and Reid. It seems that the parents with the most difficulties are the most likely to take the story into near-adulthood—or perhaps adolescence always brings more difficulties. It is instructive to see Green's and Wolff's updates in the collection *A Love Like No Other: Stories from Adoptive Parents*, since both present a somewhat less blissful picture. Green discusses at length the constant reminders that their family is nonstandard in lacking a mother. Wolff writes about her adolescent son's greater distance and the repeated evidence that he is different in many ways from her and her husband.

Perspectives beyond the Family

The older the adoptee is, the more some critics, even some other parents, are likely to say that the story is the adoptee's to tell, not the adoptive parent's. This is probably one reason why Savarese ends the book with a chapter by his son, Trimberger includes an afterword by hers, and Bates includes many reflections and memories quoted from his adopted children, as well as thoughts from each of his children about their relationship with each other.

Dorris's inclusion of Adam's chapter serves mostly as a demonstration of his continuing handicaps, although it also seems to have given Adam a sense of accomplishment to work on it.[74] The more troubled an adoption is, the more important it is to preserve the adoptee's privacy, and so Loux and Dorris give their children pseudonyms. In *Beyond Good Intentions*, quoted in the previous chapter, Cheri Register frames what she has learned from raising transnationally adopted children into adulthood and meeting other adult transnational adoptees as an advice book, rather than a memoir, and she does not name any person specifically.[75]

One of the main contrasts among adoptive parents' memoirs is how much they focus only on their relationship with their children and how much they deal with the world beyond and in what way. Reid's interest is most confined to her nuclear family. For those such as Bates, who have had family prejudice to contend with, grandparents' acceptance of their children is particularly important. Wolff expands her family to include Ari's birthmother. Trimberger meets as many of Marco's relatives as she can, wishes she had done this earlier, and forms the most lasting connection with, oddly enough, Jeanette, who was married to Marco's father when they reunited but has divorced him. Greene, especially, and Knobler, at least briefly, also make connections with children's birth family and birth country. Gammage and Prager are much concerned with China; Laskas finds this concern too difficult to maintain, but puts human adoption in the context of the animal world (eliding the political and psychological complexity of traveling internationally to care for the motherless) as well as her relation to her family of origin. Trimberger studies the epigenetics of addiction and brings this together with research on open adoption in her concluding recommendations to adoptive parents and adoption scholars. Dorris's experience with his son leads him to learn more about the Native American history they share and the serious problems FAS and fetal alcohol spectrum disorders create in the Native American community. At a certain point, he may feel that he can do nothing more for his son, but at least he can try to help prevent others from having the same problems. Rush is already involved with African American issues when she adopted, and she continues to be so; this is true of Bates in a less informed way, and he shows us more of his struggles. Green puts the personal history that leads to his second-parent adoption in the context of the history and sociology of the gay community. Marin includes his children's two older sisters in some family occasions and tells readers about immigrants' and foster children's problems and those of the child welfare system. Savarese from the beginning emphasizes his refusal of a "gated community" of adoptive parent possessiveness. He tries hard to keep DJ's connection with his birth family, and also discusses how DJ's experience shows possibilities for other people with autism—unlike Dorris, he never gives the impression that he is giving up on his son in order to attack the cause of his problems.

The suggestion of a religious perspective, generally found in memoirs by first mothers discussed in one previous chapter and in some rituals described in another, may occur here in the description of a ritual entrance by the child into a community outside the nuclear family: we see both a baptism of the adopted child of a friend and Luke's bris in *Velveteen Father* and an emergency baptism as well as two Masses, one presurgery and one a funeral, all for Savarese's baby nephew in *Reasonable People*. Bates concludes with the celebration of the wedding of his Black daughter Lynn, with his white relatives present as well as her husband's Black family; the ceremony is performed by a white Protestant pastor of a mostly Cambodian congregation. Trimberger describes a funeral for Marco's birth sister and several other church services that she attends with members of his family, as part of her attempt to connect with them. Greene, who does not portray a religious ritual, writes in an article about "parents outside religious communities who were rearing enormous families," that "many, perhaps most, adoptive parents sense a spiritual dimension to their family-building."[76] Gammage goes to a temple in China for a blessing for his child, and Wolff imagines her son's future in the context of the prophetic alliance of Martin Luther King and Abraham Heschel. She writes both that "birth is a miracle" (54) after watching her son's and of the "miracle of adoption" (96), though unlike others who use that phrase, she acknowledges that it is "bittersweet" (97). We may remember that two birthmothers felt that their delivery seemed like a miracle, but a third, Moorman, reacted with horror when she heard of an adoptive mother considering it a miracle that she would be able to adopt her child's new birth sibling. Wolff's open adoption is both a result and a cause of her empathy with birthmothers, and her use of religious language is sensitive to their feelings.

Openness in Adoption

Open versus closed—those two adjectives sometimes applied to adoption have so many different possible meanings. How much parents tell their child about their first family and with what attitude, how open they are to meeting and relationship, and how possible that is we have seen with one kind of apparent success in Wolff, another kind in Marin, another kind in Greene, another kind in Trimberger, and a fuller picture of attempts with great difficulty in Savarese. Research shows that in most cases adopted children benefit significantly from continuing relationships with one or both birthparents from an early age.[77] This is particularly difficult to accomplish with children adopted transnationally, and in fact, as Reid exemplifies, some people choose transnational adoption specifically to avoid contact with a birthmother whom they imagine will want to take her child back. Michael Phillip Grand and James Ritter, by contrast, advocate the possible benefits of adoptive parents as well as their children remaining in contact with birthparents.[78] Grand also suggests that sometimes an appropriate alternative would be guardianship by long-term foster parents.[79] On either model, continuing relationships are complicated in domestic situations if the original and the other parents differ greatly in class, or if any parents are under supervision from Child Protective Services or suffer from addiction. In a 2021 poll of over four thousand adoptive parents, the National Council for Adoption found that about 75 percent of those adopting through private domestic adoption in the previous ten years had some contact with the birthparents, though that may mean many different things. Still, at least one article found that adoptive parents whose adoption is open, when polled twenty years later, generally say that having an open adoption is a good idea, even if they have not been in touch with the birthparents for a few years.[80]

Parents are also on a spectrum of how much they are open or closed to other connections in the surrounding world, and to other journeys that children may want to make. Adoption always offers parents some paths they did not expect. So does much other parenthood, including examples discussed by Andrew Solomon in *Far From the Tree*.[81] Perhaps this is true of any kind of parenthood. But only foster, step-, or adoptive parents have the added complication of other parents whether they are known or only ghosts.

There are other ghosts looming still behind many adoptions: the voices of agencies and orphanages telling distressed mothers that their children will be better off in a two-parent family or in the United States or another developed country and the voices of laws removing children from their parents on grounds that are race-and-class biased.[82] On the other side are the voices of adoptees saying that their adoptive parents did not understand their needs, the voices of birthparents saying they were unfairly treated, the voices of committed scholars saying that much adoption depends on social inequalities and does not remedy them. We have heard from some of these voices, most emphatically from Jane Jeong Trenka. In important recent books, Margaret Homans and Laura Briggs, both adoptive parents, discuss them, and all these issues, at length. A few of the memoirists, such as Laskas and Reid, briefly allude to such critics but then are dismissive. Gretchen Sisson's ground-breaking *Relinquished* includes many interviews and analyses that help explain how the American economic, political, and social welfare systems place burdens on some child-bearing women to provide children for other families.

Many writers refer to the idea that adoption is finding parents who want children for children in need of families; however, critics say that in many cases the children already have families and the adoptive parents' wants are the primary consideration. In the memoirs of Loux, Bates, Savarese, Trimberger, and Dorris, especially, the children are indeed needy, but the adoptive parents are also in need of information and support that they do not receive, and this hurts the children as well.

Sara Dorow presents two divergent ways to see a group of Chinese children going to the United States for adoption—"the joyful intimacy of making family next to the unjust history that it might recall."[83] Dorow, like Homans, Briggs, and many others, goes far beyond individual experiences to consider the larger social and economic picture. In this book, analyzing memoirs, I focus on individual experiences, hoping that comparison of many different kinds of experience will give perspective. These are the conclusions I draw from this research, though others may strike a different balance: relinquishing leads to painful memories for many birthmothers; parents and children may be happy in an adoptive family, but life will become often challenging if parents or community has a prejudice against adoptees' heredity or if the child has suffered too much abuse or neglect; relationships between birthparents and adult adoptees may succeed if all have some flexibility, or may be too difficult to continue; some adoptive parents make heroic efforts to meet their children's needs, but others fail to educate themselves—for example from adoptees' memoirs—about what those needs might be. And adoption agencies, social workers, doctors, and orphanages often contribute to problems by not giving prospective birth or adoptive parents accurate information or adequate counseling, presenting a picture of adoption through too rose-colored a lens and later denying adoptees information that they also need.

None of these memoirs shows adoption as clearly a win-win-win solution in all respects. Adoption creates happiness for many adoptive parents, but it demands their total commitment; some of them realize that their gain is dependent on losses for birthmothers and maybe also for adoptees. Adoptees may feel that on balance they benefited from being raised by their adoptive parents rather than their birthparents but that they might have benefited even more if they had been raised with more openness or more contact with their birth family or, in the case of transracial adoptees, with others of their race. For most birthmothers, it seems, adoption is about forced sacrifice, but those who have written about it pick up the pieces as much as they can, sometimes making the need for reform a basis for finding community.

Memoirs from people in many positions say that adoption would be better with more preparation, education, and honesty from intermediaries as well as more openness in laws. But in spite of adoption's problems, these memoirists show resilience and determination. There is no single story about what adoption means, but the beginning of understanding its complexity is listening to what these and others involved are saying in their inside stories.

Concluding Thoughts

Adoption, as Gretchen Sisson writes, is about "transferring babies from those who have less social privilege to those with more" (*Relinquished* 215). In some cases the transfer is forced by welfare workers. But after many extended interviews with women who have entrusted their children to private adoption, she writes that they "have been convinced—by virtue of their poverty, their youth, or their single status, or all these—that they are poorly prepared to parent" (255). The 2022 Supreme Court *Dobbs* decision has faith in adoption; three judges who voted for it are adoptive parents. The *Dobbs* decision claims that "a woman who puts her newborn up for adoption today has little reason to fear that the baby will not find a suitable home."[1]

Many adoptions make happy families, and the memoirs analyzed in this book describe some. But this book shows the falsity of the Court's statement. In many cases the adopting families, though they may be prepared economically, are not prepared emotionally, especially not prepared for the specific children they have adopted. Some children do find suitable homes. However, an agency places A. M. Homes with a family where the mother is very depressed and finds it hard to relate to her. Korean Jane Jeong Trenka and African American Jaiya John write about agencies giving them, with no guidance, to parents who have little understanding of racial issues, and in Trenka's case, no willingness to discuss them.

Memoirs by some adoptive parents also show dubious placements and little help. In *The Limits of Hope*, Ann Kimble Loux, in an academic household with several bright young children, is given two learning-disabled siblings, traumatized from their original home and their foster care, for whom she has no relevant experience. In *Gift Children*, Douglas Bates writes that in the four years spent in foster care, no one explained to one of his adopted children that she was Black, read to her, or showed her how to brush her teeth, and the agency gives him no help on supporting his children's racial identity in lily-white Eugene, Oregon. While most of these memoirs describe the results of adoptions going through an agency with some knowledge of the birthparents, when babies are placed in so-called Safe Havens, an institution the *Dobbs* decision praises, the difficulties they and their adoptive parents or foster parents face may be even greater. Clearly many babies and children removed do not find a suitable home, and many of them languish in foster care, which may be negligent or unsympathetic, until they age out. Contrary to the *Dobbs* decision, a woman has much reason to fear that her child will not have good care, and the court fails to even mention her own likely emotional pain, which we see especially in memoirs in this book's first chapter.

The *Dobbs* decision implies a hope for more children available for adoption—an increase, quoting from the CDC report, in the "domestic supply of infants relinquished at birth or within the first month of life and available to be adopted" (34n46). This suggests a wish for more stories like those of the memoirists of that chapter, most of whom tried to get an abortion but were too late. However, Sisson's research following up Foster's 2020 Turnaway Study, suggests there may be fewer such stories in the future than expected (*Relinquished* 61).[2] Ninety-one percent of women in Sisson's study of 956 women across the United States who were denied abortion, mostly because it was late in their pregnancy, decided against adoption and chose to raise the child (*Relinquished* 32–33; "Who are the women?"). Even in the years before *Roe v. Wade*, many more women had abortions than relinquished their children (62–63). Sisson shows that women who relinquish infants for adoption now are mostly older than the memoirists in the first chapter were at the time of childbirth. They often already have children and feel they don't have enough money to support those they have.[3] But most of the women who are denied an abortion will raise their child and be under even more pressure. If they ever have the leisure to write a memoir, it will be at least twenty years in the future, and it will not be an adoption memoir.

Most people have no idea what it feels like to entrust a child to adoption and how hard it is to forget this loss. The first chapter makes this experience more vivid, showing the impact of cultural, religious, and parental pressure—it is often because of their own parents' refusal to help that these women felt "poorly prepared to parent." It also shows a range of results in what happens when birthmothers seek to reconnect. Janet Mason Ellerby seems to have an idyllic relationship with her reunited daughter, while Lorraine Dusky and Jan Waldron experience some happiness but much more strain. And while

Amy Seek's always open relationship with her adopted-out son seems good, the loss she feels from not actually raising him persists as she never expected.

What are the results for the adoptee of transfer from a less privileged to a relatively more privileged beginning? The second chapter shows a spectrum in adoptees' experiences of childhood, growing up, and life after meeting with birthparents. Sarah Saffian and Jean Strauss emphasize the closeness they felt with their adoptive parents, while Jean Paton, Florence Fisher, Betty Jean Lifton, A. M. Homes, Emily Hipchen, and Jeanette Winterson stress the distance. (Winterson's home does not seem very privileged, but her adoptive parents were married.) Saffian, Strauss, Elyse Schein, Paula Bernstein, and Craig Hickman remember early talks about their adoption and their birthparents; Hickman in particular recalls the sympathy felt for his birthmother. Lori Jakiela and Jeremy Harding feel different from their adoptive parents in some ways, Harding enjoying inventing himself; both find a few similarities that they regret. Jakiela finds her birthmother impossible, the twins' mother is long dead, and Harding doesn't trace his relationship with his past their first lunch together—all the others of these memoirists emphasize the difficulties of building a relationship with birthparents, though most find it worthwhile. These memoirists reject the idea of finding identity in heredity alone, but they wanted to learn what their heredity was.

Racial difference adds more complexity to memoirs in the third chapter. Most memoirists write that their parents were not sufficiently prepared to raise a child of color. Jackie Kay's parents are unique in the strength of their antiracist commitment, which involves hosting political comrades from Africa and giving her an Angela Davis poster. Mei-Ling Hopgood's family seem ahead of their time in their interest in Asian culture. Catherine McKinley's mother finds a Black church that she hopes will provide some support for her daughter. But even these memoirists grow up in all-white communities and go to all-white schools, and all experience prejudice from outside the family as well as racial isolation. They are bothered by looking so different from their parents and, most of them, by a sense of double or even multiple identity. Some have parents whose denial becomes explicit racism—Jane Jeong Trenka's parents never want any discussion of adoption or Korea and her father mocks her Korean boyfriend, Jaiya John's mother rebukes him for his interest in the TV miniseries *Roots*. But some of these memoirists, most notably John, Hopgood, Kay, Katy Robinson, and Deann Borshay Liem, after their search educate their parents and other relatives and bring them together with their birth family or part of it. All who meet their birthparents (all do except Lori Jakiela and Avery Klein-Cloud) find what they learn important and try a relationship. Nicole Chung and Trenka, especially, feel a strong affinity with one and John with both. Some adoptees, like Hopgood, Kay, McKinley, and Susan Harness, find very difficult birthparents but siblings with whom relationships are somewhat easier. Harness, removed from her birth family by welfare workers, makes an explicit critique of her transfer to another home that had similar problems but white-skin privilege and a father more often around. However, almost all of them, Rebecca Carroll and Jenny Heijun Wills the chief exceptions, conclude by affirming an identity that includes a synthesis of what has been passed on to them from all their families.

The fourth chapter also emphasizes many adoptive parents' lack of preparation, especially in dealing with race, disability, or a combination of both. Some parents have difficulty with racism in school, in family, in neighbors, and even in themselves. Social workers fail to tell parents about their children's previous traumatic experiences in foster and birth families and other family history, minimize the difficulties they would cause, and do not provide support when it is needed.

In a Berkeley neighborhood with more racial diversity than many (19 percent Black), Kay Trimberger raises a son who sees more Black corpses on the street than live Black family friends. She, Michael Dorris, and others believed in a "blank slate" theory of child development but change their views when they learn more about their children's heredity and/or previous traumas. Although class and racial differences make it complicated, Jana Wolff maintains an open adoption and Trimberger connects with members of her son's birth family when he is an adult, wishing she had thought of this earlier. A few adoptive parents underplay or deny the importance of their child's ancestry, but Claude Knobler, the only one who does this when his child is teenage, may be wrong to think it is just a joke when he gets the response "Is it because I'm black?" (83) when he turns down a request from his son.

Nevertheless many of these memoirs describe experiences of sheer joy, some of them simple, some of them after long struggles. Some of the greatest emphasis on happiness in adoption comes from male memoirists, whether single or married to a man or a woman, often because its intensity is a surprise. A few of these parents are explicit about writing to persuade more people to adopt, but more of them want to make sure that others understand the difficulties they have faced as well as the rewards.

Reading many memoirs, especially those by transracial adoptees and transracially adopting parents, shows that adoption practice has many problems. The failure of agencies to prepare parents, and of parents in independent adoption to prepare themselves, is devastating; agencies often are not open about the difficulties of raising children in transracial adoption because they don't want to lose customers. On the other hand, adoption by imperfectly prepared parents is better than remaining in an orphanage or in "a foster care system whose flaws have been repeatedly exposed by investigative journalists" (Glaser, *American Baby* 277) as well as in some of these memoirs.

To publish a memoir, you have to have, minimally, not just a story but some writing competence and persistence, plus time. And you have to feel there is some benefit to thinking back on your experience. Many of the women who do relinquish their children may find it too painful to write about. And so may many adoptees who have the most painful stories to tell.

But there are possible changes that might result in different kinds of memoirs. Perhaps there will be more open domestic adoptions in which the adoptee and birthparents—and maybe adoptive parents as well—stay in touch during the years the adoptee is growing up and even afterward. Perhaps there will be more guardians who help a challenged family stay together and also maintain a permanent connection with them. There may be memoirs about such bonds, and about people who try to maintain them and fail. Probably both. Contact usually diminishes as time passes, people move away, some get divorced, and lives get more complicated in other ways, but at any rate, some big questions have been answered.

And there are and will be a few open adoptions in which adoptive parents really do treat birthparents as kin. For these adoptees keeping in touch with birthparents will seem no more memoir-worthy than keeping in touch with uncles and aunts. No searches, no dramatic recognition scenes, only gradual discoveries of how you are similar to and different from all the other people in your family. But so many adoptive parents find it too difficult to keep in touch with the birth family, often across the fissures of class and race in addition to geography, that this is sounding too utopian to be frequent. Many birthparents in open adoptions, Sisson's research has discovered, find their initial hopes for family relationships are not fulfilled. For one she interviewed eleven years after the adoption, both visits and time without seeing her child are painful (*Relinquished* 165).

Transracial adoptee Angela Tucker proposes the concept of the sondersphere: "a realm where every person in an adoptee's life has a place—where birth parents and adoptive parents and biological aunties and foster parents and adoptive cousins all exist together" and "orbit around the adoptee" making "all the parts of their story visible and accessible" and enabling adoptees to see them all as "complete, complex individuals with inner depths as vast and meaningful as [their] own."[4] This would provide the material for memoirs with lots of complex character portrayal (and many pseudonyms).

But even if this concept gains some acceptance, there will probably still be some memoirs about adopting families, transnational and domestic, where adoption is a secret and eventually is discovered. And there will be memoirs about the families made with the help of sperm and egg donors and surrogacy. Some of those children won't be told; however, some of them will be raised to know their genetic or gestational relatives, and others will find some of them. As with adoption, DNA searches will be common. As with adoption, those who experience pregnancy are the most likely to remember relinquishment. But like the discoveries in the memoirs I have written about, finding your parent or your child will usually not be the end of the story.

Adoption is more frequent in the United States than in any other industrialized country. On the one hand, historians such as Melosh have credited this to the "relative openness of American society, its fluid class and social structure, its racial and ethnic diversity."[5] On the other hand, sociologist Sisson convincingly relates this to the fragile condition of our national safety net, contrasted with those of other countries that provide their citizens with many kinds of help in raising children (*Relinquished* 256).[6] However, there have been problematic adoption practices in other countries too, practices that have resonance with those in ours. And memoirs written about them.[7]

Somehow these practices seem to be from the past, not the present. Children were taken from families in Greece, Spain, and Argentina because they were on the wrong side of a national political conflict and from families in Chile because they were poor.[8] In Australia, New Zealand, Canada, Ireland, and the UK, unmarried women were pressured to give up their children, and in the first three countries, children were also removed from indigenous households.[9] The Magdalene Laundries of Ireland have had so much bad publicity that even the pope expressed sorrow about them when visiting Dublin, but the removal and adoption practices of those other countries were also traumatic enough that the heads of government of Australia and Scotland and many Anglican religious leaders have publicly apologized for the acts of their predecessors, and there have been many calls for leaders in other countries to do the same. China has ended its one-child policy. Korea has set up a Truth and Reconciliation Commission because of all the lies in its adoption records—for example, frequently claiming that children were orphans when they were not.

However, in the United States, outside the internet and the walls of adoptees' conferences, the only place I have seen apologies requested is the conclusion of *American Baby*, which quotes Australia's Prime Minister Julia Gillard's 2013 statement accepting responsibility in the estimated 150,000 forced relinquishments there in the decades after World War II. Glaser wishes that some American political figure would do the same for our 1.5 million (278–79).

I wrote this book in the hope that studying memoirs would give a deeper understanding of adoption than is generally found in media features celebrating, for example, legal finalization, arrival from another country, or meeting with birthparents—or, for that matter, in Supreme Court decisions. My hopes were that it would contribute to the argument to open access to birth records for adoptees, something desired by many memoirists discussed in my first, second, and third chapters, and that it would help searchers have more realistic expectations and adoptive parents better understand their children and therefore see the importance of making their adoption something that can be discussed.

But adoption is a much bigger topic than I expected. Its frequency in the United States is partly because we don't provide help for the basic necessities of raising children in the ways most other developed countries now do, as Sisson has shown.[10] From the language of the Supreme Court, it seems one reason is that we want to have an adoption supply. Infertility is painful, but does it really justify removing babies from their mothers? The goals I just enumerated don't touch this problem. Indeed, it's not something many memoirists mention. One exception, adoptee Paula Bernstein, writes, "As comfortable as we are in our relationship, our gain resulted from others' losses" (*Identical Strangers* 243). Adoption is something most Americans find so hard to question that efforts to promote it find unusually bipartisan support (Sisson, *Relinquished* 5). As Kathryn A. Mariner writes, "It is a profoundly individual solution to a set of deeply structural problems."[11]

Those with the worst stories can't write memoirs, so there are limits to how much memoirs will help readers understand. There are issues for which we need sociologists, anthropologists, historians, political scientists, psychologists, investigative journalists, and scholars in the new field of critical adoption studies. Still, reading about these memoirs should give more understanding than the picture of either adoption or reunion as a happy ending. Both are just beginnings. I hope that for many readers, so is this book.

Notes

INTRODUCTION

1. Nicole Chung, *All You Can Ever Know* (New York: Catapult, 2018), 74.

2. Barbara Melosh, *Strangers and Kin: The American Way of Adoption* (Cambridge, MA: Harvard University Press, 2002), 105–6.

3. One article that gives a larger social context to its critique of media treatments of adoption is Danae Clark's "Mediadoption: Children, Commodification and the Spectacle of Disruption," *American Studies* vol. 39, no. 2, Summer 1998, 65–86.

4. Gabrielle Glaser, *American Baby: A Mother, a Child, and the Shadow History of Adoption* (New York: Viking, 2021), 6. The number comes from P. L. Maza, "Adoption Trends: 1944–1975," in the Adoption History Project website. Glaser (118) refers to this system as the "adoption-industrial complex," making more general Kimberly McKee's phrase "transnational adoption industrial complex," introduced in *Disrupting Kinship: Transnational Politics of Korean Adoption in the United States* (Urbana: University of Illinois Press, 2019), 2.

5. Cf. H. David Kirk, *Shared Fate*, 1963, 2nd ed. (Port Angeles, WA: Ben Simon, 1984), which shows that adoptive parents who acknowledge the difference of their family have better communication with their children than adoptive parents who reject the idea that their families are different.

6. Glaser (100) reveals even more ethical violations in the Louise Wise adoption agency, where babies who had no legal parents to protest were tested to see their reactions to pain.

7. McKee, *Disrupting Kinship* 81.

8. Many social workers also agree that parents who adopt transracially, especially, need a better understanding of how racial issues affect their child. See Elizabeth Raleigh, *Selling Transracial Adoption: Families, Markets, and the Color Line* (Philadelphia: Temple University Press, 2018), esp. 187–201.

9. Barbara Melosh, "Adoption Stories: Autobiographical Narratives and the Politics of Identity," in *Adoption in America: Historical Perspectives*, ed. E. Wayne Carp (University of Michigan, 2002), 221–22; Soojin Chung, *Adopting for God: The Mission to Change America through Transnational Adoption* (New York: NYU Press, 2021), 138, contextualizing Helen Doss's *The Family Nobody Wanted* (1954).

10. On statistics and possible explanations, see John Gravois, "Bringing Up Babes: Why Do Adoptive Parents Prefer Girls," *Slate*, January 14, 2004; Barbara Melosh similarly suggests that prospective parents believe girls are more malleable and affectionate (*Strangers and Kin* 54–68). For analysis that might explain further why women led and lead the movement to open adoption records and why many of them write memoirs about their search and aftermath, see Susan Stanford Friedman, "Women's Autobiographical Selves: Theory and Practice," in *Women, Autobiography, Theory: A Reader*, ed. Sidonie Smith and Julia Watson (Madison: University of Wisconsin Press, 1998), 72–82.

11. See *Adoption and Mothering*, ed. Frances J. Latchford (Bradford, Ontario: Demeter Press, 2012).

12. The Adoption History Project website (https://pages.uoregon.edu/adoption/) was last updated in 2012. In 1980, according to Glaser, the estimate was "over 5 million living" (204). The CDC's most recent National Survey of Adoptive Parents, from 2007, estimated 1.8 million adopted children under eighteen, excluding stepchildren.

13. Gretchen Sisson, *Relinquished: The Politics of Adoption and the Privilege of American Motherhood* (New York: St. Martin's, 2024), 31. Upon my request, Professor Sisson generously sent me a copy of her book before publication.

14. Sisson, *Relinquished* 26.

15. John Raible, "Life-Long Impact, Enduring Need" in *Outsiders Within*, ed. Jane Jeong Trenka, Julia Chinyere Oparah, and Sun Yung Shin (Cambridge, MA: South End Press, 2006), 181.

16. Judith Penny, L. DiAnne Borders, and Francie Portnoy "Reconstruction of Adoption Issues: Delineation of Five Phases among Adult Adoptees," *Journal of Counseling & Development*, vol. 85, no. 1, 2007, 30–41, summarized in Child Welfare Information Gateway, "Impact of Adoption on Adopted Persons," August 2013, 4–5. See also David Brodzinsky, Marshall D. Schechter, and Robin Marantz Henig, *Being Adopted: The Lifelong Search for Self* (New York: Doubleday Anchor, 1993), on variability among adoptees and across their life spans.

17. H. D. Grotevant, "Coming to Terms with Adoption," *Adoption Quarterly*, vol. 1, 1997, 3–17. Of course, there are some memoirists, such as Jane Jeong Trenka, who intentionally, for much of their memoirs, stress that adoption has made their life incoherent.

18. Marianne Novy, *Reading Adoption: Family and Difference in Fiction and Drama* (Ann Arbor: University of Michigan Press, 2005).

19. This occurs in Glaser, and in Dani Shapiro's memoir *Inheritance: A Memoir of Genealogy, Paternity, and Love* (Knopf, 2019), although there the issue is unacknowledged sperm donation. See Richard Hill, "How DNA Testing Is Changing the World for Adoptees," in *Adoption Reunion in the Social Media Age*, ed. Laura Dennis (Redondo Beach, CA: Entourage, 2014), 80–88.

20. Melosh, "Adoption Stories," 218–45. Emily Hipchen and Jill Deans discuss only adoptee memoirs in "Introduction: Adoption Life Writing: Origins and Other Ghosts," *a/b: Auto/Biography Studies*, vol. 18, 2003, 163–70, while Sidonie Smith and Julia Watson, in *Reading Autobiography: A Guide for Interpreting Life Narratives*, 2nd ed. (Minneapolis: University of Minnesota Press, 2010), also have a brief discussion of birthmothers'

memoirs and even more briefly include the phrase "adoptive parent(s)" (255) and place gay adoptive fathers under the category of "filiation narrative" (270).

21. Margaret Homans, *The Imprint of Another Life: Adoption Narratives and Human Possibility* (Ann Arbor: University of Michigan Press, 2013). Three anthropologists make parallel attempts. Linda Seligmann, in *Broken Links, Enduring Ties: American Adoption Across Race, Class, and Nation* (Stanford University Press, 2013), draws on some memoirs and other writings by adoptees in addition to interviewing adoptive parents and their children, as does Barbara Yngvesson in *Belonging in an Adopted World: Race, Identity, and Transnational Adoption* (University of Chicago Press, 2010). Before most of the memoirs discussed here were published, Judith Modell *interviewed* people with all three relations to adoption, including me, and consulted adoption memoirs by Lifton and Paton, for her book *Kinship with Strangers: Adoption and Interpretations of Kinship in American Culture* (Berkeley: University of California Press, 1994). Her book does not deal with issues of racial or national difference in adoption, which were mostly less discussed when it was researched.

22. Katarina Wegar, *Adoption, Identity and Kinship: The Debate over Sealed Birth Records*. (New Haven: Yale University Press, 1997), 131.

23. S. Chung 57–118.

24. However, evangelical opposition to abortion was not absolute when Holt wrote or in the 1960s and early 1970s, according to Frances FitzGerald, *The Evangelicals: The Struggle to Shape America* (New York: Simon & Schuster, 2017), 253–556.

25. Kathryn Joyce, *The Child Catchers: Rescue, Trafficking, and the New Gospel of Adoption* (New York: Public Affairs, 2013).

26. E. Wayne Carp, *Family Matters: Secrecy and Disclosure in the History of Adoption* (Harvard University Press, 1998); Elizabeth J. Samuels, "The Idea of Adoption: An Inquiry into the History of Adult Adoptee Access to Birth Records," *Rutgers Law Review*, vol. 53, no. 2, Winter 2001, 367–436.

27. Margaret Homans discusses two more: Karen Salyer McElmurray's *Surrendered Child: A Birth Mother's Journey* (Athens: University of Georgia Press, 2004), and Meredith Hall, *Without a Map* (Boston: Beacon, 2007). Barbara Melosh's chapter discusses aspects of thirty-eight memoirs from all three positions published before 1999. She observes that adoptive parents have published the most and birthmothers the least (apart from birthfathers). I have decided not to discuss some memoirs in which adoptive parents end the story before children leave infancy and some in which adoptees focus on their career with little emphasis on search or relationships. I have limited the number of memoirs that emphasize parental cruelty or irresponsibility.

28. Andrew Ward, *The Birth Father's Tale* (London: British Association for Adoption and Fostering, 2012). Mary Martin Mason collected interviews in *Out of the Shadows: Birthfathers' Stories* (Edina, MN: O. J. Howard, 1995).

29. G. Thomas Couser, *Memoir: An Introduction* (New York: Oxford University Press, 2012), 149–50.

30. Laura Briggs, "Making 'American' Families: Transnational Adoption and U.S. Latin American Policy," in *Haunted by Empire: Geographies of Intimacy in North American History*, ed. Ann Laura Stoler (Durham, NC: Duke University Press, 2006), 346; Grotevant, quoted in note 17 of this chapter.

31. Elaine Scarry, "Poetry, Injury, and the Ethics of Reading," in *The Humanities and Public Life*, ed. by Peter Brooks with Hilary Jewett (Fordham University Press, 2014), 42, explains the argument by Pinker in *The Better Angels of Our Nature*, with which she agrees,

that the novel is in part responsible for the humanitarian reforms of the eighteenth and nineteenth centuries.

32. Adoptive mother Pearl Buck used "birth mother" in "I Am the Better Woman for Having My Two Black Children," *Today's Health*, vol. 50, Jan. 1972, 21, quoted in Richard Uhrlaub and Nikki McCaslin, "Culture, Law and Language: Adversarial Motherhood in Adoption," Latchford, *Adoption and Mothering* 200.

33. Similarly, outside of quotations I capitalize Black when referring to people of African descent, but this usage has been only recently (2020) approved by stylebooks, so the word is not capitalized in most quotations from earlier writings.

CHAPTER 1

1. Amy Seek, *God and Jetfire: Confessions of a Birth Mother* (New York: Farrar, Straus and Giroux, 2015).

2. Jan Waldron, *Giving Away Simone: A Memoir* (New York: Random House, 1995), xiii.

3. Homans 251–52. On page 262, Homans quotes Kate Livingston's "list of ill-fitting terms for what she is," in "The Birthmother Dilemma," paper presented at NWSA Conference, Cincinnati, June 2008.

4. Studies of California adoptions in 2001, for instance, show that meetings between adoptive parents and at least one birthparent occurred in at least 90 percent of nonrelative adoptions. See Susan L. Smith and Adam Pertman, "Safeguarding the Rights and Well-Being of Birthparents in the Adoption Process," rev. Jan. 2007, Donaldson Adoption Institute, Available at https://www.ncap-us.org/post/safeguarding-the-rights-and-well-bein gof-birthparents-in-the-adoption-process, 4, 18. In 1999 in fifteen states, about 80 percent of agencies offered this possibility (19); in a recent survey of over four thousand parents, the National Council for Adoption found that almost three-quarters of those who had adopted in private domestic adoptions since 2011 had some contact with the birth family.

5. Ann Fessler, *The Girls Who Went Away: The Hidden History of Women Who Surrendered Children for Adoption in the Decades Before* Roe v. Wade (New York: Penguin, 2006).

6. This was typical of their generation in the United States. See Fessler 37.

7. Dusky, Schaefer, Seek, and their parents were affected by pressure from the Catholic Church. Gabrielle Glaser, in *American Baby*, shows that even Margaret Erle (later Katz), who was about to be married, could, since she was only eighteen, be coerced into relinquishing parental rights by a social worker's threat of the reformatory (90). Margaret's situation, on which she focuses, is poignant in a different way than that of the memoirists discussed in this chapter because she and her child's father were eager to take care of their child together. Among all the memoirs considered in this book, only those by Hipchen and Saffian describe such a situation.

8. According to Smith and Pertman, now only about a quarter of women who relinquish their children are under twenty (4, 23) but the lack of counseling remains (8, 29).

9. Judith Modell, in *Kinship with Strangers* (57), suggests that in an open adoption "the birthparent can feel less the victim of circumstances—or coercion," and this is what Seek hopes, though she still suffers. Kate Livingston, in "Adoption: Experience, Research, and Activism," *ASAC News*, Fall 2010, 4–5, also discusses the pain she experienced in an open adoption, emphasizing both her grief at her loss and the lack of support from people who had been her allies in the prolife movement.

10. As Glaser notes, "the number of babies born to unmarried mothers more than tripled between the years 1940 and 1966" (39).

11. Jean Thompson (pseud.), *The House of Tomorrow* (New York: Harper & Row, 1967). On stigma, see Valerie J. Andrews, "'Unwed Mother': Sex, Stigma, and Spoiled Identity," *Adoption & Culture*, vol. 8, no. 2, 2020, 133–49.

12. Thompson even presents justification for the home's punishment of girls who gain more than fifteen pounds. See Glaser, esp. 56–66, on this and other kinds of mistreatment in maternity homes, which she compares to jails.

13. In her memoir, *Why Be Happy When You Could Be Normal?* (New York: Grove, 2011), adoptee Jeanette Winterson acknowledges that she added a friendly older woman, Elsie, to the characters in her novel about her life, *Oranges Are Not The Only Fruit*, because her actual experience without any such friend was just too painful (*Why Be Happy* 7).

14. Lorraine Dusky, *Birthmark* (New York: M. Evans, 1979), 140.

15. Carol Schaefer, *The Other Mother: A Woman's Love for the Child She Gave Up for Adoption* (New York: Soho, 1991).

16. Schaefer explicitly critiques adoption in her play, *The Sacred Virgin*, produced off-Broadway in 2002. Like *The Other Mother*, this play, set in an unwed mothers' home, places great emphasis on shame, in particular from the influence of Catholic culture.

17. Homans discusses two formally innovative memoirs from this period by birthmothers whose own mothers are damaged and cruel, McElmurray's *Surrendered Child* and Hall, *Without a Map*. Two other birthmothers created works that set their stories beside those of people with other relations to adoption: Sheila Ganz, in her film *Unlocking the Heart of Adoption* (San Francisco: Pandora's Box Productions, 2003), also discussed by Homans, and Lynn C. Franklin, *May the Circle Be Unbroken* (Harmony, 1998).

18. Lorraine Dusky, *Hole in My Heart: A Memoir and Report from the Fault Lines of Adoption* (Sag Harbor, NY: Leto Media, 2015).

19. Margaret Moorman, *Waiting to Forget: A Memoir* (New York: Norton, 1996.)

20. Karen March, in "Denial of Self: Birthmothers, Non-disclosure Adoption Laws, and the Silence of Others," Latchford, *Adoption and Mothering*, found that birthmothers she interviewed also felt they were "living a lie" (18–19).

21. Smith and Pertman quote a 1993 study in which 93 percent of British birthmothers, ranging in age from twenty-two to eighty-one, wanted information about their adopted out children (57) and a 1996 study finding that women who felt coerced, could not talk about their experience, and had no information about their children—common circumstances in the time most of our memoirists wrote and still later—had high levels of unresolved grief (47). The authors emphasize the impact of birthmothers who advocated for change (15), referring to Schaefer among other sources (24–25).

22. Sisson, *Relinquished* 176–77. The Study is described in Foster et al., "Effects of Carrying an Unwanted Pregnancy to Term on Women's Existing Children," *Journal of Pediatrics* 205, Feb 2019, 183–89. Sisson contacted the women in this study ten years later. The article compares the subsequent lives of women who were granted abortions, women denied them who relinquished their infants, and women denied abortions who raised them. I am grateful to Professor Sisson for sending me her manuscript before publication. See also Foster, *The Turnaway Study*.

23. In 2023, Dusky published a revised and expanded version, *Hole in My Heart* (Tempe. AZ: Grand Canyon Press).

24. Glaser shows Margaret Katz making such attempts many times, and the consequences of the agency's stonewalling in her son's diabetes and his fatal "cascade of illnesses" (275).

25. Fessler found overprotectiveness common among the birthmothers she interviewed who had children (218).

26. Melosh, in *Strangers and Kin*, attempts to distance Moorman from the adoption rights movement, which Melosh sees as "esoteric" (260). But Moorman recounts calling lawmakers on behalf of a bill to open records to adoptees and notes that her view on "informed consent" is in agreement with the American Adoption Congress (209–10). The movement is not as unified as Melosh believes, so Moorman can disagree with some within it, as we see shortly, and still support reform.

27. Arthur Sorosky, Reuben Pannor, and Annette Baran, *The Adoption Triangle: The Effect of the Sealed Record on Adoptees, Birth Parents, and Adoptive Parents* (New York: Anchor, 1978), draws on interviews with birthparents and adoptees. Schaefer also writes of finding that book important (245).

28. This article appeared in *New York Magazine*, July 27, 1993.

29. Schaefer also had a negative pregnancy test after a missing period.

30. She never mentions the possible impact of the alcohol she drank during that time. The Surgeon General's warning against any alcohol during pregnancy was not issued until 1981.

31. A number of Fessler's interviewees also had difficulty in forming healthy relationships between men and rushed into bad ones because they wanted another baby. Some, on the other hand, could not stand to be around babies (214–15).

32. In "Why Reunions Go Wrong," Jane Edwards, another activist who shares the blog *[Birth Mother] First Mother* with Dusky, writes, "I have come to accept that my daughter has two families." Thanks to Jane Edwards for sending me this essay.

33. Couser, *Memoir* 44–45.

34. Rickie Solinger, *Wake Up Little Susie: Single Parenthood and Race Before* Roe v. Wade (New York: Routledge, 1992), notes that in the postwar years "the shame of illicit sex and maternity was tremendously threatening to the whole family" (9–10, see also 110 and Glaser 7).

35. Glaser explicitly makes the point on page 271 and on pages 270–76 presents arguments against open records and research that generally refutes them.

36. Rebecca Carroll, *Surviving the White Gaze: A Memoir* (New York: Simon & Schuster, 2021).

37. Fessler discusses how often women felt an overwhelming change when they held their child (179). Solinger cites a 1952 study in which 60 percent of women who earlier described themselves as certain about wanting adoption became uncertain after the baby's birth (174). According to Elizabeth Samuels, in "Adoption Consents: Legal Incentives for Best Practices," *Adoption Quarterly*, vol. 10, no. 1, 2006, those concerned about best adoption practices virtually all agree that "an expectant mother should not consent to adoption before the birth because she cannot be sure of what her feelings will be after the child is born" (90).

38. Sisson, *Relinquished*, gives those examples of the range of meaning (28, 111). She quotes and discusses interviews with women in open adoptions on pages 111–234.

39. Samuels notes the "risks of conflicts of interest when the counseling is offered or arranged by the agency or individual handling the adoption" ("Adoption Consents" 92).

40. Nicole Pietsch, "Good Mothers, Bad Mothers, Not-Mothers: Privilege, Race and Gender and the Invention of the Birthmother," Latchford, *Adoption and Mothering* 36.

41. Katherine Sieger, "A Birthmother's Identity: [M]other Living on the Border of (Non) Motherhood," Latchford, *Adoption and Mothering* 53.

42. Richard Uhrlaub and Nikki McCaslin, "Culture, Law and Language: Adversarial Motherhood in Adoption," Latchford, *Adoption and Mothering* 189–206.

43. Elizabeth J. Samuels, "Surrender and Subordination: Birth Mothers and Adoption Law Reform," *Michigan Journal of Gender and Law*, vol. 20, 2013, 33–79, shows that most birthmothers want their names available to their adopted-out children.

44. Frances J. Latchford, "Reckless Abandon: The Politics of Victimization and Agency in Birthmother Narratives," Latchford, *Adoption and Mothering* 73–87.

45. Note "the beginning," a contrast to Melosh's oversimplified statement that the "credo of the search movement" is that "reunion heals the losses of the past" (*Strangers and Kin* 249). This point is discussed further in the next chapter.

46. Samuels, "Surrender and Subordination" 60–61. These or similar statistics are cited by Dusky, *Hole in My Heart* 205; Glaser 272; and Fessler 258.

47. Janet Mason Ellerby, in *Embroidering the Scarlet A: Unwed Mothers and Illegitimate Children in American Fiction and Film* (Ann Arbor: University of Michigan Press, 2015), discusses the film on pages 235–42; on page 235, she quotes Sarah Burns, "Film Review: *Mother and Child*," *CUB Communicator* Jan.–Feb. 2011, 3. For more on this film, see Diane L. Shoos, "Birth Mothers and Adoptive Mothers Onscreen: Visibility, Iconography, and Ideology in Rodrigo Garcia's *Mother and Child*," *Adoption & Culture*, vol. 8, no. 1, 2020, 33–54.

48. See also Amy Whipple, "The Dubious Ways Parents Are Pressured to Give Up Their Children," VICE, August 13, 2019, available at https://www.vice.com/en/article/qvg45m/the-devious-ways-parents-are-pressured-to-give-up-their-children-for-adoption.

49. See also Laura Briggs, *Taking Children: A History of American Terror* (Oakland: University of California Press, 2020); Joyce; Kimberly McKee, "Adoption as a Reproductive Rights Issue," *Adoption & Culture*, vol. 6, no. 1, 2018, 74–93; Dorothy Roberts, *Shattered Bonds: The Color of Child Welfare* (New York: Basic Civitas Books, 2001); ibid., *Torn Apart: How the Child Welfare System Destroys Black Families—and How Abolition Can Build a Safer World* (New York: Basic Books, 2022); E. J. Graff, "The Lie We Love," *Foreign Policy*, November/December 2008, 59–66.

50. Kay Ann Johnson, *China's Hidden Children: Abandonment, Adoption, and the Human Costs of the One-Child Policy* (Chicago: University of Chicago Press, 2016); Xinran, *Message from an Unknown Chinese Mother: Stories of Love and Loss* (New York: Scribner, 2011).

51. For all their other disadvantages, Black Americans and Native Americans have long had the tradition of open adoption among relatives. See Carol Stack, *All Our Kin: Strategies for Survival in a Black Community* (New York: Basic Books, 1974) and Christine Ward Gailey, *Blue-Ribbon Babies and Labors of Love: Race, Class and Gender in U.S. Adoption Practice* (Austin: University of Texas Press, 2010), 79–80.

52. Kate Livingston, "The Birthmother Dilemma: Resisting Feminist Exclusions in the Study of Adoption," Latchford, *Adoption and Mothering* 63.

53. Mary Lyndon Shanley, *Making Babies, Making Families: What Matters Most in an Age of Reproductive Technologies, Surrogacy, Adoption, and Same-Sex and Unwed Parents' Rights* (Boston: Beacon, 2001), 23.

CHAPTER 2

1. Adam Pertman, *Adoption Nation: How the Adoption Revolution Is Transforming Our Families—And America*, 2nd ed. (Boston: Harvard Common Press, 2011), 143.

2. Nancy Newton Verrier, *The Primal Wound: Understanding the Adopted Child* (New York: Gateway, 1993).

3. Winterson 201.

4. Jean Paton, *Orphan Voyage* (Cedaredge, CO: Country Press, 1980), 10.

5. E. Wayne Carp, *Jean Paton and the Struggle to Reform American Adoption* (Ann Arbor: University of Michigan Press, 2014), 9–14.

6. Florence Fisher, *The Search for Anna Fisher* (New York: Arthur Fields, 1973), 15.

7. Glaser 195.

8. Carp, *Family Matters* 144; Jill R. Deans, "The Birth of Contemporary Adoption Autobiography: Florence Fisher and Betty Jean Lifton," *a/b: Auto/Biography*, vol. 18, 2003, 239–58.

9. For a more recent statement, see "National Adoption Center: Open Records," in American Academy of Pediatrics, *Pediatric Clinical Guidelines and Policies*, vol. 133, no. 6, 2014, e1808.

10. Katrina Maxtone-Graham, *An Adopted Woman: Her Search. Her Discoveries. A True Story* (New York: Remi, 1983).

11. Hipchen and Deans 167.

12. Betty Jean Lifton, *Twice Born: Memoirs of an Adopted Daughter*, 1975, 3rd ed. (New York: Other Press, 2006).

13. Jean Strauss, *Beneath a Tall Tree: A Story about Us* (Claremont, CA: Arete, 2001).

14. Emily Hipchen, *Coming Apart Together: Fragments from an Adoption* (Teaneck, NJ: Literate Chigger Press, 2005), 75.

15. Craig Hickman, *Fumbling toward Divinity: The Adoption Scriptures* (Winthrop, ME: Annabessacook Farm, 2005), 363.

16. A. M. Homes, *The Mistress's Daughter* (New York: Viking, 2007), 33.

17. Elyse Schein and Paula Bernstein, *Identical Strangers: A Memoir of Twins Separated and Reunited* (New York: Penguin, 2018).

18. Records are now open without restriction in Alabama, Alaska, Colorado, Connecticut, Hawaii, Kansas, Louisiana, Maine, Massachusetts, New Hampshire, New York, Oregon, Rhode Island, and Vermont; with restrictions related to date and/or birthparent's consent in Arkansas, Arizona, Delaware, Idaho, Illinois, Indiana, Iowa, Maryland, Michigan, Minnesota, Missouri, Montana, Nebraska, New Jersey, Ohio, Oklahoma, Pennsylvania, South Carolina, Tennessee, Utah, Washington, and Wisconsin; and sealed if the adoption is out of state in Hawaii (available at htttp://www.americanadoptioncongress .org.state.php, consulted July 12, 2023).

19. Unethical behavior by Louise Wise Services, such as allowing separation of twins and other experiments on children, providing misinformation to each participant in adoption about the other, and refusing to pass on health information, is a major theme in Glaser.

20. George Eliot, *Daniel Deronda* (1876; rpt., New York: Penguin, 1995), 186.

21. In adoptee Jan Beatty's memoir *American Bastard* (Pasadena, CA: Red Hen, 2021), she remembers, "Growing up, I liked to hit things . . . I was relentless, brutal, more competitive than anyone I knew. . . . When I found out [in my thirties] that my birthfather was a professional hockey player, it all made sense (207–8)." Beatty has held many jobs, but her longest career has been teaching creative writing; she has won many awards for her poetry.

22. Is this a need for a fiction of resemblance analogous to the need for a fiction of origin discussed by Homans (113–14)?

23. Glaser 97–102; she also writes that most of the twins in this study had "a lifelong sadness" (108).

24. Cf. Novy, *Reading Adoption* 13, and Mark Jerng, *Claiming Others: Transracial Adoption and National Belonging* (Minneapolis: University of Minnesota Press, 2010), 173, on reunions in which adoptees do *not* find the key to their lives.

25. John Triseliotis, Julia Feast, and Fiona Kyle, in "The Adoption Triangle Revisited: Summary, a Study of Adoption, Search, and Reunion Experiences," British Association for Adoption and Fostering, January 2005, found similar results: hardly any reports of damage to relationships between adoptive parents and their children after meetings with birthparents. If anything, those who were already close became closer.

26. Jean Strauss, *Birthright* (New York: Penguin, 1994), 340.

27. Joyce Maguire Pavao, in *The Family of Adoption* (Boston: Beacon Press, 1998), finds adaptability a frequent characteristic of adoptees (90).

28. William Morris, "Chimera," *American Heritage Dictionary of the English Language* (Boston: Houghton Mifflin, 1969).

29. Nola Passmore, in "Helping Adults Who Were Adopted as Children" (keynote presented at Adoption Connections Training Institute, Cambridge, MA, February 19–21, 2007), emphasizes heterogeneity among adoptees; in particular, "a well-functioning adoptive family . . . can buffer adoptees against adjustment difficulties" (2). See also Penny et al. on the divide among researchers "about whether adopted adults' psychological well-being is comparable to their nonadopted peers" (4–5), seen for example in A. L. Baden and M. Wiley, "Counseling Adopted Persons in Adulthood: Integrating Research and Practice," *Counseling Psychologist*, vol. 35, 2007, 868–901.

30. A. M. Homes, interviewed by Francine Prose and Betsy Sussler, interview, *Bomb*, September 16, 2007.

31. Betty Jean Lifton, *Journey of the Adopted Self* (New York: Basic Books, 1994), 258.

32. According to Triseliotis et al., writing of experiences in Britain, where the records are open to adopted adults, "eighty-five per cent of adopted people reported that the contact and reunion experience [with birthparents] was positive for them."

33. Penny et al. report a majority in agreement on "adopted adolescents and adults being more likely to receive counseling than their nonadopted peers" (5).

34. Falsehoods (or stonewalling) by adoption agencies and orphanages to their clients in every relation to adoption often appear in these memoirs; more appear in Glaser. Glaser notes that providers of assisted reproduction, a procedure now often undertaken by people who in earlier times might have adopted, are unregulated and may make false claims about sperm and egg donors, also (277).

35. Waldron xiii.

36. *Three Identical Strangers*, dir. Tim Wardle, CNN Films, 2018.

37. Jeremy Harding, *Mother Country: Memoir of an Adopted Boy*, 2006, updated U.S. ed. (New York: Verso, 2010).

38. Jeremy Harding, *The Uninvited: Refugees at the Rich Man's Gate* (London: Profile, 2000).

39. Lori Jakiela, *Miss New York Has Everything* (New York: 5-Spot, 2006); *The Bridge to Take When Things Get Serious: A Memoir* (Chattanooga, TN: C & R Press), 2013.

40. Lori Jakiela, *Belief Is Its Own Kind of Truth, Maybe* (Madison, NJ: Atticus, 2015), 13.

41. Richard Uhrlaub and Nikki McCaslin, in "Culture, Law and Language: Adversarial Motherhood in Adoption," Latchford, *Adoption and Mothering* 200, trace this view to Marietta Spencer, "The Terminology of Adoption," *Child Welfare*, vol. 58, no. 7, July/August 1979, 454.

42. Kate Kellaway, "Loyal Hunt of the Son," *Guardian*, March 25, 2006, 36. Available at https://www.theguardian.com/books/2006/mar/26/biography.features.

43. Lillian Rubin, *Worlds of Pain: Life in the Working-Class Family* (New York: Basic Books, 1976), 208; Jerome Kagan, *What Is Emotion?: History, Meaning and Measures* (New Haven, CT: Yale University Press, 2007), 146; Timothy Kelly and Joseph Kelly, "American

Catholics and the Discourse of Fear," in *An Emotional History of the United States*, ed. Peter N. Stearns and Jan Lewis (New York: NYU Press), 259–82.

44. Jonathan H. Turner, "Emotions and Social Stratification," in *Handbook of the Sociology of Emotions*, vol. 2, ed. Jan E. Stets and Jonathan H. Turner (New York: Springer, 2014), 186; Kagan 146–47.

45. Pauric Travers, "There Was Nothing for Me There: Irish Female Emigration, 1922–71," in *Irish Women and Irish Migration*, ed. Patrick O'Sullivan (New York: Leicester University Press, 1995), 129–50; Breda Gray, *Women and the Irish Diaspora* (New York: Routledge, 2004), 107.

46. E. Wayne Carp, "How Tight Was the Seal? A Reappraisal of Adoption Records in the United States, England, and New Zealand, 1851–1955," in *International Advances in Adoption Research for Practice*, ed. Elsbeth Neil and Gretchen Wrobel (Chichester: Wiley-Blackwell, 2009).

47. Homans 113–14.

48. John McLeod, *Life Lines: Writing Transcultural Adoption* (New York: Bloomsbury, 2015), 27.

49. However, after the Brexit vote, he wrote a short essay discussing among other things whether he could get Irish citizenship and how the category of migrant could include him as a resident of France as well as both of his first parents—either he now feels sure about the identity of his father, or his mother has told him that he was another Irish migrant (Jeremy Harding, "Short Cuts," *London Review of Books*, July 14, 2016, 31).

50. Smith and Watson 255.

51. Similarly, anthropologist Elise Prébin, in *Meeting Once More: The Korean Side of Transnational Adoption* (New York: New York University Press, 2013), writes, "I often had the impression of being 'adopted back' into my birth family . . . we were building and negotiating other kinds of ties, by choice" (180).

52. But in her next memoir, Jakiela writes, after giving him *Belief* to read, "My brother and I haven't spoken lately. It's something I'm learning to accept," *Portrait of the Artist as a Bingo Worker: On Work and the Working Life* (Huron, OH: Bottom Dog Press, 2016), 111.

53. Christine Ward Gailey, "Ideologies of Motherhood and Kinship in U.S. Adoption," in *Ideologies and Technologies of Motherhood: Race, Class, Sexuality, Nationalism*, ed. Helena Ragone and France Winddance Twine (New York: Routledge, 2000), 23.

CHAPTER 3

1. The blank slate theory of human development was developed by the seventeenth-century philosopher John Locke. According to historian Barbara Bisantz Raymond, *The Baby Thief: The Untold Story of Georgia Tann, the Baby Seller Who Corrupted Adoption* (New York: Carroll and Graf, 2007), 82, in the 1920s, Georgia Tann, executive of the Tennessee Children's Home, popularized adoption by describing babies as blank slates.

2. Kim Park Nelson, "'Loss Is More Than Sadness': Reading Dissent in Transracial Adoption Melodrama in *The Language of Blood* and *First Person Plural*," *Adoption & Culture*, vol. 1, 2007, 101.

3. Marina Fedosik, "Grafted Belongings: Identification in Autobiographical Narratives of African American Transracial Adoptees," *a/b: Auto/Biography Studies*, vol. 27, no. 1, 2012, 226.

4. Buck founded the agency Welcome House, which served and placed children of mixed heritage, in 1949. In *Children for Adoption* (1964) and other publications she wrote, ahead of her time, that parents should "teach their children the value of their heritage, . . .

confront bigotry" and "help their adopted children if they wished to search for natal rela-tives" (Ellen Herman, *Kinship by Design: A History of Adoption in the Modern United States* [Chicago: University of Chicago Press, 2008], 211). Her influence and her views, most no-tably a critique of the matching system in adoption, shaped by a more liberal Protestantism than the Holts', are discussed in Soojin Chung, *Adopting for God*, 87–117. On Korean War origins, see Eleana Kim, *Adopted Territory* (Durham, NC: Duke University Press, 2010), 43–57. SooJin Pate, in *From Orphan to Adoptee* (Minneapolis: University of Minnesota Press, 2014, 23–40), traces the origin to the earlier U.S. military occupation of South Korea.

5. Jae Ran Kim, "Scattered Seeds: The Christian Influence on Korean Adoption," in *Outsiders Within: Writing on Transracial Adoption*, ed. Jane Jeong Trenka, Julia Chinyere Oparah, and Sun Yung Shin, (Cambridge, MA: South End Press, 2006) 152–58. On the Holts, see also Joyce (47–52) and S. Chung (57–85), who stresses Bertha's role. McKee em-phasizes that Holt was just one of many agencies that were part of what she calls the "Trans-national Adoption Industrial Complex" (5).

6. Rachel Raines Winslow, in *The Best Possible Immigrants* (Philadelphia: University of Pennsylvania Press, 2017), shows the minimization of racial difference in parents' memoirs and news stories in the 1950s and '60s, 132–34. S. Chung, similarly, associates Bertha Holt's view of race with the "ideology of 'colorblindness'" (83). S. Chung (130–37) and Cynthia Callahan, "Nice White Lady: Whiteness and Domestic Transracial Adop-tion in Helen Doss's *The Family Nobody Wanted*," *Adoption & Culture*, vol. 10, no. 1, 2022, 43–63, also discuss "colorblindness" in Helen Doss, who adopted twelve children domes-tically, most multiracial, and wrote a popular book about her experience. Subsequently, in this chapter, "Chung" will refer to Nicole Chung, unless S. is added.

7. McKee, in *Disrupting Kinship*, emphasizes the "assertion of adoptee agency" (79) found in *Seeds from a Silent Tree*. Tobias Hubinette, in *Comforting an Orphan Nation: Representations of International Adoption and Adopted Koreans in Korean Popular Cul-ture* (Stockholm University, 2005), 126–43, discusses the 1991 Korean film *Susanne Brink's Arirang*, adapted from a memoir published the same year by an adopted Korean woman brought up in Sweden and other earlier texts.

8. E. Kim 114–5.

9. Kristi Brian, *Reframing Transracial Adoption: Adopted Koreans, White Parents, and the Politics of Kinship* (Philadelphia: Temple University Press, 2012), 65.

10. Heather Jacobson, *Culture Keeping: White Mothers, International Adoption, and the Negotiation of Family Difference* (Nashville: Vanderbilt University Press, 2008), 4–5. M. E. Vonk, "Cultural Competence for Transracial Adoptive Parents," *Social Work*, vol. 46, 2001, 246–55, is the source of the second quotation.

11. It was produced by Mu Films and presented by the Independent Television Service.

12. Homans, 168–69 and 179–81, notes the different blindnesses of the Korean and American siblings; David Eng, *The Feeling of Kinship: Queer Liberalism and the Racial-ization of Intimacy* (Durham, NC: Duke University Press, 2010), 111–32, makes a detailed analysis of problematic family dynamics in this film, noting the limitations of any prog-ress made.

13. See Park Nelson's discussion of its reception and context in "Reading Dissent," 108.

14. Jane Jeong Trenka, *The Language of Blood: A Memoir* (Minneapolis: Borealis, 2003), 27.

15. Jenny Heijun Wills, *Older Sister. Not Necessarily Related. A Memoir* (Toronto: Mc-Clelland and Stewart), 2019.

16. State laws against transracial adoption "were held unconstitutional or overturned" after 1967, when the Supreme Court struck down laws prohibiting interracial marriage;

see Yngvesson 27. On matching and changes in the 1960s, see Herman, *Kinship by Design*, 121–33 and 230–52.

17. However, by 1951, Pearl Buck had adopted her first partly African American child (Peter Conn, *Pearl S. Buck: A Cultural Biography* [Cambridge: Cambridge University Press, 1996], 328) and then another in 1957 (Herman, 210).

18. Herman, 212–15.

19. Jaiya John, *Black Baby White Hands: A View from the Crib* (Soul Water Rising, 2005), 27. John puts this explicitly in the context of his adoptive parents' admiration for King and shock at his assassination.

20. An earlier adoption memoir involving partly African American ancestry, *Mixed Blessing* (New York: St. Martin's Press, 1985), does not fit well into a "transracial adoption" category because Doris McMillon, the memoirist, is biracial and adopted from Germany into an African American family, where the main prejudice she has to deal with is not racism but anti-illegitimacy.

21. Jackie Kay, *The Adoption Papers* (Newcastle-upon-Tyne: Bloodaxe Books, 1991).

22. For a memoir of an even more painful Black male adoptee childhood, see Harrison Mooney, *Invisible Boy* (Lebanon, NH: Steerforth Press, 2022).

23. Waldron 129.

24. Carroll 266.

25. Lyncoya died at sixteen trying to run away.

26. Laura Briggs, *Somebody's Children: The Politics of Transracial and Transnational Adoption* (Durham, NC: Duke University Press, 2012), 72.

27. Cheri Register, *Beyond Good Intentions: A Mother Reflects on Raising Internationally Adopted Children* (St. Paul: Yeong & Yeong, 2005).

28. I have not seen Trenka making the connection explicit but allusions to this Harlow appear in writing by at least two other Korean adoptees: her Minnesota contemporary Jae Ran Kim, whose blog was called "Harlow's Monkey," and, more recently, Tiana Nobile, who quotes him several times in her book of poetry, *Cleave* (Spartanburg, SC: Hub City Press, 2021).

29. Katy Robinson, *A Single Square Picture: A Korean Adoptee's Search for Her Roots* (New York: Berkley, 2002), 36.

30. Mei-Ling Hopgood, *Lucky Girl* (Chapel Hill: Algonquin, 2010), 69.

31. On Orientalism, see Jenny Heijun Wills, "Narrating Multiculturalism in Asian American Fiction," Latchford, *Adoption and Mothering* 119–31. Unlike the novels, and families in Jacobson's research, Hopgood's memoir does not specify that the Asian presence was orchestrated by her mother. Both parents were teachers and her father was an organizer of the teachers' union.

32. Catherine McKinley, *The Book of Sarahs* (New York: Counterpoint, 2002), 9–10.

33. Jenny Heijun Wills, "Fictional and Fragmented Truths in Korean Adoptee Life Writing," *Asian American Literature: Discourses and Pedagogies*, vol. 6, 2015, 50.

34. Jackie Kay, *Red Dust Road* (London: Picador, 2010), 12.

35. Kay changed some details from her life in writing *The Adoption Papers*; aspects of the interview with a social worker, for example, come from the earlier adoption of her brother. However, the poem is autobiographical enough to be treated as a memoir. See Susanna Rustin, "A Life in Writing: Jackie Kay," *Guardian*, April 27, 2012, https://www.theguardian.com/books/2012/apr/27/life-writing-jackie-kay.

36. McLeod 215.

37. Avery Klein-Cloud and Nicole Opper, coscriptwriters, *Off and Running*, directed by Nicole Opper, ITVS International, 2009.

38. For similar incidents recounted by another transracial adoptee, see John Branch, "Kaepernick's Conscience," *New York Times*, Sports, September 10, 2017, 6; for those from the perspective of an adoptive parent, see Barbara Katz Rothman, *Weaving a Family: Untangling Race and Adoption* (Beacon, 2005), 4.

39. Susan Devan Harness, *Bitterroot: A Salish Memoir of Transracial Adoption* (Lincoln: University of Nebraska Press, 2018), 17.

40. Yngvesson discusses this issue especially with regard to adoptees from Korea and Ethiopia (154–64).

41. On the frequent tendency to see Black boys as older and less innocent than white same-age peers, see Philip Atiba Goff, Matthew Christian Jackson, Brooke Allison Lewis Di Leone, Carmen Marie Culotta, and Natalie Ann DiTomasso, "The Essence of Innocence: Consequences of Dehumanizing Black Children," *Journal of Personality and Social Psychology*, vol. 106, no. 4, 2014, 526–45.

42. Others have observed how complicated it is to belong to both these categories. In *Off and Running*, Avery experiences a split between her Black and Jewish identities as she moves from one kind of school to the other. She tries to teach her new Black friends the Jewish prayer before meals. In *The Family Flamboyant: Race Politics, Queer Families, Jewish Lives* (Albany: SUNY Press, 2006), Marla Brettschneider recalls trying to teach her two-year-old daughter to say, "I am an African-American Jewish girl," and muses on the fact that there is no Library of Congress heading for "Black Jews" or "African-American Jews," 19–20).

43. For similar experiences, see Kim Park Nelson, *Invisible Asians: Korean American Adoptees, Asian American Experiences, and Racial Exceptionalism* (New Brunswick, NJ: Rutgers University Press, 2016), 121–49, and McKee, 84–85.

44. Park Nelson, "Reading Dissent," 118.

45. In 2006, after meeting her father and writing about it, she was named Member of the British Empire, national recognition of her service. In 2016, she was named Scotland's Makar, the equivalent of poet laureate or national poet.

46. Kay was also "glued to the [*Roots*] series" but remembers its strongest appeal to her as that it showed humor "as a kind of defence against racism: you can get me down but you won't get my soul" (186). From her portrayal of her parents, it seems likely that they watched with her.

47. Interviewing in the twenty-first century as more of a Korean adoptee community exists in the United States than when these memoirists first wrote, McKee reports that after an immediate sense of kinship, Korean adoptees see their heterogeneity, and one compares their community to a "dysfunctional family" (120).

48. Homans (169–70) analyzes this memoir as presenting here "nearly womb-like contact" and the bath as "enact[ing] her rebirth."

49. Bringing birth and adoptive families together in person is less often mentioned in same-race adoptee memoirs. Perhaps the racial/national contrast can make the situation less personal or less obviously a matter of class and maybe therefore less challenging for a white family. Hickman, a Black memoirist adopted by Black parents, describes one party that includes his adoptive parents and some of his birth family; nothing like this is narrated by the other memoirists in that chapter. In some cases, death intervenes, or the difficult or hostile personality of at least one parent seems too much to overcome. Saffian, in the second edition of her memoir, writes about why she does *not* invite her birth family to her wedding—no one among her friends knows them, though she has been in contact with them for years—so they would be the focus of attention.

50. Benjamin Spock, *The Commonsense Book of Baby and Child Care*, 1946, excerpted on the Adoption History Project website, writes, "The parents should, from the begin-

ning, let the fact that he's adopted come openly, but casually, into their conversations with each other, with the child, and with their acquaintances. This creates an atmosphere in which the child can ask questions whenever he is at a stage of development where the subject interests him." His book is an all-time bestseller and had its ninth edition in 2011.

51. Jacobson (5), quoting United Nations Convention on the Rights of the Child, which has been signed but not ratified by the United States.

52. Jerng discusses Robinson's identification of nation and parent (220–22).

53. Mary C. Waters, in *Ethnic Options: Choosing Identities in America* (Berkeley: University of California Press, 1990), discusses the sense of freedom that her white subjects have about their ethnic identification. Park Nelson, *Invisible Asians*, argues that race is different and there is less choice; one subject says, "as an adoptee, you're always going to be in between; you're not Asian enough and you're not White enough," 127.

54. Jane Jeong Trenka, *Fugitive Visions: An Adoptee's Return to Korea* (Saint Paul, MN: Graywolf, 2009), 186.

55. Eng notes the family trio—Liem, her husband, and their son—that is the last image of the memoir film *First Person Plural*: "this marriage allows her to create and inhabit a compensatory nuclear family structure of her own" (132). However, most of these memoirs stress mother-daughter bonds at the end rather than the traditional nuclear family.

56. John Dovidio et al., "On the Nature of Prejudice: Automatic and Controlled Processes," *Journal of Experimental Social Psychology*, vol. 33, no. 5, Sept. 1997, 510–40.

57. Peggy McIntosh, "White Privilege: Unpacking the Invisible Knapsack," *Peace and Freedom*, July–Aug. 1988, 10–12.

58. On page 216, she argues that the conversion narrative is so important that "reunions do not seem central to John's search." His "immersion in African American culture" has helped prepare for them. However, important changes come afterward, including his name change, which he sees as part of escaping "lifelong spiritual bondage" (305), supporting Fedosik's emphasis on emancipation imagery.

59. Dorothy Roberts, *Fatal Invention: How Science, Politics, and Big Business Re-create Race in the Twenty-First Century* (Nashville: Vanderbilt University Press, 2011), 203, 255.

60. Alondra Nelson, *The Social Life of DNA: Race, Reparations and Reconciliation after the Genome* (Boston: Beacon, 2016), 164.

61. See the analysis of Michael Phillip Grand, *The Adoption Constellation: New Ways of Thinking about and Practicing Adoption* (CreateSpace, 2011), 8–21. Grand's term *adoption constellation* is a replacement for *adoption triad* or *adoption triangle*, intended to include other family members, "service providers, teachers, physicians, courts, social service workers, legislators and the clergy" and "wider cultural forces," 2–3.

62. And perhaps as an infant she already had "a gentle temperament that made the task of comforting [her] quite easy," according to Grand's explanation of the active role that the infant plays in attachment (79). This may have been true of others discussed here as well.

63. The "lucky adoptee" trope appears more often in transracial than in same-race adoption memoirs, but her birthmother's rejection elicits it in Jakiela's, and Hickman recalls his mother using it.

64. Jenny Heijun Wills, in "Fictional and Fragmented Truths in Korean Adoptee Life Writing" (58), sees this as one among many of Trenka's fictionalizations. The imagined advice is part of a widespread evangelical movement, perhaps even larger now, to encourage the adoption of orphans, especially from overseas. See Joyce 39–74 and passim.

65. See also Melissa Fay Greene, "The Family Mobile," *New York Times Sunday Magazine*, August 31, 2001, 35: adoptive parents of all faiths say that the children they are

rearing "were meant to be theirs." Cf. the analysis of anthropologist Yngvesson: "Each adoption points to the contingencies of birth, to the arbitrariness of choice (which family, which nation), and to the fact that any adopted child could have had a different story: there is no 'meant to be' in adoption stories" (147). This book is a thoughtful analysis of the experience of adoptees in Sweden, where they are virtually all transracial and transnational.

66. See the discussion of the Holts and Buck in *Adopting for God*, mentioned near the beginning of this chapter.

67. Register, *Beyond* 104–6.

68. Raleigh 34.

69. Joyce; Graff 59–66; Gailey, *Blue-Ribbon Babies*. On December 18, 2019, the UN General Assembly in New York adopted the Resolution on the Rights of the Child, which signifies a major milestone in ending the institutional care of children globally. By adopting the resolution, all of the 193 member states of the United Nations have agreed, for the first time in history, that orphanages harm children and, recognizing that the vast majority of children in orphanages have living family, all children should be reunited with or supported to remain with their families. Where that's not possible, the resolution says that governments should commit to provide high-quality family and community-based alternative care for children.

70. Gailey, *Blue-Ribbon Babies* 107; Joyce.

71. McKee, *Disrupting Kinship*, 2019. Raleigh, in *Selling Transracial Adoption*, shows through analyses of many interviews by social workers how much adoption "is an industry" (3).

72. H. D. Grotevant et al, "Many Faces of Openness in Adoption," *Adoption Quarterly*, vol. 10, nos. 3–4, 2008, 79–101. Carroll does not feel this is the case with her—although she wishes that she could have known her birthfather longer. The adoptions Grotevant researched were open from a much earlier age than was hers.

73. See also quotations from adoptive parents of children from China in Seligmann 88.

74. Angela Tucker, *"You Should Be Grateful": Stories of Race, Identity, and Transracial Adoption* (Boston: Beacon Press, 2022).

CHAPTER 4

1. Winslow 122, 125, 140. See also Callahan, "Nice White Lady."

2. Melosh, "Adoption Stories," 241n1.

3. Melosh, in *Strangers and Kin*, discusses Loux's and Dorris's memoirs of special needs adoption on pages 265–67 and open adoption on pages 275–85, with a quotation from Wolff's memoir on page 280.

4. The recorded figures from the National Council for Adoption for 2020 are 95,306 domestic adoptions, 19,658 of them non-stepparent private adoptions—close to one-fifth. Private adoptions are the most likely to be of infants, but many infant adoption are unrecorded. The U.S. government no longer gathers statistics on adoption.

5. Theresa Reid, *Two Little Girls* (New York: Berkley, 2006).

6. Ralph Savarese, *Reasonable People: A Memoir of Autism and Adoption* (New York: Other, 2007).

7. Savarese, xxvii, 80, 7.

8. Larissa MacFarquhar, *Strangers Drowning* (New York: Penguin, 2015), 3.

9. E. Douglas Bates, *Gift Children: A Story of Race, Family, and Adoption in a Divided America* (New York: Ticknor & Fields, 1993); E. Kay Trimberger, *Creole Son: An Adoptive*

Mother Untangles Nature & Nurture (Baton Rouge: Louisiana State University Press, 2020); Jana Wolff, *Secret Thoughts of an Adoptive Mother* (New York: Andrews McMeel, 1997); Sharon Rush, *Loving across the Color Line: A White Adoptive Mother Learns about Race* (New York: Rowman & Littlefield, 2000).

10. Even Randall Kennedy, who thinks, in *Interracial Intimacies: Sex, Marriage, Identity, and Adoption* (New York: Viking, 2003), that Wolff and Rush rely on racism too much as an explanation for any problems they have, finds Bates and his wife "appallingly ignorant about white racism" (463, 567).

11. Researching at the beginning of the twenty-first century, at least thirty years later than Bates's adoption, Kristi Brian finds the education on racism given by one adoption agency placing children from Asia still woefully inadequate (42). Parents were anxious about openness in adoption based on what they had heard from social workers fifteen years earlier and had no idea of recent changes in professionals' approaches to adoption (120).

12. Cheri Register, *Are Those Kids Yours?: American Families with Children Adopted from Other Countries* (Free Press, 1990), calls this "seemingly benign racism" (159).

13. Rush 39.

14. Laura Briggs, in *Somebody's Children*, quotes an example of the policy of preference for heterosexual couples from the Massachusetts Department of Social Services (248).

15. Linda Seligmann, in *Broken Links, Enduring Ties*, writes, "Almost all the AA adoptive parents [adoptive parents of African American children] I spoke with considered race of far more urgent concern than adoption" (168).

16. Jana Wolff, "The First Thirteen," in *A Love Like No Other*, ed. Pamela Kruger and Jill Smolowe (New York: Riverhead, 2005), 107.

17. Jana Wolff, "Black Unlike Me," *New York Times Magazine*, February 14, 1999, 78.

18. Seligmann notes the increasing trend toward openness and quotes from interviews with several families who adopted African American children about their continuing relationship with birthparents (146–52).

19. In "The First Thirteen," Wolff writes about how her son is gaining independence, has a more direct relationship with Martie, and is different from her and her husband in ways that might come not from heredity but, alternatively, from adoption itself.

20. He is called Marco throughout *Creole Son*, but he uses "Marc" in the credit line of the afterword. This is the only time it appears in the book in combination with his last name; perhaps he is still using Marco and wants to avoid this book showing up in web searches when he applies for jobs. Or maybe he just prefers Marc. I will use Marco to describe him as portrayed in the book.

21. Trimberger's book has been particularly subject to the critique that she should have let her son tell his own story instead of telling it for him, but this does not seem to be the way he wants to exercise his agency. As the previous note suggests, it might sometimes be a disadvantage to him for other people to know his story. Dorris and Loux, who also extend the story past teenage years, deal with this potential problem by giving their children pseudonyms.

22. In this way, Trimberger's memoir resembles Michael Dorris's, discussed in the next section of this chapter, which, as Couser notes, also "involves a shift from confidence in nurture to belief in nature" (440), though Dorris believes the diseased nature was the result of bad prenatal nurture. This move is part of a larger cultural shift in ideas about child development, exemplified influentially by Steven Pinker's critique *The Blank Slate: The Modern Denial of Human Nature* (Harvard, 2002).

23. However, he did not become a victim of the violence of the drug culture; Trimberger attributes this partly to his inherited nonviolent temperament, partly to the stability of her household after he was four, and partly to luck (114).

24. She acknowledges that she did not research adoption at all beforehand, let alone transracial adoption (7). Her more recent research includes Sandra Patton's *Birth Marks* (2000), Randall Kennedy's *Interracial Intimacies*, and the memoirs of Jackie Kay and Jane Jeong Trenka.

25. Kennedy believes that Rush and Wolff attribute racism to events that have other explanations, but they are more credible than his interpretation, which sounds like that of Jaiya John's father when he says, "People stare at me all the time because of my beard" (180).

26. Seligmann 169.

27. Ann Kimble Loux, *The Limits of Hope* (Charlottesville: University of Virginia Press, 1997), 28.

28. Michael Dorris, *The Broken Cord* (New York: Harper & Row, 1989), 76.

29. Dawn's indiscriminate friendliness could be a symptom of reactive attachment disorder, owing to early neglect (see Seligmann 130), and that is how Loux comes to see it until Dawn's child, Billy Ray, is diagnosed with Williams syndrome, which also has indiscriminate friendliness as a symptom (240).

30. Briggs, *Taking Children* 117.

31. Analyzing problems with Dorris's book, Briggs, in *Somebody's Children* (106–7), cites data to show that his claims about the percentage of American Indian children harmed by maternal drinking are hyperboles and ignore the implications of 1994 research in Arizona showing that developmental delays of most of the children diagnosed with FAS could be explained by their Down's syndrome or other genetic disorders. In *Taking Children*, she sees Adam's teenage mother, dead a few years after his birth from alcohol poisoning, as herself a "hurting child" (119).

32. G. Thomas Couser, "Raising Adam: Ethnicity, Disability and the Ethics of Life Writing in Michael Dorris's *The Broken Cord*," *Biography*, vol. 21, no. 4, Fall 1998, 424.

33. In an op-ed after her book's publication, again asking for more help with such parenting, "The Catch That Came with Our Adoption," *Washington Post*, November 23, 1997, she writes that "some continued contact with their mother might have allowed [them] to see us both as real, complex people."

34. *Deej*, directed by Robert Rooy (2017). DJ was a producer and wrote the text.

35. Gailey, *Blue Ribbon Babies* 75.

36. Briggs, in *Somebody's Children*, discusses this practice with regard to lesbians and gay men (256).

37. Briggs argues that "queer folk are invited to provide a safety valve to states in their decades-long wars on impoverished people and communities of color and their ability to raise their own children" (*Somebody's Children* 268).

38. Jesse Green, *The Velveteen Father* (New York: Villard, 1999), 124.

39. Ellen Lewin, in *Gay Fatherhood* (University of Chicago Press, 2009), discusses other writers on this topic and attributes the term *homonormativity* to Lisa Duggan (6–11).

40. Lewin treats the legal ability to adopt as a sign of citizenship and does not see this as problematic. Eng does see it as problematic that "the possession of a child, whether biological or adopted, has today become the sign of guarantee both for family and for full and robust citizenship" (101). Stephen Engel, in *Fragmented Citizens The Changing Landscape of Lesbian and Gay Lives* (New York: NYU Press, 2016), on the other hand, argues that gay and lesbian people experience a mix of recognition and nonrecognition, depending on the issue and the location.

41. Margery Williams, *The Velveteen Rabbit* (1921; rpt., Running Press, 1998).

42. This objectification was not inevitable among gay people at the time: Briggs quotes from a small-circulation lesbian magazine, *Mom's Apple Pie*, to show that the queer community in the early 1990s *did* include some recognition of the pain of birthmothers, the social and political issues that would make it difficult for them to raise their children, and the need for adoptive parents and their kids to be involved in the children's culture of origin (*Somebody's Children* 256–58).

43. Ironically, Marla Brettschneider, in *The Family Flamboyant*, writes that "many Jews adopt Latinx children because they want their children to 'look like' them" (56). Six years later, in the chapter "The Holiday Hallmark Forgot," in *A Love like No Other*, ed. Pamela Kruger and Jill Smolowe (New York: Riverhead, 2005), Green associates insisting that his kids learn Spanish with nurturing "separateness and a sense of injury" (151). Green's desire for acceptance seems parallel to his distancing his children from *Latinidad*, but he hopes to be bonded with them as Jews.

44. Van R. Newkirk II, "Trump's White-Nationalist Pipeline," *Atlantic*, August 23, 2018.

45. For years, Green has been a drama critic for the *New York Times*, now the main one. He has respected his children's privacy by never mentioning them in his reviews, but I wonder if the greater Latino presence in the theater today has changed his attitude. Or has he contributed to the greater Latino presence by the plays he has reviewed?

46. I have referred to this view in discussing several memoirs by adoptees.

47. Melissa Fay Greene, *No Biking in the House without a Helmet* (New York: Farrar, Straus and Giroux, 2012), 35.

48. Joyce, *Child Catchers* 133. Many people in developing nations, Joyce writes, do not understand adoption as a permanent transfer of parental rights, but as a temporary move for education.

49. Barbara Yngvesson, in *Belonging*, quotes and discusses four transnational *adoptees*, three raised in Sweden and one in the United States, who send money to birthparents in Korea, Ethiopia, and Colombia (162–68). However, when the request for money is made by the Vietnamese birth family in the film *Daughter from Danang* the adoptee finds this very distressing.

50. Homans 57.

51. Claude Knobler, *More Love, Less Panic: 7 Lessons I Learned about Life, Love, and Parenting after We Adopted Our Son from Ethiopia* (New York: Penguin, 2014), 22–23.

52. Heather Jacobson, in *Culture Keeping*, found that "Russia-adoptive mothers work to ensure that their children have at least a superficial understanding—at an age appropriate level—of the larger social context of abandonment and relinquishment of children in Russia" (80). Reid does not seem to go this far, but possibly that is because of the age of her children at the close of the memoir.

53. Seligmann's interviewees who had adopted from Russia had an average household income of $205,800 at the time of adoption, in the early 2000s; the average household income of those who had adopted from China was $110, 853 and of those who had adopted African American children, $92,000 (17).

54. Reid resembles the business/professional adopters whom Gailey, in her research for *Blue-Ribbon Babies*, finds more narcissistic, showing "emotional distance from children if they did not fulfill parental images of what they should be like" (132–33).

55. On indiscriminate friendliness in children adopted from orphanages in Russia, see Seligmann 130. Claudia Sadowski-Smith, *The New Immigrant Whiteness* (NYU Press, 2018), critiques the lack of contextualization of this diagnosis in Reid and elsewhere.

56. Heather Jacobson, in *Culture Keeping* (157–59), and Seligmann, in *Broken Links* (115), discuss parents choosing Russian adoption for privacy but do not mention parents admitting they want to deny their adoptive status to themselves.

57. Claudia Sadowski-Smith comments on the irony of her initial disappointment at being given a blonde girl rather than one with "big dark eyes and curly dark hair," though "no one in either of our families fits this description" (27).

58. At least one third of the parents Seligmann interviewed who adopted from Russia had a previous link with the country, through ancestry, study, or travel (117).

59. The blonde hair in the first photo they see makes her think of "the anonymous hordes who persecuted Europe's Jews" (28).

60. Emily Prager, *Wuhu Diary: On Taking My Adopted Daughter Back to Her Homeland in China* (New York: Random, 2001), 4.

61. Jeanne Marie Laskas, *Growing Girls: The Mother of all Adventures* (New York: Bantam, 2006), 5.

62. Jeanne Marie Laskas, *The Exact Same Moon: Fifty Acres and a Family* (New York: Random House, 2003), 155.

63. Prager's previous experience in China was unusual among the adoptive parents Seligmann studied, though not unprecedented, 91–92. There were others in Jacobson's sample, 43.

64. Seligmann, similarly, quotes an interviewee who remembers the notary at her daughter's adoption ceremony saying to her and her husband that now, they were "members of a Chinese family" (101). The government "explicitly desires that children who are adopted by foreigners learn about and take pride in their cultural heritage."

65. Seligmann (102–4) quotes Laskas on children's rejection of Chinese cultural materials and finds many children making a similar rejection at age seven or eight.

66. Margaret Homans, in *Imprint of Another Life*, writes about how Prager creates a "complex tissue of fictions" (159) for her daughter and shows in many other cases as well that writing about searches for birthparents almost inevitably involves creating fictions. Prager's storytelling here recalls that of Jackie Kay's mother, discussed in the previous chapter.

67. This preoccupation is also found in Lori Jakiela's memoir. Could it be relevant that both grew up Catholic and, perhaps, like the birthmother Marie that Jakiela imagines, were affected by the image of the idealized Blessed Mother that, in different ways, they could not live up to?

68. Seligmann says the "orderliness and predictability" of the process in China appealed to many adoptive parents (88).

69. Her research is in *Wanting a Daughter, Needing a Son* (St. Paul, MN: Yeong and Yeong, 2004) and *China's Hidden Children*. The year the second book was published, China changed the child limit from one to two.

70. Jeff Gammage, *China Ghosts* (New York: HarperCollins, 2007), 238. Jacobson finds other cases where "the distance from birth mothers that participants reported as so attractive during the adoption process was actually mourned by some once their families were established" (36); the parent she quotes also adopted from China.

71. Jacobson found that "mothers with children from China expressed unease about their role in separating their children from China and in the resulting loss or pain that they imagine their children will experience" (78), while mothers who adopt from Russia instead focus on the loss of the birthmother (79).

72. Melosh, "Adoption Stories" 221. Winslow calculates that "30 percent of the thirteen memoirs [about international adoption] written in this era ['50s and '60s] came from

fathers" (129). In this chapter, two of the six memoirs about international adoption, those by Knobler and Gammage, come from fathers, a similar percentage, though I do not claim to be exhaustive in my selection of memoirs to discuss. Both of them emphasize that they agreed to adopt because of their wives' strong desire.

73. Latchford, *Adoption and Mothering*.

74. As Couser notes, this narrative shows that "Adam does not perceive himself as deprived and thus does not suffer the way his parents do" (436).

75. Register's first book about adoption, *Are Those Kids Yours?: American Families with Children Adopted from Other Countries*, was written in 1991, when her children were about fifteen years younger, and has more autobiographical vignettes as well as anecdotes that quote other parents of relatively young children.

76. Greene, "Family Mobile," 35. See Winslow on religious language in adoptive parents' memoirs and new articles from the 1950s and '60s (130).

77. Pertman 61–63; Grotevant et al. 79–101; Siegel, Deborah H., and Susan L. Smith, "Openness in Adoption: From Secrecy and Stigma to Knowledge and Connections," Donaldson Adoption Institute, 2012. Available at https://njarch.org/wpress/wpcontent/uploads/2015/11/2012_03_OpennessInAdoption.pdf.

78. James L. Gritter, *Hospitious Adoption* (Arlington, VA: CWLA Press, 2009); Michael Philip Grand, in *The Adoption Constellation: New Ways of Thinking about and Practicing Adoption* (CreateSpace, 2011), discusses adopting a parent and child together as an alternative to current adoption practices (144–47).

79. Grand, in *The Adoption Constellation* 142–44.

80. Deborah A. Siegel, "Open Adoption: Adoptive Parents' Reactions Two Decades Later," *Social Work*, vol. 58, no. 1, 2013, 43–52. Thanks to Joanna Mittereder for this reference and also the one to the National Council for Adoption poll.

81. Andrew Solomon, *Far from the Tree: Parents, Children, and the Search for Identity*, (New York: Scribner, 2012).

82. Roberts, *Shattered Bonds*; ibid., *Torn Apart* 202; Joyce.

83. Sara Dorow, *Transnational Adoption* (New York: NYU Press, 2016), 3.

CONCLUDING THOUGHTS

1. Samuel Alito et al., *Dobbs v. Jackson Women's Health Organization*, U.S. Supreme Court, no. 19–1392, October Term 2021, June 24, 2022. www.supremecourt.gov/opinions/21pdf/19-1392_6j37.pdf, 24.

2. Diana Greene Foster, et al., "Effects of Carrying an Unwanted Pregnancy to Term on Women's Existing Children," *Journal of Pediatrics* 205, February 2019, 183–89.

3. Gretchen Sisson, "Who Are the Women Who Relinquish Infants for Adoption: Domestic Adoption and Contemporary Birth Motherhood in the United States," *Perspectives on Sexual and Reproductive Health*, vol. 54, no. 2, 2022, 45–53; this conclusion is also in *Relinquished* 33.

4. Tucker 166.

5. Melosh, *Kinship with Strangers* 2.

6. This point was made earlier by Barbara Katz Rothman, *Weaving a Family: Untangling Race and Adoption* (Boston: Beacon Press, 2005), 17.

7. For example, Robert Dessaix, *A Mother's Disgrace* (Australia: HarperCollins, 1994); Myrl Coulter, *The House with the Broken Two: A Birthmother Remembers* (Vancouver: Anvil Press, 2011).

8. Gonda van Steen, *Adoption, Memory and Cold War Greece* (Ann Arbor: University of Michigan Press, 2019); Rita Arditti, *Searching for Life: The Grandmothers of the Plaza de Mayo and the Disappeared Children of Argentina* (Berkeley: University of California Press, 1999).

9. A few references: Margaret Jacobs, *A Generation Removed: The Fostering and Adoption of Indigenous Children in the Post-War World* (Lincoln: University of Nebraska Press, 2014); James Smith, *Ireland's Magdalene Laundries and the Nation's Architecture of Containment* (South Bend, IN: University of Notre Dame Press, 2007).

10. The United States is among the lowest of developed countries in federal spending for family benefits, childcare, and early childhood education yet has above average childcare fees as a percentage of average earnings, and it has much less generous parental leave than other such countries (Sisson 256).

11. Kathryn A. Mariner, *Contingent Kinship: The Flows and Futures of Adoption in the United States* (Oakland: University of California Press, 2019), 198.

Works Cited

MEMOIRS AND FICTION

Bates, E. Douglas. *Gift Children: A Story of Race, Family, and Adoption in a Divided America*. New York: Ticknor & Fields, 1993.

Beatty, Jan. *American Bastard: A Memoir*. Pasadena, CA: Red Hen Press, 2021.

Borshay Liem, Deann, director. *First Person Plural*. Center for Asian American Media, Mu Films, 2000.

Carroll, Rebecca Ann. *Surviving the White Gaze: A Memoir*. New York: Simon & Schuster, 2021.

Chung, Nicole. *All You Can Ever Know*. New York: Catapult, 2018.

Coulter, Myrl. *The House with the Broken Two: A Birthmother Remembers*. Vancouver: Anvil Press, 2011.

Dessaix, Robert. *A Mother's Disgrace*. Australia: Harper Collins, 1994.

Dorris, Michael. *The Broken Cord: A Family's Ongoing Struggle with Fetal Alcohol Syndrome*. New York: Harper & Row, 1989.

Doss, Helen. *The Family Nobody Wanted*. 1954; rpt Boston: Northeastern University Press, 2001.

Dusky, Lorraine. *Birthmark*. New York: M. Evans, 1979.

——. *hole in my heart: A memoir and report from the fault lines of adoption* (author's choice of lowercase). Sag Harbor, NY: Leto Media, 2015.

——. *Hole in My Heart: Love and Loss in the Fault Lines of Adoption*, 2nd ed. Tempe, AZ: Grand Canyon Press, 2022.

Eliot, George. *Daniel Deronda*. 1876. New York: Penguin, 1995.

Ellerby, Janet Mason. *Following the Tambourine Man: A Birthmother's Memoir*. Syracuse University Press, 2007.

Fisher, Florence. *The Search for Anna Fisher*. New York: Arthur Fields, 1973.

Gammage, Jeff. *China Ghosts: My Daughter's Journey to America, My Passage to Fatherhood*. New York: HarperCollins, 2007.

Ganz, Sheila, filmmaker. *Unlocking the Heart of Adoption*. San Francisco: Pandora's Box Productions, 2003.

Green, Jesse. *The Velveteen Father: An Unexpected Journey to Parenthood*. New York: Villard, 1999.

Greene, Melissa Fay. *No Biking in the House without a Helmet: 9 Kids, 3 Continents, 2 Parents, 1 Family*. New York: Farrar, Straus and Giroux, 2012.

Hall, Meredith. *Without a Map: A Memoir*. Boston: Beacon Press, 2007.

Harding, Jeremy. *Mother Country: Memoir of an Adopted Boy*. 2006. Updated U.S. edition. New York: Verso, 2010.

Harness, Susan Devan. *Bitterroot: A Salish Memoir of Transracial Adoption*. Lincoln: University of Nebraska Press, 2018.

Hickman, Craig. *Fumbling toward Divinity: The Adoption Scriptures*. Winthrop, ME: Annabessacook Farm, 2005.

Hipchen, Emily. *Coming Apart Together: Fragments from an Adoption*. Teaneck, NJ: Literate Chigger Press, 2005.

Homes, A. M. *The Mistress's Daughter*. New York: Viking, 2007.

Hopgood, Mei-Ling. *Lucky Girl*. Chapel Hill, NC: Algonquin, 2010.

Jakiela, Lori. *Belief is its own kind of truth, Maybe* (author's capitalization preference). Madison, NJ: Atticus, 2015.

———. *The Bridge to Take When Things Get Serious*. Chattanooga, TN: C & R Press, 2013.

———. *Miss New York Has Everything*. New York: 5-Spot, 2006.

———. *Portrait of the Artist as a Bingo Worker*. Huron, OH: Bottom Dog Press, 2017.

John, Jaiya. *Black Baby White Hands: A View from the Crib*. Soul Water Rising, 2005.

Kay, Jackie. *The Adoption Papers*. Newcastle-upon-Tyne: Bloodaxe Press, 1991.

———. *Red Dust Road*. London: Picador, 2010.

Klein-Cloud, Avery, and Nicole Opper, coscriptwriters. *Off and Running*. Directed by Nicole Opper, ITVS International, 2009.

Knobler, Claude. *More Love (Less Panic): 7 Lessons I Learned about Life, Love, and Parenting after We Adopted Our Son from Ethiopia*. New York: Penguin, 2014.

Kruger, Pamela, and Jill Smolowe, eds. *A Love Like No Other: Stories from Adoptive Parents*. New York: Riverhead, 2005.

Laskas, Jeanne Marie. *The Exact Same Moon: Fifty Acres and a Family*. New York: Random House, 2003.

———. *Growing Girls: The Mother of All Adventures*. New York: Bantam, 2006.

Lifton, Betty Jean. *Twice Born: Memoirs of an Adopted Daughter*. 1975. 3rd ed., New York: Other Press, 2006.

Loux, Ann Kimble. *The Limits of Hope: An Adoptive Mother's Story*. Charlottesville: University of Virginia Press, 1997.

Marin, David. *This Is US: The New All-American Family*. Exterminating Angel Press, 2011.

Maxtone-Graham, Katrina. *An Adopted Woman. Her Search. Her Discoveries. Her Story*. New York: Remi, 1983.

McElmurray, Karen Salyer. *Surrendered Child: A Birth Mother's Journey*. Athens: University of Georgia Press, 2004.

McKinley, Catherine. *The Book of Sarahs*. New York: Counterpoint, 2002.

McMillon, Doris, with Michele Sherman. *Mixed Blessing*. New York: St. Martin's Press, 1985.

Melanson, Yvette, with Claire Safran. *Looking for Lost Bird: A Jewish Woman Discovers Her Navajo Roots*. New York: Bard, 1999.

Mooney, Harrison. *Invisible Boy*. Lebanon, NH: Steerforth Press, 2022.

Moorman, Margaret. *Waiting to Forget: A Memoir*. New York: Norton, 1996.

Nobile, Tiana. *Cleave*. Spartanburg, SC: Hub City Press, 2021.

Paton, Jean. *Orphan Voyage*. Cedaredge, CO: Country Press, 1980.

Prager, Emily. *A Visit from the Footbinder*. New York: Simon & Schuster, 1982.

———. *Wuhu Diary: On Taking My Adopted Daughter Back to Her Homeland in China*. New York: Random House, 2001.

Reid, Theresa. *Two Little Girls: A Memoir of Adoption*. New York: Berkley, 2006.

Robinson, Katy. *A Single Square Picture: A Korean Adoptee's Search for Her Roots*. New York: Berkley, 2002.

Rush, Sharon. *Loving across the Color Line: A White Adoptive Mother Learns about Race*. New York: Rowman & Littlefield, 2000.

Saffian, Sarah. *Ithaka: A Daughter's Memoir of Being Found*. 1998. New York: Delta, 2006.

Savarese, Ralph. *Reasonable People: A Memoir of Autism and Adoption*. New York: Other Press, 2007.

Schaefer, Carol. *The Other Mother: A Woman's Love for the Child She Gave Up for Adoption*. New York: Soho Press, 1991.

Schein, Elyse, and Paula Bernstein. *Identical Strangers: A Memoir of Twins Separated and Reunited*. New York: Penguin, 2018.

Seek, Amy. *God and Jetfire: Confessions of a Birth Mother*. New York: Farrar, Straus and Giroux, 2015.

Shapiro, Dani. *Inheritance: A Memoir of Genealogy, Paternity, and Love*. Knopf, 2019.

Strauss, Jean. *Beneath a Tall Tree: A Story about Us*. Claremont, CA: Arete, 2001.

Thompson, Jean [pseud.]. *The House of Tomorrow*. New York: Harper & Row, 1967.

Trenka, Jane Jeong. *Fugitive Visions: An Adoptee's Return to Korea*. Saint Paul, MN: Graywolf Press, 2009.

———. *The Language of Blood: A Memoir*. Minneapolis: Borealis, 2003.

Trimberger, E. Kay. *Creole Son: An Adoptive Mother Untangles Nature & Nurture*. Baton Rouge: Louisiana State University Press, 2020.

Waldron, Jan. *Giving Away Simone: A Memoir*. New York: Random House, 1995.

Ward, Andrew. *The Birth Father's Tale*. London: British Association for Adoption and Fostering, 2012.

Wills, Jenny Heijun. *Older Sister. Not Necessarily Related: A Memoir*. Toronto: McClelland and Stewart, 2019.

Winterson, Jeanette. *Oranges Are Not the Only Fruit*. 1985. New York: Atlantic Monthly, 1987.

———. *Why Be Happy When You Could Be Normal?* New York: Grove, 2011.

Wolff, Jana. *Secret Thoughts of an Adoptive Mother*. New York: Andrews McMeel, 1997.

OTHER

American Adoption Congress. https//www.americanadoptioncongress.org/state.php.

Andrews, Valerie A. "'Unwed Mother': Sex, Stigma, and Spoiled Identity." *Adoption & Culture*, vol. 8, no. 2, 2020, 133–49.

Arditti, Rita. *Searching for Life: The Grandmothers of the Plaza de Mayo and the Disappeared Children of Argentina*. Berkeley: University of California Press, 1999.

Baden, Amanda L., and M. O'Leary Wiley, "Counseling Adopted Persons in Adulthood: Integrating Research and Practice." *Counseling Psychologist*, vol. 35, 2007, 868–901.

Branch, John. "Kaepernick's Conscience." *New York Times*, Sports, 10 Sept., 2017, 6.

Brettschneider, Marla. *The Family Flamboyant: Race Politics, Queer Families, Jewish Lives*. Albany: SUNY Press, 2006.

Brian, Kristi. *Reframing Transracial Adoption: Adopted Koreans, White Parents, and the Politics of Kinship.* Philadelphia: Temple University Press, 2012.

Briggs, Laura, "Making 'American' Families: Transnational Adoption and US Latin American Policy." *Haunted by Empire: Geographies of Intimacy in North American History,* edited by Ann Laura Stoler, Durham, NC: Duke University Press, 2006, 344–65.

———. *Somebody's Children: The Politics of Transracial and Transnational Adoption.* Durham, NC: Duke University Press, 2012.

———. *Taking Children: A History of American Terror.* Oakland: University of California Press, 2020.

Brodzinsky, David M., Marshall D. Schechter, and Robin Marantz Henig. *Being Adopted: The Lifelong Search for Self.* New York: Anchor, 1993.

Buck, Pearl S. *Children for Adoption.* New York: Random House, 1964.

———. "I Am the Better Woman from Having My Two Black Children." *Today's Health,* 5, Jan. 1972, 20–21.

Burns, Sarah. Review of *Mother and Child, CUB Communicator,* Jan–Feb. 2011, 3.

Callahan, Cynthia. "Nice White Lady: Whiteness and Domestic Transracial Adoption in Helen Doss's *The Family Nobody Wanted.*" *Adoption & Culture,* vol. 10, no. 1, 2022, 43–63.

Carp, E. Wayne. *Family Matters: Secrecy and Disclosure in the History of Adoption.* Harvard University Press, 1998.

———. "How Tight Was the Seal? A Reappraisal of Adoption Records in the United States, England, and New Zealand, 1851–1955." *International Advances in Adoption Research for Practice,* edited by Elsbeth Neil and Gretchen Wrobel, Chichester: Wiley Blackwell, 2009, 17–39.

———. *Jean Paton and the Struggle to Reform American Adoption.* Ann Arbor: University of Michigan Press, 2014.

Chung, Soojin. *Adopting for God: The Mission to Change America through Transnational Adoption.* New York: NYU Press, 2019.

Clark, Danae. "Mediadoption: Children, Commodification and the Spectacle of Disruption." *American Studies,* vol. 39, no. 2, Summer 1998, 65–86.

Conn, Peter. *Pearl S. Buck: A Cultural Biography.* Cambridge: Cambridge University Press, 1996.

Couser, G. Thomas. *Memoir: An Introduction.* New York: Oxford University Press, 2012.

———. "Raising Adam: Ethnicity, Disability, and the Ethics of Life Writing in Michael Dorris's *The Broken Cord.*" *Biography,* vol. 21, no. 4, Fall 1998, 421–44.

Deans, Jill R. "The Birth of Contemporary Adoption Autobiography: Florence Fisher and Betty Jean Lifton." *a/b: Auto/Biography Studies,* vol. 18, 2003, 239–58.

Dorow, Sara. *Transnational Adoption: A Cultural Economy of Race, Gender, and Kinship.* New York: NYU Press, 2016.

Dovidio, John, et al. "On the Nature of Prejudice: Automatic and Controlled Processes." *Journal of Experimental Social Psychology,* vol. 33, no. 5, Sept. 1997, 510–40.

Edwards, Jane Elizabeth. "Why Reunions Go Wrong, What Memoirs of Adopted Daughters Tell Mothers." October 2007. Published in *First Mother Forum* (2009) as "Why Reunions Go Awry, What Memoirs of Adopted Daughters Tell Mothers."

Ellerby, Janet Mason. *Embroidering the Scarlet A: Unwed Mothers and Illegitimate Children in American Fiction and Film.* Ann Arbor: University of Michigan Press, 2015.

Eng, David. *The Feeling of Kinship: Queer Liberalism and the Racialization of Intimacy.* Durham, NC: Duke University Press, 2010.

Engel, Stephen. *Fragmented Citizens: The Changing Landscape of Lesbian and Gay Lives.* NYU Press, 2016.

Fedosik, Marina. "Grafted Belongings: Identification in Autobiographical Narratives of African American Transracial Adoptees." *a/b: Auto/Biography Studies,* vol. 27, no. 1, 2012, 211–30.

Fessler, Ann. *The Girls Who Went Away: The Hidden History of Women Who Surrendered Children for Adoption in the Decades Before* Roe v. Wade. New York: Penguin, 2006.

FitzGerald, Frances. *The Evangelicals: The Struggle to Shape America.* New York: Simon & Schuster, 2017.

Foster, Diana Greene. *The Turnaway Study: Ten Years, a Thousand Women, and the Consequences of Having—Or Being Denied—An Abortion.* New York: Scribner's, 2020.

Foster, Diana Greene, et al. "Effects of Carrying an Unwanted Pregnancy to Term on Women's Existing Children." *Journal of Pediatrics,* vol. 205, Feb 2019, 183–89.

Franklin, Lynn, with Elizabeth Ferber. *May the Circle Be Unbroken: An Intimate Journey into the Heart of Adoption.* New York: Harmony, 1998.

Friedman, Susan Stanford. "Women's Autobiographical Selves: Theory and Practice." *Women, Autobiography, Theory: A Reader,* edited by Sidonie Smith & Julia Watson. Madison: University of Wisconsin Press, 1998, 72–82.

Gailey, Christine Ward. *Blue-Ribbon Babies and Labors of Love: Race, Class, and Gender in U.S. Adoption Practice.* Austin: University of Texas Press, 2010.

——. "Ideologies of Motherhood and Kinship in US Adoptees." In *Ideologies and Technologies of Motherhood: Race, Class, Sexuality, Nationalism,* edited by Helena Ragoné and France Winddance Twine, New York: Routledge, 2000, 11–55.

Glaser, Gabrielle. *American Baby: A Mother, A Child, and the Shadow History of Adoption.* New York: Viking, 2021.

Goff, Philip Atiba, Matthew Christian Jackson, Brooke Allison Lewis Di Leone, Carmen Marie Culotta, and Natalie Ann DiTomasso. "The Essence of Innocence: Consequences of Dehumanizing Black Children." *Journal of Personality and Social Psychology,* vol. 106, no. 4, 2014, 526–45.

Graff, E. J. "The Lie We Love." *Foreign Policy,* Nov./Dec. 2008, 59–66.

Grand, Michael Phillip. *The Adoption Constellation: New Ways of Thinking about and Practicing Adoption.* CreateSpace, 2011.

Gravois, John. "Bringing Up Babes: Why Do Adoptive Parents Prefer Girls?" *Slate,* 14 Jan. 2004. Available at https://slate.com/news-and-politics/2004/01/why-do-adoptive-parents-prefer-girls.html.

Gray, Breda. *Women and the Irish Diaspora.* New York: Routledge, 2004.

Green, Jesse. "The Day Hallmark Forgot." *A Love Like No Other,* edited by Pamela Kruger and Jill Smolowe, New York: Riverhead, 2005, 140–52.

Greene, Melissa Fay. "The Family Mobile." *New York Times Sunday Magazine,* 31 Aug., 2001, 32–65.

Gritter, James L. *Hospitious Adoption.* Arlington, VA: CWLA Press, 2009

Grotevant, H. D. "Coming to Terms with Adoption: The Construction of Identity from Adolescence into Adulthood." *Adoption Quarterly,* vol. 1, no. 1, 1997, 3–27.

Grotevant, H. D., G. M. Wrobel, L. Von Korff, B. Skinner, J. Newell, S. Friese, and R. G. McRoy. "Many Faces of Openness in Adoption; Perspectives of Adopted Adolescents and Their Parents." *Adoption Quarterly,* vol. 10, no. 3–4, 2008, 79–101.

Harding, Jeremy. "Short Cuts." *London Review of Books,* 14 July, 2016, 31.

———. *The Uninvited: Refugees at the Rich Man's Gate*. London: Profile, 2000.

Herman, Ellen. The Adoption History Project Website. Department of History, University of Oregon. Available at https://pages.uoregon.edu/adoption/index.html.

———. *Kinship by Design: A History of Adoption in the Modern United States*. University of Chicago Press, 2008.

Hill, Richard. "How DNA Testing Is Changing the World for Adoptees." *Adoption Reunion in the Social Media Age*, edited by Laura Dennis. Redondo Beach, CA: Entourage, 2014, 80–88.

Hipchen, Emily, and Jill Deans. "Introduction: Adoption Life Writing: Origins and Other Ghosts." *a/b: Auto/Biography Studies*, vol. 18, 2003, 163–70.

Homans, Margaret. *The Imprint of Another Life: Adoption Narratives and Human Possibility*. Ann Arbor: University of Michigan Press, 2013.

Homes, A. M. Interview by Francine Prose and Betsy Sussler. *Bomb*, 16 Sept., 2007.

Hubinette, Tobias. *Comforting an Orphaned Nation: Representations of International Adoption and Adopted Koreans in Korean Popular Culture*. 2005. Stockholm University, Doctoral thesis.

Isaac, Rael Jean, with Joseph Spencer. *Adopting a Child Today*. New York: Harper & Row, 1965.

Jacobs, Margaret. *A Generation Removed: The Fostering and Adoption of Indigenous Children in the Post-War World*. Lincoln: University of Nebraska Press, 214.

Jacobson, Heather. *Culture Keeping: White Mothers, International Adoption, and the Negotiation of Family Difference*. Nashville: Vanderbilt University Press, 2008.

Jerng, Mark. *Claiming Others: Transracial Adoption and National Belonging*. Minneapolis: University of Minnesota Press, 2010.

Johnson, Kay. *China's Hidden Children: Abandonment, Adoption, and the Human Costs of the One-Child Policy*. Chicago: University of Chicago Press, 2016.

———. *Wanting a Daughter, Needing a Son: Abandonment, Adoption, and Orphanage Care in China*. St. Paul: Yeong and Yeong, 2004.

Joyce, Kathryn. *The Child Catchers: Rescue, Trafficking, and the New Gospel of Adoption*. New York: Public Affairs, 2013.

Kagan, Jerome. *What Is Emotion? History, Meaning and Measures*. New Haven, CT: Yale, 2007.

Katz Rothman, Barbara. *Weaving a Family: Untangling Race and Adoption*. Boston: Beacon Press, 2005.

Kellaway, Kate. "Loyal Hunt of the Son." *Guardian*. 25 March, 2006. Available at https://www.theguardian.com/books/2006/mar/26/biography.featuresonline6/24/2018.

Kelly, Timothy, and Joseph Kelly. "American Catholics and the Discourse of Fear." *An Emotional History of the United States*, edited by Peter N. Stearns and Jan Lewis, New York: NYU Press, 1998, 259–82.

Kennedy, Randall. *Interracial Intimacies: Sex, Marriage, Identity, and Adoption*. New York: Viking, 2003.

Kim, Eleana. *Adopted Territory: Transnational Korean Adoptees and the Politics of Belonging*. Durham, NC: Duke University Press, 2010.

Kim, Jae Ran. "Scattered Seeds: The Christian Influence on Korean Adoption." *Outsiders Within: Writing on Transracial Adoption,* edited by Jane Jeong Trenka, Julia Chinyere Oparah, and Sun Yung Shin, Cambridge, MA: South End Press, 2006, 151–62.

Kirk, H. David. *Shared Fate: A Theory and Method of Adoptive Relationships*. 1964. 2nd ed. Port Angeles, WA: Ben Simon Press, 1984.

Latchford, Frances J. "Reckless Abandon: The Politics of Victimization and Agency in Birth-mother Narratives." *Adoption and Mothering*, edited by Frances J. Latchford, Bradford, Ontario: Demeter Press, 2012, 73–87.

Lewin, Ellen. *Gay Fatherhood: Narratives of Family and Citizenship in America*. University of Chicago Press, 2009.

Lifton, Betty Jean. *Journey of the Adopted Self*. New York: Basic Books, 1994.

Livingston, Kate. "Adoption: Experience, Research and Activism." *ASAC News*, Fall 2010, 4–5.

———. "The Birthmother Dilemma: Resisting Feminist Exclusions in the Study of Adoption." *Adoption and Mothering*, edited by Frances Latchford, Bradford, Ontario: Demeter Press, 2012, 58–72.

Loux, Ann Kimble. "The Catch That Came with Our Adoption." *Washington Post*, 23 Nov., 1997. Available at https://www.washingtonpost.com/archive/opinions/1997/11/23/the-catch-that-came-with-our-adoption/b1f0e401-5bd9-45cd-bd4d-94ef873aa837/.

MacFarquhar, Larissa. *Strangers Drowning: Impossible Idealism, Drastic Choices, and the Urge to Help*. New York: Penguin, 2015.

March, Karen. "Denial of Self: Birthmothers, Non-disclosure Adoption Laws, and the Silence of Others." In *Adoption and Mothering*, edited by Frances Latchford, Bradford, Ontario: Demeter Press, 2012, 11–25.

Mariner, Kathryn A. *Contingent Kinship: The Flows and Futures of Adoption in the United States*. Oakland: University of California Press, 2019.

Mason, Mary Martin. *Out of the Shadows: Birthfathers' Stories*. Edina, Minn.: O. J. Howard, 1995.

McIntosh, Peggy. "White Privilege: Unpacking the Invisible Knapsack." *Peace and Freedom*, July–August 1988, 10–12.

McKee, Kimberly. "Adoption as a Reproductive Rights Issue." *Adoption & Culture*, vol. 6, no. 1, 2018, 74–93.

———. *Disrupting Kinship: Transnational Politics of Korean Adoption in the United States*. Urbana: University of Illinois Press, 2019.

McLeod, John. *Life Lines: Writing Transcultural Adoption*. New York: Bloomsbury, 2015.

Melosh, Barbara. "Adoption Stories: Autobiographical Narratives and the Politics of Identity." *Adoption in America: Historical Perspectives*, edited by E. Wayne Carp. Ann Arbor: University of Michigan Press, 2002, 218–45.

———. *Strangers and Kin: The American Way of Adoption*. Cambridge: Harvard University Press, 2002.

Modell, Judith. *Kinship with Strangers: Adoption and Interpretations of Kinship in American Culture*. Berkeley: University of California Press, 1994.

Morris, William, ed. "Chimera." *American Heritage Dictionary of the English Language*. Boston: Houghton Mifflin, 1969.

"National Adoption Center: Open Records." *Pediatrics*, June 1, 2014, vol. 133, no. 6, e1808.

Nelson, Alondra. *The Social Life of DNA: Race, Reparations and Reconciliation after the Genome*. Boston: Beacon, 2016.

Newkirk, Van R., II. "Trump's White-Nationalist Pipeline." *Atlantic*, August 23, 2018.

Novy, Marianne. *Reading Adoption: Family and Difference in Fiction and Drama*. Ann Arbor: University of Michigan Press, 2005.

Park Nelson, Kim. *Invisible Asians: Korean American Adoptees, Asian American Experiences, and Racial Exceptionalism*. New Brunswick: Rutgers University Press, 2016.

———. "'Loss Is More Than Sadness': Reading Dissent in Transracial Adoption Melodrama in *The Language of Blood* and *First Person Plural*." *Adoption & Culture*, vol. 1, 2007, 101–28.

Passmore, Nola. "Helping Adults Who Were Adopted as Children." Keynote presented at Adoption Connections Training Institute, Cambridge, MA, Feb. 19–21, 2007. Available at https://eprints.usq.edu.au/4292/1/Passmore_3rd_Adoption_Services_Conf.pdf.

Pate, SooJin. *From Orphan to Adoptee: U.S. Empire and Genealogies of Korean Adoption.* University of Minnesota Press, 2014.

Patton, Sandra Lee. *BirthMarks: Transracial Adoption in Contemporary America.* New York: NYU Press, 2000.

Pavao, Joyce Maguire. *The Family of Adoption.* Boston: Beacon, 1998.

Penny, Judith, L. DiAnne Borders, and Francie Portnoy. "Reconstruction of Adoption Issues: Delineation of Five Phases among Adult Adoptees." *Journal of Counseling & Development*, vol. 85, no. 1, 2007, 30–41. Summarized in "Impact of Adoption on Adopted Persons," Child Welfare Information Gateway, August 2013, 4–5.

Pertman, Adam. *Adoption Nation: How the Adoption Revolution Is Transforming Our Families—and America.* 2nd ed. Boston: Harvard Common, 2011.

Pietsch, Nicole. "Good Mothers, Bad Mothers, Not-Mothers: Privilege, Race and Gender and the Invention of the Birthmother." *Adoption and Mothering*, edited by Frances Latchford, Bradford, Ontario: Demeter Press, 2012, 26–41.

Pinker, Steven. *The Better Angels of Our Nature: Why Violence Has Declined.* New York: Viking, 2011.

———. *The Blank Slate: The Modern Denial of Human Nature.* Cambridge, MA: Harvard University Press, 2002.

Prebin, Elise. *Meeting Once More: The Korean Side of International Adoption.* NYU Press, 2013.

Raible, John. "Life-Long Impact, Enduring Need." In *Outsiders Within*, edited by Jane Jeong Trenka, Julia Chinyere Oparah, and Sun Yung Shin. Cambridge, MA: South End Press, 2006, 179–88.

Raleigh, Elizabeth. *Selling Transnational Adoption: Families, Markets, and the Color Line.* Philadelphia: Temple University Press, 2018.

Rankin, Jo, and Tonya Bischoff, eds. *Seeds from a Silent Tree.* Pandal Press, 1997.

Raymond, Barbara Bisantz. *The Baby Thief: The Untold Story of Georgia Tann, the Baby Seller Who Corrupted Adoption.* New York: Carroll & Graf, 2007.

Register, Cheri. *Are Those Kids Yours?: American Families with Children Adopted from Other Countries.* New York: Free Press, 1990.

———. *Beyond Good Intentions: A Mother Reflects on Raising Internationally Adopted Children.* St. Paul: Yeong & Yeong, 2005.

Roberts, Dorothy. *Fatal Invention: How Science, Politics, and Big Business Re-create Race in the Twenty-First Century.* Nashville: Vanderbilt University Press, 2012.

———. *Shattered Bonds: The Color of Child Welfare.* New York: Basic Books, 2002.

———. *Torn Apart: How the Child Welfare System Destroys Black Families—And How Abolition Can Build a Safer World.* New York: Basic Books, 2022.

Rooy, Robert, director. *Deej.* RooyMedia, 2017.

Rothman, Barbara Katz. *Weaving a Family: Untangling Race and Adoption.* Boston: Beacon, 2005.

Rubin, Lillian. *Worlds of Pain: Life in the Working-Class Family.* New York: Basic Books, 1976.

Rustin, Susanna. "A Life in Writing: Jackie Kay." *Guardian*, 27 Apr. 2012. Available at https://www.theguardian.com/books/2012/apr/27/life-writing-jackie-kay.

Sadowski-Smith, Claudia. *The New Immigrant Whiteness: Race, Neoliberalism, and Post-Soviet Migration to the United States*. NYU Press, 2018.

Samuels, Elizabeth. "Adoption Consents: Legal Incentives for Best Practices." *Adoption Quarterly*, vol. 10, no. 1, 2006, 85.

———. "The Idea of Adoption: An Inquiry into the History of Adult Adoptee Access to Birth Records." *Rutgers Law Review*, vol. 53, no. 2, Winter 2001, 367–436.

———. "Surrender and Subordination: Birth Mothers and Adoption Law Reform." *Michigan Journal of Gender and Law*, vol. 20, no. 1, 2013, 1–14.

Scarry, Elaine. "Poetry, Injury, and the Ethics of Reading." *The Humanities and Public Life*, edited by Peter Brooks with Hilary Jewett, Fordham University Press, 2014, 41–48.

Seligmann, Linda K. *Broken Links, Enduring Ties: American Adoption Across Race, Class, and Nation*. Stanford University Press, 2013.

Shanley, Mary Lyndon. *Making Babies, Making Families: What Matters Most in an Age of Reproductive Technologies, Surrogacy, Adoption, and Same-Sex and Unwed Parents' Rights*. Boston: Beacon, 2001.

Shoos, Diane L. "Birth Mothers and Adoptive Mothers Onscreen: Visibility, Iconography, and Ideology in Rodrigo Garcia's *Mother and Child*." *Adoption & Culture*, vol. 8, no. 1, 2020, 33–54.

Siegel, Deborah H. "Open Adoption: Adoptive Parents' Reactions Two Decades Later." *Social Work*, vol. 58, no. 1, 2013, 43–52.

Siegel, Deborah H., and Susan L. Smith. "Openness in Adoption: From Secrecy and Stigma to Knowledge and Connections." Donaldson Adoption Institute, 2012. https://njarch.org/wpress/wp-content/uploads/2015/11/2012_03_OpennessInAdoption.pdf.

Sieger, Katherine. "A Birthmother's Identity: [M]other Living on the Border on (Non) Motherhood." *Adoption and Mothering*, edited by Frances Latchford, Bradford, Ontario: Demeter Press, 2012, 42–57.

Sisson, Gretchen. *Relinquished: The Politics of Adoption and the Privilege of American Motherhood*. New York: St. Martin's, 2024.

———. "Who Are the Women Who Relinquish Infants of Adoption: Domestic Adoption and Contemporary Birth Mothers in the United States." *Perspectives on Sexual and Reproductive Health*, vol. 54, no. 2, 2022, 45–53.

Smith, James. *Ireland's Magdalene Laundries and the Nation's Architecture of Containment*. South Bend, IN: University of Notre Dame Press, 2007.

Smith, Sidonie, and Julia Watson. *Reading Autobiography: A Guide for Interpreting Life Narratives*. 2nd ed. Minneapolis: University of Minnesota Press, 2010.

Smith, Susan L., and Adam Pertman. "Safeguarding the Rights and Well-Being of Birthparents in the Adoption Process." Rev. Jan. 2007. Available at https://www.ncap-us.org/post/safeguarding-the-rights-and-well-beingof-birthparents-in-the-adoption-process, Donaldson Adoption Institute.

Solinger, Rickie. *Wake Up Little Susie: Single Parenthood and Race Before* Roe v. Wade. New York: Routledge, 1992.

Solomon, Andrew. *Far From the Tree: Parents, Children, and the Search for Identity*. New York: Scribner, 2005.

Sorosky, Arthur D., Annette Baron, and Reuben Pannor. *The Adoption Triangle*. New York: Anchor, 1978.

Spencer, Marietta. "The Terminology of Adoption." *Child Welfare*, vol. 58, no. 7, July–Aug., 1979, 451–59.

Spock, Benjamin. *The Commonsense Book of Baby and Child Care*, 1946, excerpted in Adoption History Project Website.

Stack, Carol. *All Our Kin: Strategies for Survival in a Black Community*. New York: Basic Books, 1974.

Strauss, Jean. *Birthright: The Guide to Search and Reunion for Adoptees, Birthparents, and Adoptive Parents*. New York: Penguin, 1994.

Travers, Pauric. "'There Was Nothing for Me There': Irish Female Emigration, 1922–71." *Irish Women and Irish Migration*, edited by Patrick O'Sullivan. University Park, PA: Penn State University Press, 1995, 146–67.

Triseliotis, John, Julia Feast, and Fiona Kyle. "The Adoption Triangle Revisited: A Summary: A Study of Adoption, Search, and Reunion Experiences." British Association for Adoption and Fostering, Jan. 2005.

Tucker, Angela. *"You Should be Grateful": Stories of Race, Identity, and Transracial Adoption*. Boston: Beacon, 2022.

Turner, Jonathan H. "Emotions and Social Stratification." *Handbook of the Sociology of Emotions*, vol. 2, edited by Jan E. Stets and Jonathan H. Turner, New York: Springer, 2014, 179–97.

Uhrlaub, Richard, and Nikki McCaslan. "Culture, Law, and Language: Adversarial Motherhood in Adoption." In *Adoption and Mothering*, edited by Frances Latchford, Bradford, Ontario: Demeter Press, 2012.

Van Steen, Gonda. *Adoption, Memory, and Cold War Greece*. Ann Arbor: University of Michigan Press, 2019.

Verrier, Nancy Newton. *The Primal Wound: Understanding the Adopted Child*. New York: Gateway, 1993.

Vonk, M. E. "Cultural Competence for Adoptive Parents." *Social Work*, vol. 46, 2001, 246–55.

Wardle, Tim, Director. *Three Identical Strangers*. CNN Films, 2018.

Waters, Mary C. *Ethnic Options: Choosing Identities in America*. Berkeley: University of California Press, 1990.

Wegar, Katarina. *Adoption, Identity, and Kinship: The Debate Over Sealed Birth Records*. New Haven, CT: Yale University Press, 1997.

Whipple, Amy. "The Dubious Ways Parents Are Pressured to Give Up Their Children." *Vice*, 13 Aug., 2019. Available at https://www.vice.com/en/article/qvg45m/the-devious-ways-parents-are-pressured-to-give-up-their-children-for-adoption.

Wilkins, Amy C., and Jennifer A. Pace. "Class, Race, and Emotions." *Handbook of the Sociology of Emotions*, vol. 2, edited by Jan E. Stets and Jonathan H. Turner, New York: Springer, 2014, 385–409.

Williams, Margery. *The Velveteen Rabbit; or, How Toys Become Real*. 1922. Running Press, 1998.

Wills, Jenny Heijun. "Fictional and Fragmented Truths in Korean Adoptee Life Writing." *Asian American Literature: Discourses and Pedagogies*, vol. 6, 2015, 45–59.

———. "Narrating Multiculturalism in Asian American Fiction." In *Adoption and Mothering*, edited by Frances Latchford, Bradford, Ontario: Demeter Press, 2012, 119–31.

Winslow, Rachel Rains. *The Best Possible Immigrants: International Adoption and the American Family*. Philadelphia: University of Pennsylvania Press, 2017.

Wolff, Jana. "Black Unlike Me." *New York Times Magazine*, February 14, 1999, 78.

———. "The First Thirteen." In *A Love Like No Other*, edited by Pamela Kruger and Jill Smolowe. New York: Riverhead, 2005.

Xinran. *Message from an Unknown Chinese Mother: Stories of Love and Loss*. New York: Scribner, 2011.

Yngvesson, Barbara. *Belonging in an Adopted World: Race, Identity, and Transnational Adoption*. University of Chicago Press, 2010.

Index

Abortion: before Roe v. Wade, 21, 185; evangelical attitude, 193n24; after Roe, 46, 94; after Dobbs, 2

Adoptees: activism, 24; curiosity/fantasy about birthparents, 44, 55; difficulty of knowing truth about past, 50; early instability, 28, 44, 68, 82, 87, 128; experience bad judgment by professionals, 44, 184; felt different in childhood, 4, 44, 54, 104–5, 186; felt loved, 104–5, 128, 186; helped by finding community, 45, 56; invisibility/secrecy, 3, 44, 57; likeness to birthparents sometimes uncomfortable, 58–59; loss, trauma, 6, 12, 59; mirroring or lack of it, 57–59, 104; need imagination, 98; phases of development, 5; search in archives/reading gives connection, 55–56; seeking larger network, 61–62; self-invention, 55, 186; sense of injustice, 44; stereotypes, 43; stigma, 44; stress family connections at end of memoir, including their own constructions, 62, 117, 121, 122, 124, 127; writings included in parents' memoirs, 155–56, 179. *See also* Post-reunion relationships

Adoptees, Transracial: seeking and finding community, 108, 112–13; reading Black or biracial writers, 113; emotions of sadness and anger often not understood by parents, 110–11; humor as defense, 103, 166, 168, 187; supportive parents, 112; synthesize heritages, 186. *See also* Post-reunion relationships; Racial difference; Racial isolation; Racism

Adoption: "best solution—everyone wins" belief, 8; economic privilege, 29, 36, 186; extrinsic motivation for, 71, 77; idealization of, 28, 136, 139; language, terminology, 12–13, 46, 70–71; in literature, 5–6, 12; recent changes, 6; helps to convert heathen, 89, 132; rescue, 53–54, 131–32; secrecy about, 3, 188; social commitment, 139; statistics, 4, 205n4; stereotypes: idealizing or melodramatic, 3; win-win-win view questioned, 183

Adoption, open, 9–10, 17–18, 34–38, 188; benefits adoptees, 36; connections with real people rather than fantasy, 153; difficult to maintain over time, 42, 188; multiple sources of identity, 42; range of meaning, 196n38

Adoption agencies: denial of information to adoptive parents, 26; to birthparents, 23; downplaying significance of race because of market concerns, 135; lying about identity of child, 109, 135, 199n34;

Adoption agencies (*continued*)
  misrepresent meaning of adoption, 135;
  poor choice of parents or failure to
  prepare, 135, 184, 187; some improvement
  in honoring child's background by 1990s,
  but not much by Lutheran Social
  Services, 118; stonewalling, 199n34. *See
  also* Louise Wise Services
Adoption History Project, 192n12
Adoption-industrial complex, transnational
  adoption industrial complex, 29, 191n4
The Adoption Triangle, 24, 196n27
"Adoptive being," 84, 126
Adoptive fathers: abusive, 95–96, 105;
  happiness in adoption unexpected, 187;
  suspected of being fetishists when with
  Asian daughters, 101
Adoptive mothers: care emphasized in
  adoptees' memoirs, 80–81; good mother
  ideal, 178; solidarity with birthmother (as
  fantasy), 170, 171
Adoptive parents: acknowledging mistakes,
  145–46, 148; attitude to economic
  privilege, 166–67; contribute money to
  birth family, 164; denial, silence about
  adoption or openness, 2, 97; denied
  information about child and heredity,
  150; denied preparation for racism, 133,
  135, 140–42; difficulties of raising child
  with disability, 150–56; doubts about
  loving children enough, 155; might
  extend family to include child's birth
  relatives, 134; games reenacting adoption
  helpful, 172–73; give up expectations of
  control, 165; need for reciprocation, 155;
  need support networks, 154–55, 166;
  parallels with animal parenting, 172;
  talk with children about birthparents,
  honor ancestral culture, 52–53, 96–98,
  140–42, 163
"Adversarial motherhood," 38, 78, 178
African-descended children, transracial
  adoption of, 92–93
ALMA (Adoptees' Liberty Movement
  Association), 25–26, 28, 47–48, 56. *See
  also* Fisher, Florence
American Academy of Pediatrics, on
  adoptees' need to search, 47
American Adoption Congress website
  recording states with open and closed
  birth records, 198n18

American values: choice, freedom, contrast
  with Korean self-restraint, 119, 120
Asians, hostility toward, 90, 100, 101
Assimilation, 89–90, 96, 109; redefined, 146
Attachment as infant, toddler, 130, 157, 162,
  165
Autism, 140; caused by trauma, 152; child
  develops friendly interactions,
  conceptual thinking, 155; possibilities for
  others with, 180

Bates, E. Douglas, *Gift Children*, 140–46,
  185
Beatty, Jan, *American Bastard*, 198n21
Bernstein, Paula, 53–55, 57–58, 63, 190. *See
  also* Schein, Elyse, and Paula Bernstein,
  Identical Strangers
Birth certificate, adoption records: U.S.
  history of sealing, 9, 57; UK opening in
  1975, 57
Birthfathers: lack of memoirs by, 10;
  reduced to biological role, 14, 160;
  stereotyped, 6, 29, 94, 98
Birthmothers, First Mothers: activism, 17,
  19, 24, 26; ambiguity of identity, 37;
  critique of language about adoption, 20,
  40; deceived by agencies and social
  workers, 42; economic issues, 29, 40, 184,
  189, 190; expected to disappear, silenced,
  status mainly invisible, 4, 6, 16; fictional
  representations, 41; forced into coercive
  system, 2; grief, loss, trauma, 6, 16, 17;
  lack of sex education, counseling, other
  preparation, 3, 17; mystical connection
  with child, 20; prevented from giving
  adoptive parents medical history, 17;
  recent changes in acceptance, 17; reduced
  to biological role, 160; self-censorship, 35,
  38; separation anxiety with later child,
  22; stereotyped, 17
"Blank slate" idea of child development, 88,
  187, 200n1
Borshay Liem, Deann, director of *First
  Person Plural*, 90, 101, 109, 121, 135, 186
Bowlby, John, 20
Brettschneider, Marla, 203n42, 208n43
Brian, Kristi, 89, 135, 206n11
Briggs, Laura, *Somebody's Children*, on
  adoptions of Native children, 94; on
  preference for heterosexual couples,
  207n36; queer adoption as safety valve,

207n37; queer attitudes to birthmothers, 208n4; *Taking Children*, on Dorris's attitude to Adam and his mother, 207nn30–31

British culture, class emphasis, 78, 80; reticence, 80

Brodzinsky, David, et al., 192n16

Buck, Pearl, 8, 89, 132, 194n32, 200n4, 202n17

Bureau of Indian Affairs, 109–10

Burns, Sarah, 42

Callahan, Cynthia, 201n3

Campbell, Lee, organizer of Concerned United Birthparents, 13

Canada, immigration policy, 116; multiculturalism, 119–20

Carp, E. Wayne, *Family Matters*, 9, 48

Carroll, Rebecca, *Surviving the White Gaze*, 32, 33, 94, 98–100, 102, 105, 108, 113, 127

Catholic church: Charities/Social Services, 19, 36, 70–71, 72, 81, 82, 87, 151; hospital, 130; culture, tradition, 19, 75, 76, 77, 86; ritual comforting, 134; racism in Catholic school, 101, 126, 133–34. *See also* Mary, mother of Jesus

CDC (Centers for Disease Control), 185

Childbirth: without support, 30; witnessed by adoptive mother in open adoption, 144

Childhood sexual and physical abuse: at school, 152; in adoptive family, 28; of native adoptees, 112; in birth and foster home, 143, 152; by future brother-in-law in childhood, 77

Child Welfare League, 94, 133

China, adoptions from, 169–77; largest number after Korea, overwhelmingly of girls, 169–70; impact of economic insecurity, 174

The Chosen Baby, 54

Chung, Nicole, *All You Can Ever Know*, 1, 10, 91, 101, 104–5, 113, 115–18, 122, 125, 126, 129–31, 133–35

Chung, Soojin, *Adopting for God*, 89, 201n4, 201n6

Civil rights, integration, 92, 111, 140

Class: attempt to control adoptee's class identification, 71–72, 73–74; middle-class values, 147; adoptive parents, adoptees in reunion reaching across class, 78, 86, 148–49

Commodification of children: rejected, 61; in language about adoption, 53, 65

Concerned United Birthparents, 23

Conversion narrative, 124, 148, 187, 206n22

Couser, Thomas, *Memoir*, 11; "Raising Adam," 153–54, 210n74

Deans, Jill, 48

Depression, in adoptive parent, from loss of a child, from sexual abuse, 77

Disability in adopted children, adoptive parents insufficiently prepared, 150, 151; discovered by birthmother upon reunion, 26; knowledge and total dedication enables achievement, 152–56

DNA, 9, 188

DNA testing, 127, 192n19

Dobbs decision, 2; view of adoption as safe, 184; as child supply, 185

Domesticity: desire for, after Korean War, motivating desire for adoption, 89

Dorris, Michael, *The Broken Cord*, 150–55, 177, 187

Doss, Helen, *The Family Nobody Wanted*, 92, 201n6

Drug/alcohol addiction: in birthparents, 114, 131, 143, 147, 150–57; hereditary and environmental factors, 153; racist stereotypes invoked against Native Americans, 96

Dusky, Lorraine, *Birthmark*, 19, 26; *hole in my heart*, 20–22, 25–29, 36–40, 185

Economic issues in U.S. adoption, 3, 29, 179, 182, 184, 185, 189–90

Edwards, Jane, 196n32

Ellerby, Janet Mason, *Embroidering the Scarlet A*, 21; *Following the Tambourine Man*, 21, 29–31, 36–39, 40

Emancipation narrative, 124

Empathy, especially for birthparents, increase in adoptees, 59, 62–63, 124, 128, 131; in adoptive parents, 121, 144, 153, 178. *See also* Sympathy for birthparents

Eng, David, 201n12, 204n55, 207n40

Engel, Stephen, 207n40

Ethiopian children, adopted to Greene's family, reassured by Atlanta's Black population, 163; visits to birth family, financial support, 164–65

Evangelical Protestantism, 8, 133; Fundamentalism, 94. *See also* Pentecostals

Facilitated communication, for nonspeaking child with autism, 152, 154
Fate, God's will, 8; language used to justify loss and inequity in adoption, 133–34
Fedosik, Marina, 89, 107, 204n58
Fessler, Ann, *The Girls Who Went Away*, 17, 41, 195n25, 196n31
Fetal Alcohol Syndrome, 150, 151, 152–54, 155, 178–80
Fictions about origins: created by adoptee, 72–73; by adoptive mother, 96–98
Fisher, Florence, *The Search for Anna Fisher*, 25, 28, 40, 46–48, 57
FitzGerald, Frances, 193n24
Florence Crittenton Homes, 4, 22, 24, 29
Forgiveness, 68, 115, 118, 119, 127, 128
Foster, Diana Greene, Turnaway Study, 21, 185, 195n22
Foster care system, 157, 159, 185
Franklin, Lynn C., 195n17
Friedman, Susan Stanford, 192n10

Gailey, Christine Ward, 87, 197n51, 208n54
Gammage, Jeff, *China Ghosts*, 175–77, 178, 179, 181
Ganz, Sheila, 195n19
Garcia, Rodrigo, director, *Mother and Child*, 41–42
Gay people as adoptive parents, 159–60
Gender issues: Women as writers, activists about adoption, 2–3; prejudice against female sexuality; girls more desired as adoptees, 3; gender roles in parenting critiqued, 158–59, 177; accepted—Good Mother ideal, 177–78; prejudice against males adopting, 156–57, 159
Genealogy, 51
Genetics, heredity, 7, 9, 11, 22, 24, 26, 28, 36–40, 44, 58, 122–23, 126–27, 186
German ethnicity, 79, 80, 111, 119
Gillard, Julia, former Prime Minister of Australia, 189
Glaser, Gabrielle, *American Baby*, 2, 29, 41, 187, 189, 194n7, 194n10, 195n12, 195n24, 196n35, 196n37, 198n19, 199n34
Grand, Michael Phillip, *The Adoption Constellation*, 136, 204nn61–62, 210n78

Gratitude, 112; expected of adoptee, 131–32, 136
Gravois, John, 192n10
Green, Jesse, *The Velveteen Father*, 158–61, 208n45; comparison with *The Velveteen Rabbit*, 160
Greene, Melissa Fay, *No Biking in the House Without a Helmet*, 162–64, 166, 177, 178, 179, 181
Grotevant, Harold, 136
Guardianship, 188

Hair, African American, issue in transracial adoption, 8, 98, 103, 107, 141–42
Hall, Meredith, *Without a Map*, 193n27, 195n17
Harding, Jeremy, *Mother Country*, 69–87, 186, 200n49; *The Uninvited: Refugees at the Rich Man's Gate*, 70, 84
Harlow, Harry, 20, 95
Harness, Susan Devan, *Bitterroot: A Salish Memoir of Transracial Adoption*, 95–96, 103–10, 112–16, 126, 131, 136, 186–87
Herman, Ellen, *Kinship by Design*, 201n4, 201–2n16
Heteronormativity/homonormativity, 159
Hickman, Craig, *Fumbling Toward Divinity*, 50- 51, 53, 56, 58, 61–62, 186, 203n49
Hill, Richard, *Guide to DNA Testing*, 192n19
Hipchen, Emily, *Coming Apart Together*, 50, 55, 58, 186
Holt, Bertha and Harry, Holt Adoption Agency, 8, 89
Homans, Margaret, *Imprint of Another Life*, 6, 40, 41, 59, 83, 100, 113–14, 115, 121, 165, 167–68, 203n48, 209n66
Homes, A. M. *The Mistress's Daughter*, 51, 54, 57, 58, 61, 62, 63, 65–66, 126, 184, 186
Homophobia, 51, 152, 158, 159
Hopgood, Mei-ling, *Lucky Girl*, 91–92, 96, 99–101, 104, 110, 113, 115, 120–21, 126, 130, 135, 186, 202n31
Hubinette, Tobias, 201n7

Identification of country and parent, 119–120
Identity: double or multiple identity vivid for transracial adoptee, 106; can one be Black/ Scottish/ Jewish? 107–8, 110;

choosing Blackness, 108; Korean adoption in United States as re/birth contrasted with image of reunion as coming back to life, 109; name changes, 109; conflict between American and ancestral, 119–20; outsider when returning to origin, 126; exile, 120; reconstruction of identity after search, 64, 85; rejection of finding in origin alone, 70, 126, 186; related to food, 120; as traveler, 124, 126, 130; working-class, 67, 71, 75; complexity universal, 126

Illegitimacy: increased by World War II, 16, 18; stigma, 46, 55, 202n20

Indian Adoption Project, 94

Indian Affairs, Bureau of, 94

Indian Child Welfare Act, 136

Indigo, link to all families and teacher for McKinley, 125

Infertility, 4, 14, 16, 190

Irish immigrants, Irishness, 67, 73, 75–76, 82, 119

Jacobson, Heather, 70, 209n56, 209n71

Jakiela, Lori, *Belief is its own kind of truth, Maybe*, 69–87; *Miss New York Has Everything*, 70, 75, 79; *The Bridge to Take When Things Get Serious*, 70, 200n52, 209n67

Jerng, Mark, 198n24

Jewish tradition, 47, 125; identity, 72, 80, 93, 99, 107–8, 160; schools, 99; Jewish adoption of Latinx children because of similarity, 208n43; Jewish identity prioritized, 160–61; Jewish/Black mix, 107–8, 125, 203n42

John, Jaiya, *Black Baby White Hands*, 92, 93, 102–3, 105–7, 111–12, 113, 123–24, 184, 186, 202n19

Johnson, Kay Ann, 42, 174, 176

Joyce, Kathryn, *The Child Catchers*, 8, 133

Kay, Jackie, *The Adoption Papers*, 93, 97, 112; *Red Dust Road*, 94, 97–98, 102, 110, 112, 113, 114, 122–23, 126, 128–30, 131, 134–35, 186

Kellaway, Kate, 80, 82

Kim, Jae Ran, 201n5, 202n28

Kirk, H. David, et al, 191n5

Klein-Cloud, Avery, co-scriptwriter of *Off and Running*, 93–94, 99, 111, 125

Knobler, Claude, *More Love, Less Panic*, 165–66, 178, 179, 187

Korean adoptees, 89–90, 108–9; like dysfunctional family, 126; Korean history, 133; history and heredity lead to different temperament than Scandinavian and German parents, 111

Korean War, began large-scale adoption of Asians, 89

Laskas, Jeanne Marie, *Growing Girls*, 170–72, 174, 177–80; *Exact Same Moon*, 170, 171, 174, 176, 178

Latchford, Frances, *Adoption and Mothering*, birthmothers who did not feel coerced to give up children, 41

Latinos: often placed with single or gay males, 158; prejudice against, 158–60

Learning/cognitive disability, 26, 151–52

Lewin, Ellen, 207n39

Lifton, Betty Jean, *Twice Born*, 49, 52, 54–63, 67, 81, 86, 87, 186; *Journey of the Adopted Self*, 67

Livingston, Kate, birthmother in/on open adoption, 16, 42, 194n3, 194n9

Losses related to adoption, 10, 16, 17, 31, 40, 48, 59, 64, 69, 128, 131

Louise Wise Services, 56, 57, 60, 63, 69

Loux, Ann Kimball, *The Limits of Hope*, 150–51, 153–56, 184–85

Luck in adoption: generalization or individual cases, 8, 126, 131–32

Lutheran Social Services, 118, 132

Lyncoya, 94

MacFarquhar, Larissa, 139

Magdalene Homes, 76, 189

Marin, David, *This is US*, 156–61

Mariner, Kathryn, *Contingent Kinship*, 190

Mary, mother of Jesus: ritual veneration, statues in shrine and cathedral helpful, 20, 125; statues in maternity home intimidating in fantasy, 72, 75–76

Mason, Mary Martin, ed., *Out of the Shadows*, 193n28

McElmurray, Karen Salyer, 193n27, 195n17

McKee, Kimberly, 2, 109, 126, 191n4, 201n5, 203n47

McKinley, Catherine, *The Book of Sarahs*, 92–93, 96, 100, 102, 105, 107, 108, 111, 113, 115, 186

McLeod, John, Life Lines, 84, 85, 123, 125, 126, 129, 222
McMillon, Doris, with Michele Sherman, Mixed Blessing, 202n20
Melanson, Yvette, Looking for Lost Bird, 127–28
Melosh, Barbara, Strangers and Kin, 1, 6, 48–49, 189, 191n2; 192n10; 196n26, 197n45, 210n5; Adoption Stories, 137–38, 192n9, 193n27
Melting pot ideology in United States, 89, 94, 109
Memoirs: and civil rights movements, 12, 49; coming of age plot; continuing after reunion, 49; counter-stories, 2; filial narratives; help author's identity development, 5; intended readers, 11; involve multiple stories, 5; self-published; showing changes of view, 5; speak to each other, 8–9, 12
Modell, Judith, Kinship with Strangers, 193n21, 194n9
Mooney, Harrison, 202n22
Moorman, Margaret, Waiting to Forget, 21–25, 27, 28–29, 37, 38, 40, 196n26

National Association of Black Social Workers, 93
Native American ancestry, 104, 123, 127–28
Native children, adoption of, 94–95
Nature vs. nurture, 6, 7, 28, 51, 59–61, 88, 165, 206n22; nature/culture opposition transcended, 71
Neglect, abuse: by foster parents, 143, 151; by birthparents, 129, 143, 151, 156; by adoptive father, 95; in an orphanage or hospital, 68, 129; causes indiscriminate friendliness in children, 207n29
Nelson, Alondra, 127
Neubauer, Peter, 62
Nigeria, 94, 112
Nightmares, birthmother's about lost child, 31; adoptee's about earlier life in Korea, 90
Nobile, Tiana, 202n28

Oedipus, 6, 154
"Open Records," 198n18
Orphan, self-image of adoptee, 46, 54, 60, 73

Orphanages: mistreatment of birthmothers, 42; critique by UN, 205n69; deceptive about identity, 90, 109, 135; about living parents, 135, 164; memoirists' time in, 87; religious affiliations, 133
Orphan crisis, 8; ambiguity, deceptiveness of term "orphan" 8, 29, 133, 135, 161–62, 164; in Ethiopia, caused by AIDS, 163

Park Nelson, Kim, 88, 109
Passmore, Nola, 199n29
Pate, SooJin, 201n4
Paton, Jean, Orphan Voyage, 43, 44–46, 186; assembled interviews in The Adopted Break Silence, 45
Pavao, Joyce Maguire, 199n29
Penny et al, 199n29, 199n33
Pentecostals, 52. See Evangelical Protestantism
Photographs, in rituals of identity, 125, 127
Pietsch, Nicole, 37
Pinker, Steven, 193–94n31, 206n22
Post-reunion relationships: birthmother's viewpoint, 20, 26–27, 30–33, 36–40; adoptee's viewpoint, 44, 45, 49, 51, 59, 60–61, 63, 86, 94, 95, 114–20, 122–27, 128–29; transracial adoptee educating adoptive parents, 121, 123–24, 130–31, 186
Prager, Emily, Wuhu Diary, 170–75, 177–80
Prebin, Elise, 122, 200n51
Pseudonyms: used in first adoptee memoir and first narrative of life in a maternity home, 3; used by memoirists in writing about birth families, 62; in writing about children, 180, 188, 206n21

Racial difference from parents, 33; observed by child, 97, 104, 105, 172
Racial identity, pride, 96; search for, 103, 107–8, 163, 175
Racial integration. See Civil rights, integration
Racial isolation, 32, 93, 94, 95, 96, 98, 99, 100, 101, 102, 103, 106, 186; resulting internalized racism, discomfort with appearance, 90, 92, 101, 109, 135, 175
Racism, dramatized in transracial adoption, 7, 12; in family, 100, 102; by stalker, 100; by fetishists, 101; hostility in school, 101–2, 103–4; in community, 100, 102,

103; "friendly" racism, 166; implicit bias, 124; lack of education of white parents about, 102, 104; stress transferred genetically, 149; perception of Black boys, 203n41

Raible, John, transracial adoptees' development over life span, 10

Raleigh, Elizabeth, 135

Raymond, Barbara Bisantz, 200n1

Register, Cheri, *Beyond Good Intentions: A Mother Reflects on Raising Internationally Adopted Children*, 110; *Are Those Kids Yours?*, 210n75

Registry, mutual consent, for adoptees and birthparents, started by Fisher, 48, 62

Reid, Theresa, *Two Little Girls*, 139–40, 166–69, 177, 178, 179, 180

Religion, spirituality: in birthmothers' memoirs and survey, 38–39; connection to eloquence, 8; ecumenical vs. dogmatic, 8, 133, 8; language for gratitude, 8, 38; mysticism, mystical convergences, 20, 38; promoting adoption, 8, 21, 133; religious language, 39, 56; rituals of inclusion, 8; shame and social control, 8, 86. *See also* Catholic church; Evangelical Protestantism; Fate, God's will; Jewish identity; Rituals

Reproductive technology, 188

Reunions of adoptees with birthparents: healing losses or not, beginning of relationship, requires change in worldview, 60–61; as rebirth, 109. *See* Post-reunion relationships

Rituals, private, familial, religious, or tribal, near conclusion of transracial adoptees' memoirs: John, 125; McKinley, 125; Kay, 126, 129; Harness, 126; Chung, 196; refused, Trenka, 119

Roberts, Dorothy, 126–27

Robinson, Katy, *Single Square Picture*, 91, 92, 95, 96, 100, 101, 104, 113, 115, 116, 117, 119, 122, 186

Roe v. Wade, 185

Romani ancestry, 162

Roots, TV adaptation of Alex Haley's book, 111, 186, 203n46

Rothman, Barbara Katz, 203n38, 210n6

Rush, Sharon, *Loving Across the Color Line*, 177, 178, 179, 180, 182

Rustin, Susanna, 202n35

Sadowski-Smith, Claudia, 208n55, 209n57

Safety net, lacking in United States, 189, 190

Saffian, Sarah, *Ithaka*, 50, 52–61, 64, 78, 85, 186, 203n49

Samuels, Elizabeth, 196n37, 196n39, 197n45

Savarese, Ralph, *Reasonable People*, 139–40, 177, 179, 180, 181

Scarry, Elaine, 193n31

Schaefer, Carol, *The Other Mother*, 19–20, 23, 29, 30, 32, 40, 195n16, 195n21, 196n29

Schein, Elyse, and Paula Bernstein, *Identical Strangers*, 50–65. See Bernstein, Paula; Louise Wise Services; Twins

Searchers, professional, 72, 113

Seeds from a Silent Tree, 89

Seek, Amy, *God and Jetfire*, 16, 17, 34, 37–38, 39, 40, 186

Seligman, Linda, 135, 193n21, 206n18, 207n29, 208n53

Shame: in birthmothers, 17–18, 19, 21, 30, 70, 72; in adoptees, 55, 63, 65, 82; class, 70, 72, 74, 77; from sexual abuse, 70, 77; converted to depression, 77, 87; in transracial adoptees, from hair problems, 195n16, 196n34

Shanley, Mary Lyndon, 42

Shapiro, Dani, *Inheritance*, 192n19

Sieger, Katherine, 37

Sisson, Gretchen, *Relinquished*, 21, 29, 35, 40, 182, 184, 185, 188, 189, 192nn13–14, 195n22, 196n38, 210n3, 211n11

Smith, Sidonie, and Julia Watson, 192n20

Smith, Susan, and Adam Pertman, 194n4, 194n8, 195n21

Social workers, failing to prepare parents who adopt transracially, 133, 135

Solinger, Rickie, 196n37

Spock, Dr. Benjamin, 118, 203n50

Stack, Carol, 197n51

Stigma: birthparents, 4, 195n11; infertility, 4; adoptees, 44; racial prejudice, 11, 44. *See also* Shame

Strauss, Jean, *Beneath a Tall Tree*, 50, 52–54, 56, 60–66, 85; *Birthright*, 50, 56, 63–64

Supreme Court decisions, 94, 184, 210n1

Sympathy for birthparents, 98, 155. *See also* Empathy

Thompson, Jean (pseud.), *House of Tomorrow*, 18–19

Three Identical Strangers, film, 69

TRACK (Truth and Reconciliation for the Adoption Community of Korea) 133, 189

Trauma: of adoptees: "primal wound," 67–68; from neglect in orphanage, hospital, foster care, 68, 87; from stalking, 101; from childhood sexual abuse, 112–13; lack of understanding, 110–11

Trenka, Jane Jeong, *The Language of Blood*, 90–91, 95, 96, 97, 100–101, 105, 109, 114, 116, 118, 119, 120, 121, 127, 128, 129, 131–32, 134; critique of Korean adoption system and activism, 132–33; imagines continuing connections between American adopting and Korean relinquishing families, 134, 184–86, 192n17, 203n48; *Fugitive Visions*, 120, 133

Trimberger, Kay, *Creole Son*, 178, 179, 180, 181, 182, 187, 206n21

Triseliotis et all, 11, 195n25, 195n32

Tucker, Angela, *You Should be Grateful*, 136

Turnaway Study. *See* Foster, Diana Greene

Twins: separate adoptions arranged by Louise Wise Adoption Agency, 44, 51, 57, 60, 62, 64–65, 69; image of lost Korean identity of sisters for Trenka, 90

UN Resolution on Rights of the Child, 205n69

Velveteen Rabbit, 160

Verrier, Nancy, *Primal Wound*, 44, 67, 82–83

Waldron, Jan, *Giving Away Simone*, 16, 32–33, 37, 39, 40, 69, 185. *See* Carroll, Rebecca, *Surviving the White Gaze*

Ward, Andrew, *Birth Father's Tale*, 193n28

Wegar, Katarina, *Adoption, Identity and Culture*, 192n22

Welcome House, 132, 133

Welfare system, problems of, 134, 135, 157

Whipple, Amy, 197n48

White privilege, transracial adoptees' ambiguous relation to, 88

Williams syndrome, overfriendly, specific mental and physical disabilities, 155, 207n29

Wills, Jenny Heijun, *Older Sister. Not Necessarily Related*, 92, 96, 100, 101, 109, 111, 113, 114, 115–16, 117–20; "Fictional," 97, 204n64

Winslow, Rachel Raines, 201n6

Winterson, Jeanette, *Why Be Happy When You Could Be Normal?*, 44, 52, 54–55, 57, 59–61, 63, 66–69, 81, 84, 186, 195n13; *Oranges are not the Only Fruit*, 52

Wolff, Jana, *Secret Thoughts of an Adoptive Mother*, 178, 179, 181, 187; "The First Thirteen," 206n19

Yngvesson, Barbara, 127, 193n21, 201–2n16, 205n65